# TEACHING READING TO DISABLED AND HANDICAPPED LEARNERS

# TEACHING READING
# TO DISABLED
# AND HANDICAPPED LEARNERS

*By*

**HAROLD D. LOVE, ED.D.**

*Professor*

*and*

**FREDDIE W. LITTON, ED.D.**

*Chair and Professor*

*Special Education Department*
*University of Central Arkansas*

CHARLES C THOMAS • PUBLISHER
*Springfield • Illinois • U.S.A.*

*Published and Distributed Throughout the World by*

CHARLES C THOMAS • PUBLISHER
2600 South First Street
Springfield, Illinois 62794-9265

© *1994 by* CHARLES C THOMAS • PUBLISHER

ISBN 0-398-05909-8

Library of Congress Catalog Card Number: 94-3917

*With* THOMAS BOOKS *careful attention is given to all details of manufacturing
and design. It is the Publisher's desire to present books that are satisfactory as to
their physical qualities and artistic possibilities and appropriate for their particular
use.* THOMAS BOOKS *will be true to those laws of quality that assure a good
name and good will.*

*Printed in the United States of America*
*SC-R-3*

**Library of Congress Cataloging-in-Publication Data**

Love, Harold D.
    Teaching reading to disabled and handicapped learners / by Harold
D. Love and Freddie W. Litton.
        p.    cm.
    Includes bibliographical references and index.
    ISBN 0-398-05909-8
    1. Learning disabled children—Education—Reading.   2. Reading—
United States—Remedial teaching.   I. Litton, Freddie W., 1946–
.  II. Title.
LC4704.88.L68     1994
371.9'0444—dc20                                                                  93-3917
                                                                                        CIP

# PREFACE

This book is concerned with helping the many children, adolescents, and adults who encounter difficulty with reading. Designed as a text for undergraduate and graduate students, it guides prospective and present special education teachers in assisting and teaching handicapped learners to read.

This book combines time-tested materials with newer, more innovative items. It is important for today's teachers to be familiar with traditional methods of diagnosis and instruction. In education, the recent research in reading gives us a clearer picture of the new reading process. We need to know about the new innovative diagnostic methods and teaching strategies. This text integrates traditional methods with newer perspectives to provide an effective reading program in special education.

This text also compares handicapped children with the average and above average children. It tells the student how to adapt methods and materials for atypical learners. It also introduces the student to specialized remedial reading techniques for the handicapped learner.

The authors wish to thank Mrs. Jean Thompson for her invaluable contributions in the making of this book.

# CONTENTS

# TEACHING READING TO DISABLED AND HANDICAPPED LEARNERS

# Chapter 1

# DISABLED AND HANDICAPPED LEARNERS

In the public schools of America, the organization into grades for all children of the same age is based on the assumption that they are all alike and that all children learn at the same rate and by the same methods. Nothing could be further from the truth. The American tradition of equality has been confused with identical learning ability and identical learning style. Actually, children differ biologically, psychologically, and socially, and all children learn differently and at different rates. It is for this reason not all seven-year-old children learn to read at the second grade level and not all children can master first grade reading material at the age of six. It is also for this reason that many children in kindergarten are ready to learn to read, but a majority of the children in kindergarten are not ready to learn to read. Too often we push academics in kindergarten when we are doing a disfavor to a large group of children. Some kindergartens now actually start teaching the basic components of reading to all children as though they all learn at the same rate and as though they all learn by the same senses and by the same methods. For a particular child, we do not know what his potential for reading is unless we give him a battery of tests. The schools cannot afford to give every child a battery of tests to determine what his learning potential is. Our objective, therefore, must be to provide every child with the widest possible opportunities and to remove any obstacles inhibiting the child's ability to learn to read.

This book is concerned with the teaching of reading to children who are handicapped learners. These children deviate from the norm in their learning patterns and have been often referred to as slow learners, mentally retarded, specific learning disabled, dyslexic, minimal brain dysfunction, perceptually handicapped, or atypical learners.

The classification and labeling of children has its advantages and disadvantages. An advantage to a label would be the child who is classified as hearing-impaired by an otologist. The child is referred to the school for the deaf and is admitted to this school. There, the personnel in the school for the deaf forget the label of hearing-impaired and proceed to evaluate the child for educational purposes. At that school for the deaf, they know this child is hearing-impaired and they are going to do everything possible to help this child. An example of a disadvantage to labeling a child would be to test an immature child when he's five years old and label him mentally retarded. Here we have the looking glass theory at work because the child finds out what the teachers think about him and he reacts to the way that they think he should be. In other words, he tries to be like they think he's going to be. We also have by this label the self-fulfilling prophesy, "What will be is going to be." This child is expected to be a failure because he has been labeled mentally retarded, therefore, he will fulfill this prophesy and become a failure.

## DEFINITIONS AND CLASSIFICATION

### Mental Retardation

People with mental retardation have been studied for centuries, by a variety of professional people. The most widely accepted definition of mental retardation is that of the American Association on Mental Retardation (AAMR). The AAMR definition states that "Mental Retardation refers to significantly subaverage general intellectual functioning resulting in or associated with concurrent impairments in adaptive behavior, and manifested during the developmental period" (Grossman, 1983, p. 11). The essential features of this definition have also been adopted by the American Psychiatric Association.

**Intelligence.** Significantly subaverage general intellectual functioning is determined through the use of a standardized intelligence test. On an intelligence test, a person's score is compared to the statistical average of age mates who have taken the same test. The statistical average for an intelligence test is generally set at 100. In other words, the mean IQ of Americans is 100. We say that a standard deviation of 15 or 16 is common among the two most used intelligence tests. A standard deviation measures the dispersion of scores in a distribution. A score that deviates more than two standard deviations from the mean of 100 is considered to be significantly different. An individual who scores two standard deviations below the average on one of the Wechsler tests would have an IQ of 70 or less and would be mentally retarded. The person who scores two standard deviations below the mean on the Stanford-Binet would have an IQ of 68 or less and would be considered mentally retarded.

**Adaptive Behavior.** Impairments in adaptive behavior are defined by the AAMR as significant limitations in a person's ability to meet standards of maturation, learning, personal independence, and social responsibility that would be expected of another individual of comparable age level and cultural group (Grossman, 1983). Adaptive behavior can also be measured by standardized tests. These tests are more often referred to as adaptive behavior scales, and generally use structured interviews or direct observations to obtain information. Adaptive behavior scales generally compare an individual to an established norm or measurement.

**Developmental Period.** In the AAMR definition, the developmental period is defined as "the period of time between birth and the eighteenth birthday" (Grossman, 1983, p. 1). The reason for the inclusion of a developmental period within the definition is to clearly distinguish mental retardation from other conditions that may not originate until the adult years, such as head injuries or strokes.

## Slow Learners

The term slow learner is used in a generalized sense in this book to include children who are borderline in intelligence. These children were once classified as dull-normal, but now most people use the word slow learner. Slow learners require much repetition in order to learn and they require a more systematic instructual procedure. These children do not reach the levels of reading achievement of other children their age. Ordinarily, we say a child who has an IQ of 70–90 would be classified as a slow learner. According to the manual of the Wechsler Intelligence Scale for Children—III, this group of children makes up approximately 22 percent of the population. These children will always function below grade level in reading, but in most cases, they will not have a reading problem. These children as well as all children only have a reading problem when their mental age is higher than their reading proficiency or reading age.

## The Learning Disabled Child

Probably the most common accepted definition is that endorsed by the federal government:

"Specific learning disability" means a disorder in one or more of the basic psychological processes involved in understanding or in using language, spoken or written, which may manifest itself in an imperfect ability to listen, think, speak, read, write, spell, or to do mathematical calculations. The term includes such conditions as perceptual handicaps, brain injury, minimal dysfunction, dyslexia, and developmental aphasia. The term does not include children who have learning problems which are primarily the result of visual, hearing, or motor handicaps, of mental retardation, of emotional disturbance, or of environmental, cultural, or economic disadvantage (*Federal Register,* 1977, p. 65083).

## The National Joint Committee for Learning Disabilities Definition

The National Joint Committee for Learning Disabilities (NJCLD), made up of representatives of the American-Speech-Hearing Association, the Association for Children and Adults with Learning Disabilities, the Council for Learning Disabilities, the Division for Children with Communication Disorders, the International Reading Association, and the Orton Society, has issued an alternative definition:

Learning disabilities is a general term that refers to a heterogeneous group of disorders manifested by significant difficulties in the acquisition and use of listening, speaking, reading, writing, reasoning, or mathematical abilities. These disorders are intrinsic to the individual, presumed to be due to central nervous system dysfunction, and may occur across the life span.

Problems in self-regulatory behaviors, social perception and social interaction may exist with learning disabilities but do not by themselves constitute a learning disability.

Although learning disabilities may occur concomitantly with other handicapping conditions (for example, sensory impairment, mental retardation, serious emotional disturbance) or with extrinsic influences (such as cultural differences, insufficient or inappropriate instruction), they are not the result of these conditions or influences.

## VISUAL IMPAIRMENTS

### Definitions

The term visual impairment describes people with a wide range of educational, social, and medical needs directly related to a partial or complete loss of sight. Warren (1989) suggested that visual impairments encompass people who have never had any visual function, those who had normal vision for some years before becoming gradually or suddenly partially or totally blind, those with disabilities in addition to the visual loss, those with selective impairments of parts of the visual field, and those with a general degradation of acuity across the visual field (p. 155).

## Blindness

Blindness has many meanings. In fact, there are over 150 citations for blind in an unabridged dictionary. Legal blindness is defined by the Social Security Administration as visual acuity of 20/200 or worse in the best eye with the best correction or a visual field of 20 percent or less. This definition of blindness employs two basic criterion which are visual acuity and the field of vision.

**Visual Acuity.** The person of normal eyesight is defined as having 20/20 vision. However, if an individual is able to read at 20 feet what a person with normal vision can read at 200 feet, then his or her visual acuity would be described as 20/200. Most people who are legally blind have some light perception and only about 20 percent of legally blind people are totally without sight.

A person is also considered legally blind if his or her field of vision is limited at its widest angle to 20 degrees or less. A restricted field is also referred to as tunnel vision and this vision restricts a person's ability to participate in athletics, read, or drive a car.

**Partial Sighted.** People who are partially sighted have a visual acuity greater than 20/200, but not greater than 20/70 in the best eye after correction. The person who is partially sighted may need a work area that does not have an unnecessary glare and any obstacles should be removed that could impede mobility. This individual might also need large print books and special lighting to enhance visual opportunities. In most states, the State Department of Education will furnish a special education teacher or a regular classroom teacher with large-print basal readers and other books for reading, spelling, and other academic subjects.

## PREVALENCE

Reynolds and Birch (1982) indicate that at least 20 percent of the population has some visual problems, but most of these defects can be corrected to a level where they do not interfere with reading. LaPlante

(1991) estimated that approximately 1,438,000 individuals of all ages have visual impairments which are significant enough to limit their activities. The U.S. Department of Education's 13th Annual Report to Congress (1991) approximates that there are 22,960 school-age children with visual impairments severe enough to receive special services in the U.S. public schools.

## CHARACTERISTICS

A visual impairment present at birth will have a more significant effect on an individual's academic performance and later performance in life than if the individual becomes blind after birth. Useful visual imagery may disappear if sight is lost prior to the age of five. If sight is lost after the age of five, it is possible for the person to retain some visual frame of reference. We call this "in the mind's eye." Total blindness that occurs before the age of five has the greatest negative influence on the functioning of the individual.

**Intelligence.** For the child with a visual impairment, his or her perceptions of the world may be based on input from senses other than vision. If the child is born blind or becomes blind shortly after birth, his experiences are significantly restricted by the lack of vision. The only valid way to compare the intellectual capabilities of children who are visually impaired is to compare them on a verbal test and not on a performance test of intelligence.

**Speech and Language Skills.** For children with limited sight, speech and language development occurs primarily through the integration of visual experiences and the symbols of the spoken word. The child who does not have this sight must depend on other senses to associate words with objects. The child who is limited severely in sight will have to use the auditory sense more so than any other sense in developing reading skills. The child with limited vision can also use the tactile and kinesthetic methods for learning to read. With the auditory channels working for this child and the tactile and kinesthetics working, this child should be able to learn to read as well as a sighted child.

**Educational Placement.** Historically, we have placed these individuals in specialized residential facilities. At the present time, we are placing more and more visually-impaired children in the resource room for the handicapped throughout the public schools in America. The child will go to the regular classroom for a certain period of the day and then will spend a specified period of time in the resource room with the resource teacher generally doing work in reading, math, and other academic subjects. The public schools generally offer the use of consulting teachers, resource rooms, part-time special classes, or full-time special classes. Placement of a student into one of these programs depends on the extent to which the visual impairment affects his or her overall educational achievement. Hardman, et al. (1993) offer these tips for the regular classroom teacher when helping the visually impaired child:

- Remove obstacles in the classroom that may interfere with the mobility of students with visual impairments, including small things like litter on the floor, to desks that are blocking aisles.
- Place the child's desk as close as necessary to you during group instruction. He or she should also sit as close as possible to visual objects associated with instruction (e.g., blackboard, video monitor, or classroom bulletin board).
- Be consistent in where you place classroom materials so that the child with a visual impairment can locate them independently.
- When providing instruction, always try to stand with your back to the windows. It is very difficult for a person with a visual impairment to look directly into a light source.
- Work closely with a vision specialist to determine any specialized mobility or lighting needs for the student with a visual impairment (e.g., special desk lamp, cassette recorder, large-print books, personal reader).
- Help the student gain confidence in you by letting him or her know where you are in the classroom. It is especially helpful to let the student know when you are planning to leave the classroom.

## HEARING IMPAIRMENTS

### Definitions

A hearing impairment is defined according to the degree of hearing loss. This may be accomplished by assessing a person's sensitivity to loudness and pitch. Loudness is defined as sound intensity and pitch is defined as sound frequency. The unit used to measure sound intensity is the decibel (db), and the range of human hearing is approximately 0–130 db. Sounds louder than 130 db are extremely painful to the ear. Table 1.1

illustrates the various common environmental sounds and their measured decibel levels.

Table 1.1 **Estimated Decibel (db) Levels of Common Environmental Sounds.**

| Decibel Level (sound intensity) | Source of Sound |
|---|---|
| 140 db | Jet aircraft (80 feet from tail at takeoff) |
| 130 db | Jackhammer |
| 120 db | Loud thunder |
| 110 db | Rock concert/Personal cassette player |
| 100 db | Chain saw |
| 90 db | Street traffic |
| 80 db | Telephone ring |
| 70 db | Door slam |
| 60 db | Washing machine |
| 50 db | Conversational speech (40–60 db) |
| 40 db | Electric typewriter |
| 30 db | Pencil writing |
| 20 db | Watch ticking |
| 10 db | Whisper |
| 0 db | Lowest threshold of hearing for the human ear |

**Deaf and Hard of Hearing.** The term hearing impairment is generally used to describe the entire range of hearing loss, from mild to profound conditions. There are two terms which we use, deaf and hard of hearing.

Deaf describes those individuals whose hearing impairment is in the extreme range of loss—90 db or greater. Even with the use of hearing aids or other forms of amplification, the individual's primary means for developing language and communication is through the visual channel. Deafness, as defined by the Individuals with Disabilities Education Act (IDEA), means: "A hearing impairment which is so severe that the child is impaired in processing linguistic information through hearing, with or without amplification, which adversely affects educational performance." A child who is deaf is unable to recognize sound or the meanings of sound pressure waves.

The definition for persons classified as hard of hearing or hearing impaired, is "A person who is hard of hearing is one who, generally with the use of a hearing aid, has residual hearing sufficient to enable successful processing of linguistic information through audition" (Brill, MacNeil, & Newman, 1986, p. 67).

The distinction between deaf and hard of hearing, based on the functional use of residual hearing, is not as clear as many traditional definitions imply. There are new breakthroughs in the area of hearing which have made it possible for many children labeled as deaf to use their hearing functionally under limited circumstances.

As far as teaching academics, and specifically reading, the age of onset for the hearing impairment is extremely important. A hearing impairment may be present at birth (congenital) or acquired at any time during life. The distinction between congenital and acquired impairments is an important one. The age of onset will be a critical variable in determining the type and extent of intervention necessary to minimize the effect of the individual's disability. This is particularly true in relation to speech and language development. Of course, reading is a part of language and the child who is born deaf will not be able to learn the words in our language incidentally. He will not be able to hear the sounds and by the time he enters first grade he will know several thousand fewer words than the child born with average intelligence and normal hearing. For this reason, the deaf child gains only approximately two reading months per year in a 10-month schooling. For example, a fourth grade child with normal hearing goes through the fourth grade and gains 10 months of reading skills. The same child who is deaf and in the fourth grade goes through the fourth and gains only two months of reading skills. As a reader can see, it only takes a few years for the deaf child to be extremely far behind in reading and other academic skills. By the time the deaf child goes to college, he is generally reading at the beginning ninth grade level. This is true of the deaf children from the schools for the deaf in America who are above average in intelligence and functioning ability.

## PREVALENCE

It is extremely difficult to determine the prevalence of hearing impairments. Estimates of hearing loss in the United States go as high as 28 million, or 11 percent of the total population. It has also been estimated that there are 836,000 people with hearing impairments so severe that they need specialized services.

The most accurate data may well be the U.S. Department of Education in its Thirteenth Annual Report to Congress (1991). This report stated that there are 57,555 students who are hard of hearing or deaf between the ages of six and 21 who are receiving specialized treatment in the schools of the United States. These students account for approximately

1.4 percent of the over four million students labeled as disabled and who are receiving special services in the public schools in America.

## BEHAVIOR DISORDERS

There are a number of terms which have been used to describe individuals with emotional, social, and behavioral problems. These terms include behavior disorders, social maladjustment, emotional disturbance, and others. Childhood adolescence and adult behavior problems can frequently be grouped into two broad but overlapping categories: externalizing and internalizing disorders. The latter category refers to behaviors that seem to be directed more at the self than at others. Depressions and phobias are examples of behaviors that we would place in the internalizing category. Some clinicians would describe the individuals with these conditions as being emotionally disturbed. Children who exhibit externalizing disorders can be described as engaging in behaviors which are directed more at others than at themselves. These behaviors may have greater observable impact on parents, siblings, and teachers. The juvenile offender who chronically engages in crimes that involve damaged property or injuries to others might be identified as being socially maladjusted. This author will use the term behavior disorders to describe children and adults with both external and internal problems.

### Definitions

A variety of definitions have been created to describe children with behavior disorders. The definition used by this author comes from the Individuals with Disabilities Education Act (IDEA), is as follows:

(i) The term means a condition exhibiting one or more of the following characteristics over a long period of time and to a marked degree, which adversely affects educational performance:
   (A) An inability to learn which cannot be explained by intellectual, sensory or health factors;
   (B) An inability to build or maintain satisfactory relationships with peers and teachers;
   (C) Inappropriate types of behavior or feelings under normal circumstances;
   (D) A general pervasive mood of unhappiness or depression, or
   (E) A tendency to develop physical symptoms or fears associated with personal or school problems.

(ii) The term includes children who are schizophrenic (or autistic). The term does not include children who are socially maladjusted, unless it is determined that they are seriously disturbed (U.S. Department of Health, Education and Welfare, 1977, p. 42478).

A large number of children who have reading problems also have emotional problems. Many years ago, Dr. Arthur Gates (1941) reported that 75 percent of the disabled readers he studied showed personality maladjustment. Robinson (1946) reported that 40.9 percent of her disabled readers had a significant degree of emotional maladjustment, but she believed that it was an anomaly that caused reading failure in only 31.8 percent of her cases. Albert Harris and Edward Sipay (1980) reported that of several hundred reading disability cases seen in the Queens College Educational Clinic during a 15-year period, almost 100 percent showed some kind of emotional maladjustment. Harris and Sipay report that emotional maladjustment was a causal factor in approximately 50 percent of the cases in this group.

Researchers (Quay, 1975, 1979; Von Isser, Quay & Love, 1980) identified four distinct categories of behavior disorders in children. They are:

1. Conduct disorders involve such characteristics as overt aggression, both verbal and physical; disruptiveness; negativism, irresponsibility; and defiance of authority—all of which are at variance with the behavioral expectations of the school and other social institutions.
2. Anxiety-withdrawal stands in considerable contrast to conduct disorders, involving, as it does, overanxiety, social withdrawal, seclusiveness, shyness, sensitivity, and other behaviors implying a retreat from the environment rather than a hostile response to it.
3. Immaturity characteristically involves preoccupation, short attention span, passivity, daydreaming, sluggishness, and other behavior not in accord with developmental expectations.
4. Socialized aggression typically involves gang activities, cooperative stealing, truancy, and other manifestations of participation in a delinquent subculture (Von Isser et al., 1980, pp. 272–273).

## Prevalence

Estimates of the prevalence of behavior disorders vary greatly from one source to another. The prevalence ranges from 0.05 to 15.0 percent. The U.S. Office of Education estimated that 2 percent of the children in this country have serious behavior disorders. However, Bower (1982) indicated that approximately 10 percent of children in schools have moderate to severe emotional problems. Kauffman (1985) suggested that 6–10 percent of the school-age population need specialized services because of behavior disorders.

## Academic Achievement

Several studies have been conducted to assess the academic characteristics of children with behavior disorders. Tamkin (1960) evaluated the achievement of children in institutions who had been classified as having behavior disorders. He found that 41 percent were academically advanced in comparison to their actual grade level and 32 percent were performing below grade level. Reading achievement for the group as a whole was higher than math performance. Coutinho (1986) found that children with behavior disorders had subaverage performance in reading at the secondary level. Stone and Rowley (1964) found that 59 percent of the children studied were reading below grade level. Graubard (1964) found that emotionally disturbed children were severely disabled in reading and math in relationship to their mental ages.

This author thinks that we can safely say that many emotionally disturbed children have reading problems. It is also fair to say that reading problems make the emotional problems worse. Children who have reading problems are often made fun of in school and absolutely hate to read aloud. Every time this child reads aloud, his fears and problems are multiplied. Also, children who are thinking more about their problems than academic achievement will have greater problems in academics and especially in reading. Children who have behavior problems also fail to get their homework at night and parents constantly bicker and fuss at them, which makes the emotional problems and the reading problems worse.

## PHYSICAL DISORDERS

Physical disorders are impairments that often interfere with an individual's mobility and coordination. These disorders may also affect his or her capacity to communicate, learn, and adjust to life. The Individuals With Disabilities Education Act (IDEA) uses the term orthopedically-impaired to describe children with physical disorders. These disorders are physical impairments which are usually diagnosed by a physician early in a child's life. As a child with these physical disorders or health problems grows older, his or her treatment program may involve professionals from many different disciplines, including medicine, psychology, education, and vocational rehabilitation. The discussion here will evolve around traumatic brain injury, cerebral palsy, spina bifida, spinal cord injuries, amputations, and muscular dystrophy. The author would like to make it clear that any child with amputations who does not have a learning problem should not be placed in special education. Just because a child has a limb that is deformed or amputated does not mean that the child will have a reading problem or that the child will have any problems academically. In special education and regular education, some provisions must be made for certain disorders. However, because this book is about reading and mental retardation and learning disabilities have already been discussed, it should be pointed out that just because a child has amputations there is no reason to adapt his education or the educational plan as far as reading is concerned.

Traumatic brain injury (TBI) is a new category that appeared in IDEA. In children, TBI consists of "rapid acceleration and deceleration of the brain, including shearing (tearing) of nerve fibers, contusion (bruising) of the brain, tissue against the skull, brain stem injury, and edema (swelling)" (Lehr, 1990, p. 15). When the injury does not involve penetration of the skull, it is referred to as closed-head or generalized head injury. Children's head injuries are usually of this type. Focal or open-head injuries, such as a gunshot wound, are not common in children.

Two types of brain damage, primary and secondary, have been described by the medical people. Primary damage is a direct outcome of the initial impact to the brain. For example, a child who is hit accidentally with a baseball in the head may develop a hematoma, an area of internal bleeding within the brain. This can be called a primary damage. However, as time passes, the brain's response to the initial injury may be swelling, which will cause additional insult to the brain. This is referred to as secondary damage.

The child with TBI who does not have a learning problem should not be placed in special education. Very often though, this child will have a learning problem due to brain damage and must receive special help in reading and other academic subjects. The type of reading instruction that this child receives will depend on how poorly he reads and what type of channels he uses in learning to read. For example, if the child can learn best through the visual channel, then this will be stressed and possibly the Phonovisual Approach to teaching reading can be used. If the child learns best through the auditory channel, then a program such as DISTAR should be used. If the child needs a phonics program, we can resort to the METRA Program, DISTAR, Open Court, or several others. If the child needs a combination approach, we can use a method such as Phonovisual and Open Court. SRA Corrective Reading is also a good approach if the child needs a combination approach.

## Cerebral Palsy

Cerebral palsy is a disability resulting from damage to the brain before, during, or after birth. It is often evidenced by motor problems, general physical weakness, lack of coordination, and speech disorders. A child who has cerebral palsy and is a quadriplegic (all four extremeties and usually the trunk are involved) may need special provisions made in the classroom for academics. The child may need some kind of board so that he can indicate by a mouth stick what letters and what words he wants put into a sentence. If the child has speech, then, of course, he can talk and tell the teacher his responses. If the child does not have a learning problem and is not mentally retarded, then it is very possible that he can remain in the regular classroom and not go to special education at all.

## Spina Bifida

Spina bifida is a birth defect characterized by an abnormal opening in the spinal column. Spina bifida occulta is a very mild condition in which there is a small slit in one or more of the vertebral structures. Spina bifida cystica is a malformation of the spinal column in which a tumor-like sac grows on the infant's back. Many children with spina bifida also suffer from hydrocephaly and mental retardation. If the child suffers from mental retardation, he should be treated in the area of academics just like a mentally retarded child. If he has a specific learning disorder, then he should be treated just like a child with specific learning disabilities.

The same is true with the child who has spinal cord injury. If he does not have anything wrong with his learning, then he may very well remain in the regular classroom. If he has some type of learning problem, he should be treated just like children with learning problems as far as reading and other academics are concerned.

## Muscular Dystrophy

**Definitions**

The U.S. Department of Health and Human Services tells us that "muscular dystrophies are a group of chronic, inherited disorders characterized by progressive weakening and wasting of the voluntary skeletal muscles." They affect the muscles of the hips, legs, shoulders, and arms. Individuals with muscular dystrophy progressively lose their ability to walk and also the effective use of their arms and hands. The loss of this ability is attributable to fatty tissue that gradually replaces the muscle tissue. Heart muscle may also be affected, in which case symptoms of heart failure often occur. The seriousness of the different dystrophies is influenced by heredity, age of onset and the rate at which the condition progresses.

The exact cause of the various forms of muscular dystrophy remain unknown. Approximately 200,000 people are affected by muscular dystrophy and other related disorders. Some estimates indicate that 0.14 in 1,000 people develop muscular dystrophy. There is no known cause for this disease and the focus of treatment is maintaining or improving the individual's functioning and preserving his or her ambulatory independence for as long as possible.

As far as reading is concerned, if the child does not have a learning problem, he will remain in the regular classroom as long as possible. When the child becomes too weak to remain in the regular classroom, the special education resource room is the place for this child. The teacher can work with him on a one-to-one basis in reading and other academic subjects while he can still ambulate and even after he is in a wheelchair, he still needs to be in an educational setting. Later when he can no longer come to school but must remain at home, the school should send a home-bound teacher to help this type of child.

## SUMMARY

The authors have discussed many disabling conditions in which handicapped learners need special help, especially in the area of reading. In this chapter, we see that there are various methods to improve the reading ability of children who have different types of handicaps. One child may need an auditory approach while another child needs a visual approach in learning to read. There are some children who can use a combination approach as far as modality, and these approaches have been included in this chapter.

The children discussed in this chapter who have handicaps which may cause reading problems constitute approximately 10 percent of the school-age population. This is a very large percentage and many teachers will be required to teach reading and other academic subjects to the many handicapped children in the public schools of America.

## BIBLIOGRAPHY

Brill, R. C., MacNeil, B., & Newman, I. R. (1982). Framework for appropriate programs for deaf children. *American Annals of the Deaf, 131*(2), 65–77.

Coutinho, M. (1986). Reading achievement of students identified as behaviorally disordered at the secondary level. *Behavior Disorders, 11*(3), 200–207.

Gates, A. J. (1941). The role of personality maladjustment and remedial reading. *Journal of Generic Psychology, 59,* 77–83.

Graubard, P. S. (1964). The extent of academic retardation in a residential treatment center. *Journal of Education Research, 58,* 78–80.

Grossman, H. J. (Ed.) (1983). *Manual on Terminology and Classification in Mental Retardation.* Washington, DC: American Association on Mental Deficiency.

Hardman, M. L., Drew, C. J., Egan, M. W., & Wolf, B. (1993). *Human Exceptionality: Society, School, and Family* (4th ed.). Boston: Allyn and Bacon.

Harris, A. J., & Sipay, E. R. (1980). *How to Increase Reading Ability* (7th ed.), New York: Longman.

Kauffman, J. M. (1985). *Characteristics of Children's Behavior Disorders* (3rd ed.). Columbus, OH: Merrill.

Lehr, E. (1990). *Psychological Management of Traumatic Brain Injuries in Children and Adolescents.* Rockville, MD: Aspen.

Quay, H. C. (1975). Classification. In H. C. Quay & J. S. Werry (Eds.), *Psychopathological Disorders of Childhood* (2nd ed.). New York: Wiley.

Reynolds, M. C., & Birch, J. W. (1982). *Teaching Exceptional Children in All America's Schools.* Reston, VA: Council for Exceptional Children.

Robinson, H. (1946). *Why Pupils Fail in Reading.* Chicago: University of Chicago Press.

Stone, F., & Rowley, V. N. (1964). Educational disability in emotionally disturbed children. *Exceptional Children, 30,* 423–426.

Tampkin, A. S. (1960). A survey of educational disability in emotionally disturbed children. *Journal of Educational Research, 53,* 313–315.

U.S. Department of Education. (1991). To assure the free appropriate public education of all handicapped children. *Thirteenth annual report to Congress on the implementation of the Education of the Handicapped Act.* Washington, DC: Division of Educational Services, Special Education Program.

U.S. Department of Health, Education, and Welfare. (1977, August 23). Education of

Handicapped Children (Implementation of Part B of the Education of the Handicapped Act). *Federal Register, 42*(173), 42478.

Von Isser, A., Quay, H. C., & Love, C. T. (1980). Interrelationships among three measures of deviant behavior. *Exceptional Children, 46,* 272–276.

Warren, D. H. (1989). Implications of visual impairments for child development. In M. C. Wang, M. C. Reynolds, & H. J. Walberg (Eds.), *Handbook of Special Education: Research and Practice. Vol. 3. Low incidence conditions* (pp. 155–172). Oxford, England: Pergamon Press.

# Chapter 2

## READING READINESS

Children who have a slow rate of learning, children who have a lag in maturation, and children who have an atypical manner of learning need help in acquiring the skills which enable them to benefit from reading instruction. The term *readiness* refers to a state of development that is needed before a skill can be learned. There is readiness for walking and this requires a certain level of development of the central nervous system, adequate muscle strength, and the development of certain motor skills. An infant cannot learn to walk until he has these abilities. In a different area of learning, an individual must have certain mathematical skills and knowledge before he can profit from a course in calculus. The term *reading readiness* refers to a collection of integrated abilities, skills, and traits which the child needs before he can learn the complex process we call reading.

Reading readiness skills may be picked up in an incidental fashion by the normal learner and reinforced in a regular kindergarten program. However, slow and disabled learners require special attention in terms of both diagnosis and teaching. Many schools have developed programs to identify "high-risk" youngsters at the preschool level. These children are three-, four-, and five-year-olds who show potential for learning problems and can be discovered through screening and assessment techniques. Special teaching programs are then needed to help these children who are likely to fail in academics unless prerequisite skills and abilities for reading are taught at an early age.

Research and observation of educators and psychologists tell us that many factors contribute to reading readiness. Among these factors which are important are mental maturity, visual abilities, auditory abilities, speech and language development, thinking skills, physical fitness and motor development, social development, emotional development, and interest and motivation.

Many of these skills interact and interrelate with each other. For example, thinking skills are closely related to auditory, visual, and

20

language skills. Physical fitness and motor development often are interrelated with mental maturity and visual abilities.

Disabled and handicapped learners are likely to be deficient in several of the components shown in Figure 2.1.

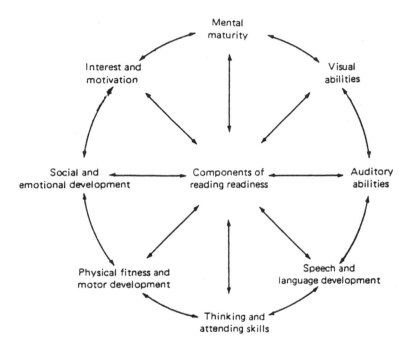

Figure 2.1. A systems network of components of reading readiness.

Many educators have found these factors to be highly correlated with learning to read; however, a single factor has not been found to be a cause of reading failure. Just because a child requires a prerequisite skill does not assure that the child will learn to read; it does mean, however, that the child is better able to benefit from reading instruction.

## MENTAL MATURITY

Mental Maturity refers to the overall Intellectual development of the child and, therefore, is related to all the other readiness skills. It is unlikely that children with low intelligence can learn to read by the time they reach the chronological age of six. Most authorities tell us that a mental age between 6-0 to 6-6 is considered to be the minimal mental age required for learning to read. We know that there will always be exceptions to this rule.

The authors of the Distar program (discussed in another chapter) taught children with a mental age of 4-0 to read. The decision about when to teach children to read should never be based on a single predictor such as mental age. The teacher should take many of the predictors into consideration in determining a time for teaching a child to read.

## Mental Age

Jensen (1979) defines mental age as a developmental measure that indicates a level of cognitive functioning. It can also be conceived of as a level of achievement that may indicate a child's readiness to learn and level of cerebral development.

## Comment on MA Scores

Sattler (1988) believes that the mental age (MA) or age-equivalent score obtained on an intelligence test provides useful information about the child's repertoire of knowledge; it reflects a more absolute level of performance than does the IQ, as it is the test-score equivalent of the 50th percentile rank in a given norm group. In contrast, the standard score of an intelligence test (or Deviation IQ, Composite Score, or IQ) provides no information about the size of the individual's repertoire of skills and knowledge. Unlike other writers, Humphreys (1985) believes that the MA concept should be retained because it provides some understanding, albeit coarse, of the individual's absolute level of performance. Sattler (1988) supports Humphrey's position.

## The Nature Versus Nurture Controversy

In the early part of the twentieth century proponents of the viewpoint that genetics determines intellectual development largely held sway. The classic study of Skeels and Dye (1939), however, did much to strengthen the position of the environmentalists. Skeels and Dye investigated the effects of stimulation on the development of infants and young children, most of whom were classified as mentally retarded and were in an orphanage. One group of children remained in the typical orphanage environment, but the other group was given stimulation. For the latter group, nurturance was provided by retarded teenage girls who were institutionalized. The effects were clear-cut: Average IQs for members of the group given stimulation increased, whereas the other children's IQs decreased. Even more dramatic were the results of Skeel's follow-up study, done twenty-one years later:

> In the adult follow-up study, all cases were located and information obtained on them, after a lapse of 21 years. . . .
>
> All 13 children in the experimental group were self-supporting, and none was a ward of any institution. . . . In the contrast group of 12 children, one had died in adolescence following continued residence in a state institution for the mentally retarded, and four were still wards of institutions, one in a mental hospital, and the other three in institutions for the mentally retarded.
>
> In education, disparity between the two groups was striking. The contrast group completed a median of less than the third grade. The experimental group completed a median of the 12th grade. Four of the subjects had one or more years of college work, one received a B.A. degree and took some graduate training.
>
> Marked differences in occupational levels were seen in the two groups. In the experimental group all were self-supporting or married and functioning as housewives. The range was from professional and business occupations to domestic service, the latter the occupations of two girls who had never been placed in adoptive homes. In the contrast group, four (36 percent) of the subjects were institutionalized and unemployed. Those who were employed, with one exception, were characterized as "hewers of wood and drawers of water." . . .
>
> Eleven of the 13 children in the experimental group were married: nine of the 11 had a total of 28 children, an average of three per family. On intelligence tests, these second generation children had IQs ranging from 86 to 125, with a mean of 104. In no instance was there any indication of mental retardation or demonstrable abnormality. . . .
>
> In the contrast group, only two subjects had married. One had one child and subsequently was divorced. Psychological examination of the child revealed marked mental retardation. . . . Another male subject had a nice home and a family of four children, all of average intelligence. (Skeels, 1966, pp. 54–55)

For many years theoreticians tended to view the nature—nurture issue as an either—or perspective—either you believed that heredity held the key to determine intellectual development or you held that the environment was the most important factor. However, by the 1980s most authorities believed that both genetics and environment are equally critical determinants of intelligence. Causes of retardation in individuals classified as moderate and profoundly retarded are more easily determined than for those in the mild range of retardation. One of the most convincing studies was conducted by Capron and Duyme (1989) who compared the IQs of four groups of adopted children: (1) children whose biological and adoptive parents were both of high socioeconomic status (SES), (2) children whose biological parents were of high SES but whose adoptive parents were of low SES, (3) children whose biological and adoptive parents were both of low SES, and (4) children whose biological parents were of low SES but whose adoptive parents were of high SES. The average IQs of the four groups were 119.60, 107.50, 92.40, and 103.60, respectively. Confirming the importance of the environment, it was found that the average IQ of the adoptees was about 12 points higher (111.60 vs. 99.95) when they were raised by parents of high SES (Groups 1 and 4) rather than low SES (Groups 2 and 3). Confirming the importance of heredity, the average IQ of the adoptees was about 16 points higher (113.55 vs. 98.00) when their biological parents were of high SES (Groups 1 and 2) compared to low SES (Groups 3 and 4).

The more scientists study genetic and environmental determinants of intelligence, the more they realize that this is a very complex picture. They do not know if the effect of SES is related to access to quality education, the variety and complexity of intellectual stimulation in the home, the parent's press for scholastic achievement, or some other factor that differentiates between high and low SES homes (McGue, Shinn, & Ysseldyke, 1982).

Children do not inherit an IQ. They collect a collection of genes referred to as a genotype for intelligence. The expression of the genotype, called the phenotype (the observable performance of the individuals), results from an interaction of the genotype with environmental experiences (Sattler, 1988). Genes set the upper and lower limits of the phenotype, but the environment determines where in this reaction range the final IQ value will fall. The current nature-nurture controversy is reducible to the single issue of how wide the range of reaction is. Those who favor environmental explanations . . . argue for a wide reaction range of 50, 70, or even 100 IQ points. Those who acknowledge genetic determinants assert that the reaction range [within which environmental variables operate] is more narrow, generally around 25 points. . . . (Zigler & Farber, 1985, p. 400).

## Heritability Estimates of Intelligence

Sattler (1988) tells us that heritability estimates for human intelligence are obtained by examining the correlations between groups of individuals of different degrees of kinship, such as monozygotic and dizgotic twins. Figures on heritability must remain estimates because experimental manipulations of human matings cannot be performed. Although refinements in estimation techniques have taken place recently, heritability estimates differ among researchers. Plomin and DeFries (1980), for example, suggest that heritability accounts for 50 percent of phenotypic variability in intelligence, while Vandenberg and Vogler (1985) indicate that heritability accounts for 30 to 40 percent of the phenotypic variance. Thus estimates indicate that at least 50 percent, and perhaps as much as 70 percent, of the variation in general intellectual ability is not related to genetic influences; therefore, some degree of external or environmental control over the development of intelligence is possible. Table 2.1 shows that the more similar people are genetically, the more highly related their IQs are.

## The Relationship of Measured Intelligence to Reading Achievement

Intelligence tests give educators information about the child's rate of mental development and his level of mental maturity. Although the tests do not tell the teacher much about a specific education program they do help to determine educational placement.

**IQ.** The IQ is a figure that gives the rate of mental growth. A child whose mental age is 5-0 and whose chronological age is 10-0 is considered to be developing at one-half the normal rate. In this child the ratio of mental age to chronological age is $5/10 = .50$. This is multiplied by 100 to express the intelligence quotient. Thus a child who grows mentally one-half a year each year would have an IQ of 50, while a child who grows three-fourths a year each year would have an IQ of 75 and a child who grows one year each year would have an IQ of 100.

The average or mean score on an IQ test is 100. Theoretically, 50 percent of the population is expected to fall in the average range of intelligence. On the WPPSI–R and WISC-3 2.27 percent of the population is expected to fall two standard deviations (IQ = 70) or more below the mean. This expectation is based on the assumption that intelligence is distributed along a "normal curve."

Figure 2.2 shows the hypothetical normal curve of intelligence. This curve is split into eight areas by means of standard deviations. On the WISC-3, where one standard deviation equals 15 points (the standard deviation on the Stanford-Binet is 16 IQ points), 34.13 percent of the population score between 85 and 100. Likewise, 34.13 percent score between IQ 100 and 115. Figure 2.2 indicates that 2.14 percent have IQs between 55–70 while 2.14 percent have IQs between 130–145.

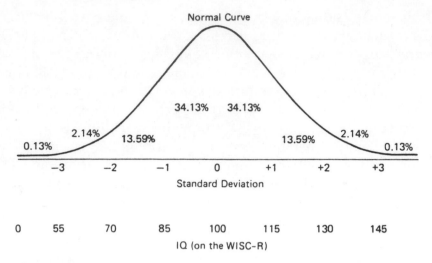

Figure 2.2. Theoretical distribution of IQ scores based on normal curve.

## Reading Disability

Reading (Stanovich, Cunningham, & Freeman, 1984) is a highly complex process that involves a variety of cognitive functions. These include attention, concentration, ability to form associations within and between sensory modalities, and such overlapping subskills and abilities as phonological awareness, rapid decoding, verbal comprehension, and general intelligence. Sattler (1988) informs us that phonological awareness (awareness of the sound characteristics of a word) likely underlies the ability to segment and analyze speech, an ability particularly important in decoding unknown words. Rapid decoding is the ability to recognize words quickly and automatically. This helps the child process information rapidly, thereby freeing the child to attend to comprehending the material rather than to decoding or recognizing the words. Verbal comprehension is necessary for the child to understand words and word order which is a critical skill underlying reading. And general intelligence relates to overall reading skill.

### Etiology of Reading Disability

Research on possible causes of reading disability is inconclusive with respect to etiology of reading disorders (see Table 2.2). Sattler (1988, p. 604) says that "like learning disabilities in general, reading disability

**Table 2.1. Environment and IQ: A Summary of Findings.**

| Area | Findings |
|---|---|
| | *Prenatal and Early Developmental Influences* |
| Complications of labor and delivery | Obstetrical complications do not appear to be related to IQ. |
| Birth weight | Birth weight has a minimal correlation with IQ (e.g. $r = .08$ with 7-year IQ). |
| Anoxia | Anoxia has a minimal correlation with IQ (e.g., $r = -.05$ to $-.06$) and results in a 4.6 point IQ deficit on average. |
| Childhood illnesses | Measles, pertussis, rubella, mumps, and scarlet fever show no relationship to test scores; the relationship between these diseases and mental subnormality is inclusive. |
| Lead poisoning | The influence of low-level lead exposure on children's IQs remains undetermined. |
| | *Malnutrition and Famine* |
| Vulnerability to malnutrition | Malnutrition, at least at the level experienced in developed economies, does not have a substantial impact on intelligence. For individual children, however, malnutrition may result in stunted mental and physical growth and death. |
| | *Family Background and IQ* |
| Biological families | Background characteristics of biological families (e.g., income, education, occupation, and home atmosphere) correlate significantly with children's IQs (e.g., range from .18 to .58). |
| Nonbiological families | Family background characteristics influence adoptive children's IQs, but only to a modest extent (e.g., range from .09 to .21). |
| | *Specific Home Environmental Factors* |
| Home environmental variables | Specific home environmental factors—such as press for achievement motivation, press for language development, and provisions for general learning—correlate highly with children's IQs. |
| | *Family Configuration and IQ* |
| Inequality of schooling and IQ | There is no firm evidence that the quality of primary and secondary education is a major source of individual differences in IQ. |
| Amount of schooling and IQ | The correlation between adult IQ and schooling completed is about .69. |
| Preschool enrichment programs | Preschool enrichment programs influence IQ, but long-term effects appear to be small. |

Original Source: Bouchard and Segal (1985). Adapted from Sattler (1988).

is likely to be multifactorial in origin—much remains to be learned about the mysteries of reading disability."

**Table 2.2. A Summary of Research Findings on
Etiological Components of Reading Disability.**

| *Etiological component* | *Findings* |
|---|---|
| *Physiological Factors* | |
| Brain damage | Studies suggest that moderate to severe brain damage is likely associated with reading disability. The degree of association is not strong, however. Many children with mild or subtle neurological damage do not have reading difficulty. |
| Maturational lag | Studies indicate that children with reading disability display lags on psychological and other behavioral tests. Studies are unclear, however, about whether children with reading disability will catch up to their peers. We do not know whether the lags reflect true maturational delay or are symptoms of a general neurological dysfunction. |
| Genetic inheritance | Studies in this area have been poorly designed. Therefore, it is difficult to estimate the degree to which genetic factors affect reading disability. It is unclear whether genetic factors affect reading independent of intelligence or whether reading difficulty is part of a more pervasive picture influenced in part by low intelligence. |
| Cerebral dominance | Studies indicate that few generalizations can be made about the role of cerebral asymmetry in reading disorders. Conceptual and methodological problems plague this area of research. |
| Ocular factors | Studies indicate that there is little evidence that peripheral ocular factors play an important role in reading disorders. |
| *Nonphysiological Factors* | |
| Environmental causes | Studies indicate that environmental conditions—such as social class, family size, geographical location, child-rearing practices, family history of reading problems, economical disadvantage, school factors, level of parents' education, overcrowding, broken home, and motivational factors—are clearly associated with academic attainment, which depends on reading proficiency. The findings are not proof of a cause-effect relationship, however. Some environmental factors also are associated with genetic influences. |
| Behavioral factors | Studies clearly indicate that children with specific reading disorders frequently have behavioral and emotional problems, including hyperactivity, inattention, and conduct problems. Although behavioral factors may not necessarily cause reading disorders, they may play a role in sustaining reading difficulties. |

Source: Adapted from Aman and Singh (1983).

**Intelligence and Reading Ability**

Stanovich et al. (1984) informs the reader that reading ability is significantly related to intelligence test scores. The correlations increase with age; typical values are in the .30 to .50 range for early elementary grade children, the .45 to .65 range for middle grade children, and the .60 to .75 range for adults. Sattler (1988) reports that median correlations between reading scores and scores on the WISC–R and (WISC) and the Stanford-Binet Intelligence Scale: Forms L–M are .44 and .46, respectively. The verbal portions of these two intelligence tests tap many subskills critical for reading, such as use of real-world knowledge, inferential skills, memory strategies, and vocabulary. Future reading performance is more accurately predicted by current reading achievement scores than by intelligence test scores, however.

**Rank order of WISC-3 subtests for reading-disabled children.** Trends are emerging from studies that have evaluated the rank order of WISC-3 subtest scores in heterogeneous groups of reading-disabled children. An inspection of 30 studies indicates that, based on the average scores of inadequate readers, the subtest rank as follows, from easiest to most difficult:

1. Picture Completion
2. Picture Arrangement
3. Block Design
4. Object Assembly
5. Similarities
6. Comprehension
7. Vocabulary
8. Coding
9. Digit Span
10. Arithmetic
11. Information

The four most difficult subtests form the acronym ACID (Arithmetic, Coding, Information, and Digit Span). Sattler states that in nearly every study that reported Verbal Scale and Performance Scale IQs, Verbal Scale IQs were *lower* than Performance Scale IQs. This discrepancy is consistent with the rank order data, which indicate that the four easiest subtests are Performance Scale subtests. Low scores on Coding may reflect failure to use an effective labeling strategy as a memory aid, which increases the time needed to complete the task (p. 610).

### Underachievement vs. Learning Problems

All children who are underachieving or who function in reading and other subjects below grade placement are not learning disabled. There are many factors which contribute to underachievement and learning disabilities is just one of them. Figure 2.3 shows the major causes of underachievement in school children. On the left are the intrinsic conditions such as mental retardation, sensory handicaps (blindness, deafness), serious emotional disorders, and learning disabilities.

On the right side of the figure are the extrinsic or environmental factors which can lead to underachievement: lack of opportunity to learn, cultural disadvantages, economic disadvantage and inadequate instruction.

There are several different types of learning disorders and they can all lead to reading problems. Figure 2.4 shows that the major components of learning disorders are: attention, memory, perception, and perceptual-motor disorders, and thinking and language disorders.

**Defining a severe discrepancy.** The indicator most frequently used to identify learning disability in children is an ability-achievement discrepancy. Children who are low achievers in school, yet of average or above average intelligence, are candidates for identification based on this

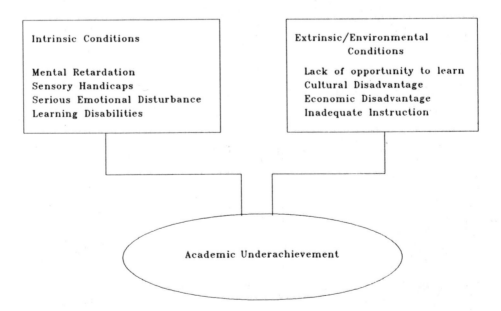

Figure 2.3. Conditions leading to academic underachievement. Original source: Kirk and Gallagher *Educating Exceptional Children* (1986).

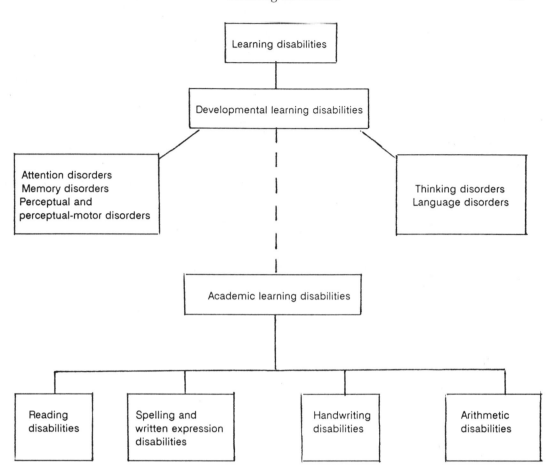

Figure 2.4. Types of learning disabilities. Original source: Kirk and Gallagher *Educating Exceptional Children* (1986).

criterion. The major classification problem centers on how to define a severe discrepancy between *ability,* usually defined by an intelligence test score, and *achievement,* usually defined by a reading, arithmetic, or spelling test score or by an overall achievement score (Sattler, 1988).

1. *Deviation from grade or age level.* Underachievement is most simply defined as a discrepancy between the child's grade-equivalent score on an achievement test and his or her grade placement. For example, a sixth-grade child who obtains a grade-equivalent score that is at the third-grade level would be characterized as being three years below grade placement. Some definitions use a graduated deviation criterion in which the amount of deviation required between grade placement and achievement varies as a function of current grade placement. The dis-

crepancy may be one year in first and second grades, one and a half years in third and fourth grades, two years in fifth through eighth grades, and three years in ninth through twelfth grades.

2. *Expectancy formulas.* Expected grade equivalent, rather than actual grade placement, may be used in the computation of an ability-achievement discrepancy. Expectancy formulae are based on the child's mental age (MA) and chronological age (CA). Examples of expectancy formulas follow:

The Mental Grade Method (Harris, 1961)

This is the simplest method. To estimate reading expectancy, five is subtracted from the mental age.

RE (reading expectancy) = MA (mental age) − 5

Jimmy is 10-0 and has a mental age of 12-0. His reading expectancy is therefore grade 7.

7 (RE) = 12 (MA) − 5

If Jimmy reads at the 3.0 grade level, he has a four-year discrepancy in reading.

Years-in-School Method (Bond & Tinker, 1967, pp. 198–203)

This method takes into account the school exposure the child has had.

$$RE \text{ (reading expectancy)} = \frac{\text{years in school} \times IQ}{100} + 1.0$$

Ten-year-old Jimmy is in the middle of fifth grade, that is, he has been in school for 4.5 years. His IQ score is 120. Using this formula, we find that his reading expectancy grade is 6.4.

$$RE = \frac{4.5 \times 120}{100} + 1.0 = 6.4$$

Since Jimmy reads at the 3.0 grade level, the discrepancy between expectancy and achievement levels is 3.4 years.

Learning Quotient Method (Myklebust, 1968)

This method determines discrepancy in terms of a quotient, that is, what percentage of his or her ability to learn has the child fulfilled? There are two steps in this method:

(1) EA (expectancy age) = $\dfrac{MA + CA + GA \text{ (grade age)}}{3}$

(2) LQ (learning quotient) = $\dfrac{AA \text{ (achievement age)}}{EA \text{ (expectancy age)}}$

Note that in this method, all scores are converted from grade scores to age scores (grade score + 5 = age score). What is Jimmy's learning quotient with this method?

(1) $EA = \dfrac{12.0 + 10.0 + 10.5}{3} = 10.8$

(2) $LQ = \dfrac{8.0}{10.8} = 7.4$

### Visual Abilities

There are two areas of visual abilities which are of concern whenever we discuss reading readiness. One is peripheral visual functions, the condition of the eye; the other deals with central visual function, the various functions of perception, association, and memory.

**Peripheral Visual Function.** Vision is the sensory pathway through which printed words are transmitted to the brain for interpretation. Poor visual acuity could very well impair a child's ability to see clearly. Any dysfunction of the eyes such as a defective visual acuity might cause difficulty in learning to read unless the child compensates for the defect. The legal definition for blindness involves assessment of visual acuity and field of vision. The legally blind person has visual acuity of 20/200 or less in the better eye even with correction or has a field of vision so narrow that its widest diameter subtends an angular distance no greater than twenty degrees. The fraction 20/200 means that the person sees at twenty feet what a person with normal vision sees at two hundred feet. (Normal vision acuity is thus 20/20.) The inclusion of a narrowed field of vision in the legal definition means that a person may have 20/20 vision in the central field but has a severely restricted peripheral vision. In addition to this medical classification of blindness, there is also a category known as partially sighted. Partially sighted individuals, according to the legal classification system, have visual acuity falling between 20/70 and 20/200 in the better eye with correction. In addition to acuity the child must be able to coordinate the two eyes, including following the line of print from left to right and fusing into one the images of words seen by both eyes. It is very important to detect any defects of either visual acuity or eye muscle imbalance in binocular vision through a visual screening examination also through teacher observation. Significant symptoms that include possible visual difficulties include: behavior; rubs eyes excessively, shuts or covers one eye, tilts head, or thrusts head forward, has difficulty in reading or in other work requiring close use of eyes, blinks more than usual or is irritable when doing close work, holds books close to eyes, is unable to see distant things clearly, squints eyelids together or frowns. The child's appearance in the following ways might indicate visual problems: crossed eyes, red-rimmed, encrusted, or swollen eyelids, inflamed or watery eyes, or recurring styes. The following complaints from children could indicate visual problems: eyes itch, burn, or feel scratchy, cannot see well, dizziness, headaches, or nausea following close eye work, or blurred or double vision.

**Central Visual Function.** If the child is able to see and there is nothing wrong with the child's eyes, we then examine the various components of the central visual functions. There are children whose eyes are apparently normal but who have disorders in their central visual function, that is, in interpreting, remembering, and recognizing what is seen.

**Visual Discrimination.** Visual discrimination refers to the ability to visually discriminate likenesses and differences in objects, geometric designs, letters, words, and pictures. In order for a child to learn to read he must be able to visually discriminate the difference between *d* and *b* or *moose* and *horse* or *house* and *horse.* Visual discrimination also indicates directional orientation. When a child reads he must learn to discriminate between *on* and *no, was* and *saw, top* and *pop,* etc. During the child's growing process he learns to visually discriminate differences in the things found in his or her environment and the child learns to make the fine visual discrimination needed in reading. If the child has difficulty discriminating these fine visual differences it is necessary that this ability be developed during the early phases of reading instruction.

**Visual Reception.** Visual reception refers to the ability for one to understand the significance of what is seen. There are children who find it difficult to translate visual symbols into meanings or to grasp the meaning of pictures. In early reading experiences sentences are reinforced with pictures that are interpreted by the child. Therefore, it is necessary for the child to understand and interpret pictures. If the child cannot do this adequately remediation is directed toward helping attach meaning to words and other written symbols and to interpret gestures.

**Visual Association.** Visual association refers to a child's ability to relate two or more things that have been presented visually. For example, at the age of three years, a child can often identify and claim her tricycle from a group of tricycles and bicycles even though she is not able to tell you exactly how she made this identification. Later, two or more coins much the same size bearing different symbols will not confuse children. The need of children to make fine visual discrimination in reading is self-evident since the symbols that they must read are visual stimuli. Even a quick examination establishes that many words look very much alike. A child who cannot differentiate among the various words in a passage cannot possibly get meaning from that passage or sentence. The widely accepted definition that reading is getting meaning from printed symbols is true but does slight some of the other sensory skills.

**Visual Closure.** Visual closure refers to the ability to identify a common object from an incomplete visual presentation. When reading the good reader will use visual closure because he or she needs to see only part of a printed word to recognize or interpret the whole word or even the sentence.

**Visual Memory.** Visual memory refers to the ability to remember what is seen. To remember what is seen and to retain what is seen is an extremely important part of the reading process.

## Auditory Abilities

Auditory abilities include peripheral auditory functions and central auditory functions. These functions include certain subabilities such as auditory discrimination, auditory reception, auditory association, auditory closure, sound blending, and auditory memory.

**Peripheral auditory functions.** Auditory acuity is the ability to hear sounds and words of varying pitch and loudness. Children who have a degree of hearing loss generally miss much of what goes on around them. They may miss some of the language and communication in their environment; they often miss parts of words and they may not hear such environmental sounds such as bells, cars, dogs. Also hearing impaired children are frequently handicapped in varying degrees in educational achievement. Reading ability, which relies heavily on language skills and is probably the most important aspect of academic achievement, is the most affected. A number of surveys over the years, taken as a whole, paint a gloomy picture of academic progress of hearing impaired students, particularly deaf students.

**Signs of Difficulty.** Signs of difficulty and hearing acuity include difficulties in understanding spoken language and/or in speaking, frequent absences because of earaches, sinus congestion, allergies, and related conditions. Also inattention and daydreaming could indicate that the child is not hearing properly as well as disorientation and/or confusion, especially when noise levels are high. The child who has a hearing problem might also have difficulties in following directions and he might frequently imitate other students' behaviors in the classroom. The child who is having a hearing problem might misunderstand simple directions or turn the radio or stereo or TV up too high. An audiometric examination or hearing test is needed to check the child's auditory acuity if the parent or teacher becomes suspicious.

**Central Auditory Functions.** Many children who do not have a hearing loss do have difficulty with their central auditory functions. They have difficulty listening because they cannot concentrate or they have difficulty interpreting what is heard, although there is nothing wrong with their mechanism. The several components of the central auditory functions are listed below:

**Auditory Discrimination.** Auditory discrimination refers to difficulty in differentiating similar sounds such as a doorbell and a telephone ring, or similar sounds such as *pan* and *pin.* It is necessary for a child to be able to discriminate between words and sounds if he or she is to learn to read not only by the oral methods but also by the auditory methods. If the child has a hearing impairment he or she must learn by a visual method and it will be at a much slower rate than do children who can hear.

**Auditory Reception.** Children with difficulty in this area have difficulty deriving meaning from spoken language and other auditory symbols. This ability is closely related with the language abilities, therefore remedial techniques for auditory reception overlap with those of language development and this is particularly true when it comes to receptive language. Disabilities in this area are often referred to as receptive aphasia or specific learning disabilities.

**Auditory Association.** This is the ability to relate concepts which are presented orally to the child. When children have a deficit in this area they need help in organizing and integrating ideas that are received through the auditory channel. A lot of information is verbal; therefore, this area overlaps with language skills especially the comprehension of language.

**Auditory Closure.** There are many children who are deficient in the ability to recognize and use common units of auditory experience when only parts of those units are presented or heard by the child. These children must be helped by the teacher in identifying what is heard and to fill in the missing parts of what is partially heard.

**Sound Blending.** This is the ability to synthesize isolated sounds into words and it is essential in learning to read. Children hear but cannot pronounce isolated sounds such as *r-a-t* cannot synthesize these words into the word *rat.* These children are likely to have difficulty learning to read unless they are taught by the visual whole-word method and they should not depend on phonics.

**Auditory Memory.** Many children have difficulty remembering what is heard long enough to repeat it back to the teacher. These children who have this deficiency in short-term auditory memory often have difficulty imitating words and sentences. Learning to talk depends a great deal on the child's ability to imitate words or sentences in his or her environment. Failure in this area often is a cause of delayed speech.

**Speech and Language Development**

Communication is such a natural part of our everyday lives that we seldom stop to think about it. We have social conversations with family, friends, and casual acquaintances and this is normal and so effortless and pleasant that it is hard to imagine anyone having difficulty with it. Most of us have feelings of uncertainty about the adequacy of our speech or language only if we are put in stressful or unusual social situations.

Speech is the ability to articulate or pronounce clearly the sounds of our language system and to use appropriate voice and rhythm patterns. If a child has faulty speech he may confuse sounds that are associated with the printed word.

When people think of language they typically think of an oral language most of us use. Language disorders include problems in the comprehension and use of language for communication, regardless of the symbol system used (spoken, written, or other).

The newborn makes few sounds other than cries. The fact that within a few years the human child can form the many complex sounds of speech, understand spoken and written language, and express meaning verbally is one of nature's great miracles. At about the same time children learn to walk and to feed themselves—roughly between 10 and 18 months—they normally say their first words. At age two they may have a vocabulary of several hundred words; by the age five, they know many more, and their vocabulary continues to increase at a rapid rate. By the time they begin school, they are fluent speakers and have mastered most of the basic morphological characteristics of language. They can construct word forms such as plurals, verb tenses, and compound words correctly. By the time they are eight or ten years old, they have mastered the phonemic components of language (their articulation of the speech sounds is correct).

Both speech disorders and language disorders are to some degree related to reading problems. The incidence of speech and language problems is higher among handicapped children. Furthermore, children with severe reading problems are often deficient in underlying oral language skills. An important element in preparing children for reading, therefore, is training in speech and language skills.

**Thinking Skills**

The cluster of skills which are needed for reading is collectively referred to in this book as thinking skills. Thinking skills, or you may want to call them cognitive skills, are a collection of mental abilities which enable one to know and to be aware, to conceptualize and use abstractions, reason, judge, criticize, and also be creative. It is difficult to discuss thinking skills apart from all the other things which correlate reading readiness because the growth of cognitive abilities cannot be separated from the basic growth of the individual. Thinking skills are very much a part of auditory and visual perception, language ability, memory, and also areas of motor and social learning. Nevertheless, a cluster of thinking skills is a prerequisite for children to be able to learn to read.

**Attending**

This refers to the ability of a child to concentrate on a task for a prolonged period of time. Attentional abilities are essential if the child is to receive necessary information and to retain this information in order to learn to read. Many of our handicapped readers exhibit characteristics of distractibility, impulsivity, and a lack of perseverence and patience.

Attentional deficits are viewed as most critical in the area of the learning disabled child not being able to learn to read. Numerous studies have documented existence of attention problems in hyperactivity in a large percentage of learning disabled children. These estimates have ranged from as low as 33 percent to as high as 80 percent. Even the lowest estimates suggest attention disorders and hyperactivity are frequently encountered problems in children who have reading problems. Similarly, although a child can have attention problems and hyperactivity without also having a learning disability, the prevalence of learning disability is considerably higher in children who are inattentive and hyperactive.

**Disorders of Memory and Thinking**

Many children with learning disabilities demonstrate memory deficits for both auditory and visual stimuli. These children are deficient in using strategies that nondisabled children use in situations requiring memory. For example, most children when presented with a list of words to memorize will rehearse the names to themselves. They will also make use of categories by rehearsing words in groups that go together. Children with learning disabilities, however, do not generally use these strategies spontaneously.

Children with learning disabilities and reading disorders find it especially difficult to remember verbal material because they have particular problems with phonological information. Phonology refers to the sounds, or phonemes, that make-up words.

**Concepts**

Concepts, according to Kirk, Kliebhan, and Lerner (1978) are symbols that stand for a class of objects or events with common properties. For example, the word *dog* does not stand for a particular dog, such as a collie, chow, or dachshund, but for an essense that is common to all of these dogs. The readers' experiential inconceptual backgrounds are extremely important in vocabulary development. Background experiences enable readers to develop, expand, and refine concepts represented by words. Vocabulary knowledge is developmental and is related to background experiences. Holdaway (1986) notes two phases in the learning of concepts. The first phase is the formation of concepts in relation to attributes which they refer to as prototypes. These attributes make connections with existing concepts. The second phase is using procedural knowledge, which is, the classification skills of generalizing and discriminating between newly encountered instances of associated concepts. In phase one, individuals may undergeneralize or overgeneralize due to their limited experiences with the concept. This is often evident in young children when they call horses cows and water, Coke®, milk, or juice. In phase two, the individuals can distinguish between horses and cows and milk and water and Cokes, etc. Some children have more difficulty though with more abstract symbols such as between, fairness, result, yet. Children who lack concepts need environmental and educational experiences which will help them build the needed concepts.

## Organization and Classification Abilities

In order for children to associate and relate information they must be able to organize and have classification abilities. Each new piece of learning and bits of learning must be related to what the child already knows or it will be quickly forgotten. In other words, we have to have a base in order to remember things. We have to be able to associate in other words.

## Physical Fitness and Motor Development

If the child is going to learn properly, he must be alert, be able to concentrate, and to have energy. The child who tires easily or is listless may have underlying problems. The problems may be medical or it may be that the child stays up too late at night or is not eating properly.

There are a lot of educators who think that adequate motor development is a prerequisite of reading achievement. According to many authors, motor learning is a foundation for cognitive learning and without adequate motor development the child is not ready to acquire the cognitive skills needed in reading. The child not only needs gross motor skills but also fine motor skills. Gross motor skills involve walking, running, jumping, hopping, skipping, etc. The fine motor skills involve hand/eye coordination such as using two hands, cutting, pasting, tracing, writing, etc. It is very common for reading readiness programs to include both gross motor and fine motor activities.

## Social and Emotional Development

The child must be socially and emotionally well adjusted in order to get along with peers and teachers. The child who is not is often a loner and ostracized by his peers. This interferes with the self-esteem that each child acquires and this self-esteem is important in academic achievement. One cannot emphasize the importance enough of self-esteem in the learning process. The child must be able to control his temper, he must be able to help himself, in other words to be self-relient, he must be able to participate in group activities. This author believes that self-confidence and self-esteem are prerequisites for learning to read. The child who is overdependent, intolerant, aggressive, unhappy, overly shy, or who often has temper tantrums is hindered in the reading readiness process.

## Interest and Motivation

Learning to read requires hard work and effort, therefore, the child must be interested and motivated to learn this difficult task. One of the essential elements of learning to read is the desire to acquire this skill. (Donnie was a first grade child who showed little desire to learn to read. When questioned by the teacher it was found that Donnie did not have breakfast and was hungry. Donnie explained that he could not keep his mind on the book when his stomach was feeling empty and growling.) One of the essential elements of learning to read then is that the child must have a strong inclination to learn and to put forth effort.

## Tests for Assessing Readiness

There are several kinds of measures which can be used to assess the child's readiness for reading. This section discusses the use of: (a) intelligence tests, (b) reading readiness tests, and (c) tests of specific mental functions.

## Using Intelligence Tests to Assess Readiness

General intelligence tests give us a global picture of the child's mental age and IQ. We must also analyze the subtest to determine a child's major abilities and disabilities. Tests of specific mental functioning are also needed to show if there are imbalances in mental abilities. A child may score high on one of the Wechsler tests in the performance areas and low in the verbal areas. This child could very well have a reading problem but still be able to work puzzles and have good manipulative skills. However, when we average the scores, the IQ may come out to be 100, yet the child is not ready to learn to read at this time.

## Reading Readiness Tests

A number of tests are designed specifically to assess readiness for reading. Reading readiness tests are generally given to all children during the kindergarten year or at the beginning of the first grade before the formal teaching of reading begins. Sometimes placement in first grade reading groups is based on the results of the readiness test. These tests generally measure visual discrimination, vocabulary, number ability, sentence comprehension, knowledge of the names of the letters of the alphabet, and so on. Commonly used reading readiness tests include:

Comprehensive Tests of Basic Skills, Readiness Tests (1977)

Cooperative Preschool Inventory (English Edition, 1970), (Spanish Edition, 1974)

Metropolitan Readiness Test (two levels, 1976)

Test of Basic Concepts-Revised (1985). New York: The Psychological Corporation, Forms C and D. Intended Level: Kindergarten and Grades One and Two

Bracken Basic Concept Scale. (1984). Columbus, OH: Merrill. Forms A and B. Intended Level: Ages 2½ to 8

Concepts About Print Tests (Clay, 1972, 1979), Exeter, NH: Heinemann

Tests of Specific Mental Functions

Some formal tests are useful in assessing specific mental functions that are prerequisites to learning to read. Some of those follow:

SRA Primary Mental Abilities Test

The Detroit Test of Learning Aptitude

The Illinois Test of Psycholinguistic Abilities

Goldman Fristoe-Woodcock Test of Auditory Discrimination

Lindamood Auditory Conceptualization Test

Test of Auditory Comprehension of Language—Revised

## SUMMARY

Readiness refers to a state of development that is needed before a skill can be learned. Reading readiness, therefore, is the collection of integrated abilities, traits and skills a child needs before he can learn the complex process called reading.

Components of reading readiness include mental maturity, visual and auditory ability, speech and language development, thinking skills, physical fitness, motor development, social and emotional development, and interest and motivation.

Many experts and much research have determined that a mental age of 6.0 to 6.6 is required for the majority of children to learn to read. However, it is difficult to know when any particular child is ready to try to learn and read until he appears to be ready. This is true regardless of mental age.

It would appear that there are many factors and these factors in combination must be present for a reading disability to develop. We know that low intelligence is correlated with reading disability. We know that high intelligence is correlated with early ability to read. However, there are many bright children who do not learn to read when they are six years old. I doubt seriously if any mentally retarded child has ever learned to read before the age of six. We must assume that intelligence is important in learning to read. However, between the IQ of 85 to 105, there are many other correlates involved in the reading process. Any combination of these correlates could cause a reading disability. Other than intelligence, seldom does one correlate cause disability. Therefore, we can assume that several of these correlates must interact with each other for a disability in reading to occur.

## REFERENCES

Aman, M. G. & Singh, N. N. (1983). Specific reading disorders: Concepts of etiology reconsidered. In K. D. Gadow & I. Bealer (Eds.), *Advances in Learning and Behavioral Disabilities* (Vol. 2, pp. 1–47). Greenwich, CT: JAI Press.

Bouchard, T. J., Jr., & Segal, N. L. (1985). Environment and IQ. In B. B. Wolman (Ed.), *Handbook of Intelligence: Theories, Measurements, and Applications* (pp. 391–464). New York: Wiley.

Capron, C. & Duyme, M. (1989, August 17). Assessment of effects of socio-economic status on IQ in a full cross-fostering study. *Nature,* pp. 552–553.

Harris, A. (1961). *How to Increase Reading Ability* (4th ed.). New York: David McKay.

Holdaway, D. (1986). The visual face of experience and language: A metalinguistic excursion. In D. B. Yaden, Jr. and S. Templeton (Eds.), *Metalinguistic Awareness and Beginning Literacy: Conceptualizing What It Means to Read and Write* (pp. 13–19). Portsmouth, NH: Heinemann.

Humphreys, L. G. (1985). General intelligence: An integration of factor, test, and simplex theory. In B. B. Wolman (Ed.), *Handbook of Intelligence: Theories, Measurements, and Applications* (pp. 201–224). New York: Wiley.

Jensen, A. R. (1979b). The nature of intelligence and its relation to learning. *Journal of Research and Development in Education, 12*(2), 79–95.

Kirk, S. A. & Gallagher, J. J. (1986). *Educating Exceptional Children* (3rd ed.). Boston: Houghton Mifflin.

Kirk, S. A., Kliebhan, S. J. M. & Lerner, J. W. (1978). *Teaching Reading to Slow Learners.* Boston: Houghton Mifflin.

Myklebust, H. (1968). "Learning Disabilities: Definition and Overview." In *Progress in Learning Disabilities* (Vol. 1, pp. 1–15). New York: Grune & Stratton.

McGue, M., Shinn, M., & Ysseldyke, J. (1982). Use of cluster scores on the Woodcock-Johnson Psycho-Educational Battery with learning disabled students. *Learning Disabilities Quarterly, 5,* 274–287.

Plomin, R. & DeFries, J. C. (1980). Genetics and intelligence: Recent data. *Intelligence, 4,* 15–24.

Sattler, J. (1988). *Assessment of Children* (3rd ed.). San Diego: J. M. Sattler.

Skeels, H. (1966). *Adult Status of Children from Contrasting Early Life Experiences*

(Monographs of the Society for Research in Child Development, No. 31). Chicago: University of Chicago Press.

Skeels, H. & Dye, H. (1939). A study of the effects of differential stimulation on mentally retarded children. *Proceedings of the American Association on Mental Deficiency, 44,* 114–136.

Stanovich, K. E., Cunningham, A. E., & Freeman, D. J. (1984). Intelligence, cognitive skills, and early reading progress. *Reading Research Quarterly, 19,* 279–303.

Vanderberg, S. G. & Vogler, G. P. (1985). Genetic determinants of intelligence. In B. B. Wolman (Ed.), *Handbook of Intelligence: Theories, Measurements, and Applications* (pp. 3–57). New York: Wiley.

Zigler, E. & Farber, E. A. (1985). Commonalities between the intellectual extremes: Giftedness and mental retardation. In F. D. Horowitz and M. O'Brien (Eds.), *The Gifted and Talented: Developmental Perspectives* (pp. 387–408). Washington, DC: American Psychological Association.

# Chapter 3

# DEVELOPMENTAL READING
# METHODS AND MATERIALS

Developmental reading refers to the patterns and sequence of normal reading growth and development and also to the methods and materials used in the regular classroom for children who are learning to read at a normal pace. When we find what a normal pace is for the children in the regular classroom, we can then compare our handicapped children with the rate of growth that a normal child would have. The teacher who desires to help children with reading problems must have an excellent knowledge of developmental reading. Once the teacher understands how the normal child grows and develops in reading, modifications of developmental methods can be made for the handicapped learner. In addition, the teacher of slow and disabled learners must be competent in the special and remedial methods that have been developed over the years to help handicapped learners with the difficult skill of reading.

Probably there has been more effort, research, and debate in the area of teaching reading than in any other area of the curriculum. Despite this effort, research into methods of teaching reading has failed to prove that one method is superior to the other. Most children can learn to read by using any method. However, there are a few children who must be given special methods or they will not learn to read. The one variable that we cannot discount is the teacher. A good teacher will find a method to teach all the children to read at some degree or level. What we must realize is that some children will only read at the first grade level even with the best instruction. We will find other children who will read at the fifth or sixth grade even with the best instruction. Some of our SLD children can learn to read at the expected level or grade placement or even above grade placement with excellent teaching and with specified methods and materials.

We are concerned in this book with teaching reading to handicapped learners. This does not mean that we cannot take materials which have been developed over the years for the average or normal learner and use them with atypical learners. Most of the materials developed for the average or normal learner can be used for the atypical learner. Also, it should be pointed out that research has not shown that certain methods should be used exclusively with one type of exceptionality such as mentally retarded youngsters or specific learning disabled children. Each classification of exceptionality comprises a heterogeneous group of learners. In other words, we have individuals who need different methods and materials that fall into each group of exceptionalities. It is very important that teachers who work with atypical learners be familiar with the many methods and materials which have been developed over the years in the teaching of reading.

During the early years of education in the United States, an alphabet method of teaching reading was utilized. Children first learned the alphabet, then started to read by spelling words. When this author attended school in the 1930s and early 1940s, a method of teaching reading using the alphabet was used. The children would name the letters, c—a—t, and then pronounce the word "cat." This was a slow and laborious process, but it was used successfully in the schools in America in the 1930s and early 1940s, and even before that. Let's go back to the Old Deluder Satan Act, though, which was an act in Massachusetts which stated that all towns of a certain size should have an elementary school. The first method of teaching reading in the first elementary schools was the alphabet method. I have already stated that it was slow and laborious and the teachers decided to add phonics whereby children learned the sound rather than the name of the letter. They were able then to decode words, and thus they learned to read faster with the alphabet and phonics than they did with just the alphabet. Later, educators discovered that children could learn words as wholes without learning either the alphabet or phonics. It was also observed that during the initial stages of reading, children could learn simple phrases and simple sentences without knowing the phonic elements. It should be stressed here, though, that for the first two years of reading, this author believes that phonics is imperative.

# DEVELOPMENT STAGES IN THE READING PROCESS

In spite of all the research on reading, there is still a great controversy about the phonics method, the experience method, the linguistic method, or some other approach. From generation to generation, different methods have been favored and many people swear by the method used when they were children.

These controversies arise because the various experts are dealing with a different part of the problem, namely, each child's particular stage of development as it pertains to the reading process.

In 1940, Kirk (1940) applied the theories and stages of development proposed by the biologist, Coghill (1929), to the process of reading. Kirk concluded that studies in biology and psychology indicate that the general process of human development follows three stages, namely: (1) mass action, (2) differentiation, and (3) integration. He stated (Kirk, 1940) that when you apply these to the reading process, these developmental stages become: (1) reading wholes, (2) learning details, and (3) reading without awareness of details.

## STAGE I: READING WHOLES

In this stage, children rely heavily on memory and configuration. One of the weaknesses of the mentally retarded child is that his memory is poor and, therefore, he cannot rely on it very well. Also the child who suffers from a specific learning disability often cannot use his memory as well as average children and this becomes a handicap. Regardless, all children are presented with a short written passage usually based on their own experience. They must then use their memory so that they can understand what is being said by the teacher when she reads the sentences as wholes. The child will get a visual picture of each word and each sentence and recall it as the teacher is reading it. When the teacher outlines the configuration of the sentence, this can help the child immensely.

In other words, a child's first impression is of whole sentences or of a short story, which they remember. These children are only vaguely aware of the blocks and gaps between words and they do not necessarily recognize the separate words or letters in a passage.

After whole sentences or paragraphs are recognized in this manner, children can then gradually be lead into the second stage of reading which is learning details.

## STAGE II: LEARNING DETAILS

After the child has successfully gone through Stage I: Reading Wholes, he is then ready for Stage II: Learning Details. The initial phase of Stage II is word discrimination. Attention is called to the separate words that make up the sentence by having children see each word as a whole. We know that many average and superior children need little instruction in learning the details, but we also know that most children in special education do need instruction in learning a specific method as they go from wholes to details.

In the secondary phase of Stage II the child must learn to discriminate between words such as *dog* and *beautiful.* But, the child must also learn to discriminate between words such as *dog* and *boy* and this is more difficult. The configuration of the words is the same but it is still more difficult to discriminate between *dog* and *boy* than between *dog* and *beautiful.* Therefore, in the second phase of Stage Two the child must learn the components of each word.

## STAGE III: AWARENESS OF DETAILS

In Stage III, the child must learn to read without awareness of details. The purpose of reading is to comprehend through units without being aware of the details on the printed page. This process, according to Kirk (1940), is known as cue reduction. For example, a child who is learning to read gets to the point that he does not think and it just becomes mechanical. Then he has mastered Stage III. Naturally, before we get to Stage I, which was reading wholes, the child must have mastered the letters of the alphabet.

Kirk, Lerner, and Kliebhan (1978) state:

> According to the three-stage model of reading (reading wholes, learning details, and reading without awareness of details), the alphabet and phonics methods emphasize Stage II rather than Stage I at the beginning of reading instruction. The three-stage model, however, suggests that only after the child has experience in perceiving objects, pictures, and words as wholes should direct instruction be given in observing details through the use of phonics and word analysis. Larger thought units can be introduced later so that the child, through the process of cue reduction, can read without noting the details of words or sentences, yet can fall back on them if necessary. It should be noted, however, that some reading authorities believe that teaching reading should begin with the teaching of phonics.
>
> Teachers of atypical learners have a more difficult task than teachers of normal children, since slow and disabled learners are likely to be deficient in

making inferences, in learning by themselves, and in using cue reduction. The teacher, therefore, must be alert to detect the stage at which the child is reading and must intensify the instruction to aid the slow learner in some of the steps that the average child learns without instruction. Teachers who recognize the three stages of reading can formulate a method to fit the process of reading at each particular stage" (p. 73).

# METHODS OF READING INSTRUCTION

## Meaning Emphasis Versus Code Emphasis

In 1967, Chall tells us that reading generally falls into two main groups and these two reflect differences in the instructional approach used. The first group is based on the "meaning emphasis" approach, while the second is based on the "code emphasis" approach. In the meaning emphasis, stress is placed on the immediate acquisition of meaning through learning whole words, and paragraphs at sight. The phonetic instruction is introduced later. In this group, most of the basal reading series that emphasize story content are included. On the other hand, the code emphasis approach stresses the early introduction of the sound-symbol system and the principles of phonics, with individualized instruction emphasized. In general, code emphasis approaches place greatest stress on word recognition skills and less on meaning. Several methods of teaching reading combine elements of both the meaning and code-emphasis approaches. Below, methods that stress meaning will be treated first.

### MEANING-EMPHASIS APPROACH

There are many approaches of reading instruction that are primarily meaning-emphasis approaches. The basal reader, individualized reading, and language-experience methods are presented here.

### Conventional Basal Readers

The conventional basal reading approach is one of the most commonly used in the schools today. It is not an approach that should be used exclusively in special education, but it can be used along with some of the other approaches. One reason for its popularity is the convenience provided a teacher in the materials which go along with the basal reader. In this approach, initial emphasis is on the development of a minimum sight vocabulary. If the teacher in special education uses the basal reader approach, he or she should remember that the criterion of success is not the number of pages covered, but rather how well the child has mastered the reading task at hand. One of the criticisms of the basal reader is that it is more designed for girls than boys and that it does not fit the experiences of the children. Once again, if the teacher uses the basal reader, he or she should use one or two other approaches for teaching reading.

**Individualized Reading**

The individualized reading method permits each child to read material at his or her own choosing and at his or her own rate. Emphasis is placed on comprehending the meaning of words and sentences from the beginning even before word analysis is begun.

A wide variety of reading material at different levels of difficulty are made available to the children. Each child can bring from home a book, magazine, or newspaper that he or she wishes to read independently. The child can ask the teacher for any help and ask the teacher to answer questions as often as is needed. The teacher will have a conference with each child and ask the child to read part of a story orally to check on comprehension. The child works individually and supplements the individual reading with some group activities and workbooks. This method is of questionable value with the slow learning, retarded or learning disabled child.

**Language-Experience Method**

The language experience method of teaching reading utilizes the child's own experiences and vocabulary. The teacher uses an experience chart and writes a story with the children furnishing the details. The teacher already knows the story that she is going to write on the experience chart, but she gets the children to present the story the way she wants it to go on the chart. For example, after a field trip to a farm, the teacher may ask the class to begin a story on "where we went yesterday and what we found on the farm." After the story is written on the chart, each line and word of the story are pointed out by the teacher while the children repeat the story in unison. Clearly, this represents Stage I of the reading process-reading wholes. After the children can read each sentence meaningfully, they are asked to match or identify single words. The teacher uses a pointer and points to single words and calls a child's name and the child identifies that word. Attention is thus called to Stage II-learning details.

### Code-Emphasis Approach

Below, the author will present some of the code-emphasis approaches:

**Phonics Methods.** There are many phonics methods that are published today which a teacher can use with the handicapped learner. Most phonics methods teach children to associate speech sounds with letters or groups of letters to help them pronounce unfamiliar words. The teaching of phonics should be started early and last through the first two years. After that, all the reading approaches have enough phonics in them to be sufficient for most of our handicapped readers.

**Linguistic Methods.** Findings from the field of linguistics have given us a better understanding of the reading process. The linguistic approach differs from the conventional basal reader approach in that breaking the written language code is emphasized rather than meaning. It also differs from phonics approaches in that the sound elements are not presented in isolation. In linguistic reading material, words are read as wholes, beginning with words that have a regular spelling pattern and then go into words that do not have a regular spelling pattern. The linguistic approach assumes that children are able to discover for themselves the relationship between sounds and letters. A sample of linguistic reading materials is the Initial Teaching Alphabet (ITA).

This approach was used a few years ago and it had 54 characters with each symbol representing one speech sound in the English language. The Initial Teaching Alphabet is discussed in another chapter in this book, but it was popular for a while in the United States in the latter part of the 1960s and early part of the 1970s. It is still a good approach, but many people have gone on to newer approaches and left the older ones behind. The reader should be advised that just because an approach is 30 or 40 years old does not mean that it is not a good approach.

## A PROGRESSION OF READING SKILLS

Vernon (1979) tells us that learning to read involves the successive acquisition of a number of hierarchically organized skills that are finally integrated. Vernon (1979) also lists the stages in learning to read:

1. Differentiating and identifying the individual letter shapes or graphemes. This process involves abstracting and generalizing significant features and ignoring irrelevant features.
2. Learning to associate graphemes with appropriate phonemes and breaking whole words down into sounds.
3. Gradually grasping the variations in grapheme-phoneme association in different word contexts.
4. Sampling the most significant words while scanning a sentence without directly perceiving all of them. One understands the whole sentence by integrating the semantically and syntactically related words into meaningful units of thought.

Sattler (1988) further talks about the stages in the reading process:

Children with reading difficulties may be stuck at different stages in the reading process, for reading difficulties may be associated with deficiencies in information processing skills connected with any of these stages. The processes most often affected are analyzing complex perceptual patterns, attending to and extracting their significant characteristic details, organizing these details, and generalizing these organizations conceptually. As reading progresses, these processes are applied to more complex material, and word meanings must be integrated in the reading process. Reading difficulty, then, typically is a form of cognitive deficiency manifested by different individuals at different stages in learning to read.

Siegel and Linder (1984) also discuss research about the learning stages of children:

Research suggests that younger learning-disabled children (8 to 9 years of age) have a deficiency in phonological coding, whereas older learning-disabled children (10 to 13 years of age) use a phonemic code but have a more general deficit in short-term memory, particularly in the context of language processing. These findings are important because they suggest that a phonemic code does develop in the short-term memory of learning disabled children, albeit more slowly.

The following poem illustrates some of the complexities involved in learning how to read English (Author unknown):

### Our Incredible Language

When the English tongue we speak
Why is "break" not rhymed with "freak?"
Will you tell me why it's true
We say "sew" but likewise "few?"
And the maker of a verse
Cannot cap his "horse" with "worse."
"Beard" sounds not the same as "heard."
"Cord" is different from "word."
Cow is "cow," but low is "low."

"Shoe" is never rhymed with "roe."
Think of "hose" and "dose" and "lose."
And think of "goose" and yet of "choose."
Think of "comb" and "tomb" and "bomb."
"Doll" and "roll" and "home" and "come."
And since "pay" is rhymed with "say,"
Why not "paid" with "said," I pray?
We have "blood" and "food" and "good,"
"Mould" is not pronounced like "could."
Wherefore "done" but "gone" and "lone."
Is there any reason known?
And, in short, it seems to me
Sounds and letters disagree.

## INDIVIDUAL DIFFERENCES IN PERCEPTUAL–COGNITIVE PROCESSES RELATED TO READING ABILITY

Research on the relationship between perceptual-cognitive processes and reading ability suggests the following (Sattler, 1988):

1. Deficient eye movement patterns do not appear to cause reading problems.
2. Visual processing abilities—such as iconic memory (brief initial representation of an external stimulus), feature extraction (identification of relevant features of an external stimulus), visual segmentation (isolation of relevant aspects of the visual field)—are at best weakly related to reading fluency.
3. Phonological awareness and phonological coding skills are strongly linked with early acquisition of reading ability.
4. Difficulty in accessing the name code of a symbolic stimulus is only weakly linked to reading deficits.
5. "The ability to recognize words automatically is related to reading skill, but a strong relationship is only present in the early stages of reading acquisition" (Stanovich, 1985, p. 200).
6. "Skilled readers are adept at [using] contextual strategies to facilitate comprehension, but skilled and less skilled readers are equally adept at using context to facilitate word recognition. . . . Poor readers may fail to show contextual effects in situations where their deficient word recognition skills have rendered the context functionally useless: (Stanovich, 1985, p. 193).

Table 3.1.
**A Summary of Research Findings on Etiological Components of Reading Disability.**

| *Etiological component* | *Findings* |
| --- | --- |
| | *Physiological Factors* |
| Brain damage | Studies suggest that moderate to severe brain damage is likely associated with reading disability. The degree of association is not strong, however. Many children with mild or subtle neurological damage do not have reading difficulty. |
| Maturational lag | Studies indicate that children with reading disability display lags on psychological and other behavioral tests. Studies are unclear, however, about whether children with reading disability will catch up to their peers. We do not know whether the lags reflect true maturational delay or are symptoms of a general neurological dysfunction. |
| Genetic inheritance | Studies in this area have been poorly designed. Therefore, it is difficult to estimate the degree to which genetic factors affect reading disability. It is unclear whether genetic factors affect reading independent of intelligence or whether reading difficulty is part of a more pervasive picture influenced in part by low intelligence. |
| Cerebral dominance | Studies indicate that few generalizations can be made about the role of cerebral asymmetry in reading disorders. Conceptual and methodological problems plague this area of research. |
| Ocular factors | Studies indicate that there is little evidence that peripheral ocular factors play an important role in reading disorders. |
| | *Nonphysiological Factors* |
| Environmental causes | Studies indicate that environmental conditions—such as social class, family size, geographical location, child-rearing practices, family history of reading problems, economic disadvantage, school factors, level of parents' education, overcrowding, broken home, and motivational factors—are clearly associated with academic attainment, which depends on reading proficiency. The findings are not proof of a cause-effect relationship, however. Some environmental factors also are associated with genetic influences. |
| Behavioral factors | Studies clearly indicate that children with specific reading disorders frequently have behavioral and emotional problems, including hyperactivity, inattention, and conduct problems. Although behavioral factors may not necessarily cause reading disorders, they may play a role in sustaining reading difficulties. |

*Source:* Adapted from Aman and Singh (1983).

7. Short-term memory is related to reading ability. "Poorer readers are less adept at employing the active, planful memorization strategies (e.g., verbal rehearsal, elaboration) known to facilitate memory performance" (Stanovich, 1985, p. 195). Strategy deficiency cannot explain all of the memory difficulties experienced by poor readers, however. Some memory problems may be due to inadequate phonological coding.

8. Less skilled readers have comprehension deficits that are independent of their decoding skills, such as depressed listening comprehension and poor use of general comprehension strategies (for example, inefficient comprehension monitoring, inefficient manner of approaching text [for example, too much passivity], inefficient text-scanning strategies, less sensitivity to text structure, and less elaborate encoding of text.

## ETIOLOGY OF READING DISABILITY

Sattler (1988) tells us that research on possible causes of reading difficulty—including brain damage, maturational lag, genetic factors, right-hemisphere dominance, ocular factors, environmental factors, and behavioral factors—is inconclusive with respect to the etiology of reading disorders (see Table 3.1). Like learning disabilities in general, reading disability is likely to be multifactorial in origin. Much remains to be learned about the mysteries of reading disability.

## REFERENCES

Cassidy, V. M., & Stanton, J. E. (1959). *An Investigation of Factors Involved in the Educational Placement of Mentally Retarded Children: A Study of Differences Between Children in Special and Regular Classes in Ohio.* U.S. Office of Education Cooperative Research Project, No. 032. Syracuse, NY: Syracuse University Research Institute.

Coghill, G. E. (1929). *Anatomy and the Problem of Behavior.* New York: Macmillan.

Individuals with Disabilities Education Act (IDEA) (PL 101-476).

Kelly, E. M. (July 1934). The improvement of reading in special classes for mentally retarded children. *Proceedings, American Association Mental Deficiency, 39,* 67–73.

Kirk, S. A. (1940). *Teaching Reading to Slow Learning Children.* Boston: Houghton-Mifflin Co.

Kirk, S. A. (1936). *Manual of Directions for Use with the Hegge-Kirk-Kirk Remedial Reading Drills.* Ann Arbor, MI: George Wahr.

Kirk, S. A., Kliebhan, S. J. M., & Lerner, J. W. (1978). *Teaching Reading to Slow and Disabled Learners.* Boston: Houghton Mifflin.

Sattler, J. M. (1988). *Assessment of Children* (3rd ed.). San Diego: Jerome M. Sattler.

Selz, M. (1981). Halstead-Reitan Neuropsychological Test Battery for Children. In G. W. Hynd & J. E. Obrzut (Eds.), *Neuropsychological Assessment and the School-Age Child: Issues and Procedures* (pp. 195–235). New York: Grune & Stratton.

Selz, M., & Reitan, R. M. (1979). Neuropsychological test performance of normal, learning-disabled, and brain damaged older children. *Journal of Nervous and Mental Disease, 167,* 298–302.

Siegel, L. S., & Linder, B. A. (1984). Short-term memory processes in children with reading and arithmetic learning disabilities. *Developmental Psychology, 20,* 200–207.

Stanovich, K. E. (1985). Cognitive determinants of reading in mentally retarded individuals. *International Review of Research in Mental Retardation, 13,* 181–214.

Stanovich, K. E. (1978). Information processing in mentally retarded individuals. *International Review of Research in Mental Retardation, 9,* 29–60.

Stanovich, K. E., Cunningham, A. E., & Cramer, B. B. (1984). Assessing phonological awareness in kindergarten children: Issues of task comparability. *Journal of Experimental Child Psychology, 38,* 175–190.

Stanovich, K. E., Cunningham, A. E., & Freeman, D. J. (1984). Intelligence, cognitive skills, and early reading progress. *Reading Research Quarterly, 19,* 278–303.

Vernon, P. E. (1979). *Intelligence: Heredity and Environment.* San Francisco: W. H. Freeman.

# Chapter 4

# ADAPTATION OF METHODS AND MATERIALS
# FOR ATYPICAL LEARNERS:
# EARLY STAGES OF READING

O ne of the outcomes of the noncategorical movement in special education is an emphasis on the commonality rather than the differences among the various categories of handicapped children. The message from this noncategorical movement is that there is not a specific approach for teaching the mentally retarded, another for the specific learning disabled, another for the slow learning child. Instead, diagnostic and teaching methods cut across all the categories of handicapping conditions. It should be further pointed out that noncategorical positions suggest that more important than the category of the handicap are the factors such as the child's abilities and disabilities in learning, the present developmental levels, the functioning ability of the child, and his attitude toward learning. In short, there is a tremendous overlap in the ways of teaching reading to children who are identified as handicapped.

## LEVELS OF LEARNING PERFORMANCE
## FOR ATYPICAL LEARNERS

The mentally retarded and children having IQ's between 70 to 90 who are called slow learners vary in degree only of the retardation. Disabled learners exhibit differences in abilities and can only reach a limited reading level. Retarded children sometimes can reach the third grade level in reading performance and will not go further than their capabilities indicate. Children with severe learning disabilities may have difficulty achieving high reading performance, but some of them do read up to their ability after a great deal of instruction. Nevertheless, certain reading functions are needed and can be set as realistic goals by the special education teacher. It should be pointed out that there are three levels of performance: (1) reading for protection, (2) reading for information or instruction, and (3) reading for pleasure. It should be stated by the author that we don't have a way of knowing what the ceiling is for each child. We must keep the door open for further achievement.

### Reading for Protection

Children having IQ's below 50 can learn to read only simple words and phrases. We call these children moderately and profoundly retarded and it would be frustrating to the teacher and the child to try to achieve more than this. For such a child, the aim of reading instruction is to help him read certain signs and certain information for self-protection.

The child should learn to read such phrases as the following: *exit, doctor, ladies, restroom, boys, stop, go, keep out, danger, bus station, no trespassing.*

### Reading for Information or Instruction

Most of the mildly retarded will be able to learn to read for information and instruction. They can be taught to look up names in a telephone book, to read parts of the newspaper, to follow directions, and to read official signs and warnings.

### Reading for Pleasure

Many of the children having IQ's between 50 and 70 can learn to read for pleasure. Certainly the slow learning children with IQ's between 70 and 90 can learn to read certain books for pleasure. The teacher should be able to help children attain this goal.

## SPECIFIC DIRECTIONS FOR INSTRUCTION IN THE INITIAL STAGES OF READING

When we teach beginning reading to a nine- or ten-year-old retarded child who has failed to learn to read during the previous school year, we have a different problem than the beginning teaching to a six-year-old normal child who has not been faced with school failure. By the time the mentally retarded child is ready to learn to read, he has already faced a great deal of failure. For example, a nine-year-old child with an IQ of 70 is about ready to learn to read. In many cases this child has not only been badgered by teachers and parents, but other children because he has not been able to grasp the concept of reading. In all probability this child will not even know the letters of the alphabet. To teach such a child to read, the teacher must (1) establish the child's self-confidence, (2) introduce a great deal of repetition in the child's school life to letters of the alphabet and the early stages of reading, (3) use different modalities to teach the child, and (4) prolong each period of training for each stage of reading. Assessment of the child should be done on a weekly basis to determine if new material can be introduced.

After the child has been given all the preprimer and primer materials the teacher will then determine whether the child can profit from further instruction in reading. This can be determined by several methods and by knowing the child's mental ability.

## The Incidental Method

This method of teaching reading refers to the presentation of words and phrases related to the immediate experiences of the child. With the mentally retarded and specific learning disabled children as well as with slow learners, the Incidental Method can be used to help determine the readiness of the child for reading. The Incidental Method alone will not teach slow and disabled learners to read. The Incidental Learning Method though should be used as a method to help the child learn the words he uses in his environment.

During the course of the prereading activities, the teacher can gradually introduce words that are not in the child's present environmental living. If the child is beginning to learn these words, the teacher will then know that the child is ready to learn to read and that in all probability he has a mental age between 6.0–6.6.

During this beginning reading stage, a great deal of learning can be absorbed by the Incidental Learning Method. For example, the teacher can use signs around the building that the child is familiar with such as *boys, girls, exit,* and labels that we use on bulletin boards as well as other materials found in the school.

1. **Bulletin Boards** — A bulletin board can be utilized for incidental reading. We can place the names of the children on the bulletin board and simple directions for their participation in activities can be written on a bulletin board. For example, if Harold, Tom, and Betty are selected to perform various tasks, the teacher writes the name Harold, Tom, and Betty and their duties on the bulletin board. The children will learn to

recognize not only their names, but possibly some words and phrases. Later on the teacher may use the bulletin board to display new items and directions for the various activities engaged in by the children.

2. **Labels** — The teacher can use labels during the prereading period as well as during the beginning reading period. The teacher can place the word *chair* on a chair. Likewise labels can be made for *table, desk, door, wall,* and so forth and this gives the children a concrete example of a symbol. The teacher can then remove the labels and allow the children to replace them on the proper objects and this is when incidental learning takes place.

3. **Pictures** — Children can bring pictures of animals and children from magazines, newspapers, etc. and they can be hung on the wall. These pictures serve as a valuable tool in incidental learning and may be used with words, phrases, or sentences.

4. **Assignments** — During beginning reading, the children can be given certain assignments outside of the reading period. If the children are about to engage in hand work, the teacher may discuss what each child is going to do and write on the Experience Chart the directions, such as *Billy will sit at the table, Johnny will draw a picture,* and *Sally will set the table.*

5. **Greetings** — Greetings and other statements by the teacher may occasionally be written on the board in place of oral instructions. When the children come into the classroom, the teacher does not say anything except, with a pointer, she points to the directions on the board. She can write things like *"Good morning children," "Sit in your chairs," "Cross your legs," "Boys look at girls,"* and *"It is a good morning, children."*

6. **Rules** — The rules of health, cooperation, and classroom activities can be placed on printed cards and posted around the room. For example, the teacher can write *We brush our teeth* and statements like this and place them around the room. She then asks the children to go and point to various rules and this is incidental reading. The cards should be changed as frequently as the children learn them.

## The Language Experience

When reading is taught to slow learning, learning disabled, and mentally retarded children, we should use the Language Experience Method. The teacher will write on the Experience Chart and put the names of the students in the stories. The stories can be about any activities the students have been engaged in at a recent time. The teacher will ask the children to start a story and she will begin writing. The children will talk and the teacher will write. When the teacher is through, she takes a pointer and has the children read aloud. Then she goes and underlines certain words and with the pointer, has the children call the words out loud when she calls the name of the child. The typical sequence of six steps are used in the Language Experience Method and are described below:

**Step 1.** The teacher should first be sure that the children are ready to read. They should have a mental age between 6.0 and 6.6 and have a vocabulary and other abilities needed in reading plus the desire to read.

**Step 2.** The children should tell a story based on their immediate experiences.

**Step 3.** The paragraph that has been written on Day One is copied onto tablets by the children. On Day Two, the children continue telling the stories and the teacher continues writing on the Experience Chart. The children continue each day making their own tablet of the story that goes on the Experience Chart.

**Step 4.** On succeeding days, new paragraphs should be written on the Experience Chart. These stories can be made up in the form of a large book by the children.

**Step 5.** The teacher gives more presentations to the children who are slower. Each child will make his or her own book of stories. After the stories have been made from the Experience Chart, the teacher tells the children to continue writing and adding to the stories that the entire group has made on the Experience Chart.

An overhead projector or slide projector should be used by the teacher. Also a teacher can use a recorder so that the children can read the stories aloud and then listen to the recorder play them back.

**Step 6.** After the children have acquired a sight vocabulary through reading stories about their own experiences, the teacher can then help them become aware of details by teaching them how to recognize other words.

In special education some severely disabled readers will know hardly any words at all. When this occurs, the methods used in the Language-Experience Approach are often quite successful. Furthermore, the Language-Experience Approach, in its latter stages, can also be used with great success with average or even better than average readers. Smith (1985) pointed out "A computer when used as a word processor can be exciting for students and enhance the value of the Language-Experience

Approach." In using the Language-Experience Approach with a group of disabled readers, a method similar to the following may be used:

1. Discuss some event of great interest.
2. As the students dictate the story, write it on the Experience Chart
   a. use manuscript or cursive writing whichever is common to the age grade level of the group,
   b. use a heavy writing instrument such as a felt-tip pen,
   c. use the language of the students; do not attempt to alter it,
   d. make sure the students see the words as they are being written,
   e. use one line sentences for the severely disabled readers and gradually increase sentence length if the teacher notices any improvement,
   f. when the teacher begins a new sentence, emphasize the fact that you start from the left and proceed to the right, and
   g. emphasize the return sweep from the end of one sentence to the beginning of the next.

When the story is finished, the teacher should read it aloud. Then she should try to get the students to try to help her as a choral exercise.

As the students' reading ability grows, the teacher should let each student write and illustrate his or her own story. A great deal of emphasis should also be placed on rereading materials that were written earlier. After sight vocabulary begins to grow, the students can begin a library or to trade books.

The Language-Experience Approach appears to be especially appropriate for disabled readers because it becomes immediately meaningful to them. They are writing about events and experiences in their own lives and using their own speaking vocabulary. Another advantage is that it develops a feeling of security and the child feels successful because he is telling the story. It also gives meaning to reading because students begin to associate printed words with stories.

Although the Language-Experience Approach offers a number of advantages to disabled readers, there are some disadvantages of which the teacher should be aware. There is no step-by-step teacher's manual and there is no scope and sequence found in a teacher's manual. The teacher must be familiar with word lists and also must be able to diagnose each student's word analysis skills. There may also be difficulty in transferring the student's from reading material written by them to reading material written by adult authors. Many of the problems, though, that we encounter in the Language-Experience Approach can be overcome if the teacher is well trained.

## THE BEGINNING READING PERIOD: DURATION AND MATERIALS

If our children learn in a normal fashion, the chart reading period is usually planned for the first six to twelve weeks of the first grade. During this period, many charts and stories are read aloud by the teacher. The children gradually acquire a sight vocabulary of 100 or more words before preprimers and primers are given to them.

For the disabled learner, though, the beginning reading period requires more than six to twelve weeks. Let's assume that the child is nine years old and ready to learn to read. He has been bombarded with so much academics that he is very much afraid of learning. The teacher will have to gradually gain his confidence and make him believe that he is not going to be forced and that the teacher is not going to put a great deal of stress on him. This may require a prolonged chart—reading period, but in the long run, it will be helpful for the child. After a substantial chart—reading period, the children will find that books are not too difficult for them. In this way, encouragement will be there and discouragement may be avoided.

### Basal Readers

Most basal readers have been designed for average children. If we use them for the disabled reader, they will need modification.

The introduction of new vocabulary is often too rapid and frequently there is not enough repetition for the disabled reader. We need overlearning to assure mastery for the disabled reader and we need that repetition. To this end, some type of program such as DISTAR or duplicated stories that utilize words occurring in the first readers may be used over and over again. The teacher may also want to use a phonic's program such as Phono-Visual Approach. Our children in special education may enjoy reading preprimers and primers. However, as they get older and still read at the first and second grade level, they will find that these stories are too immature for them. That is when we need other reading material for exceptional children and we should keep the following points in mind:

1. We must continue chart reading and use duplicated stories and the overhead projector even after book reading has begun.

2. We must stress accuracy rather than speed with the slow and disabled learner. The children need to use a tape recorder because they like to hear their voices and, with the teacher's help, can pick up their mistakes.

3. When book learning has been introduced, we should find a variety of simple books which have high interest and low vocabulary for our atypical learners to read.

Many publishers of primary books are supplementing the regular basal reader with other reading material which comes at the same grade level for handicapped children who need more repetition of the same vocabulary. The Code Book Series which was first published by Lippincott Company in 1975 is a teacher-directed working text activity for slow learning children who will be experiencing difficulty in reading. This series can be used as a supplement or as an independent program. It can also be used for individual remediation by the regular class teacher, special education teacher, or remedial reading teacher. Rand, McNally and Company published a curriculum motivation series in 1972 which was devised for the less able readers. It is a supplementary material which follows the basal reading program. MacMillan Company published Solo Books in 1975 which is a supplement to the basal reader. Ginn and Company published its 720 Series in 1976. All of these companies still have supplementary programs which go along with the basal reader.

When we use supplementary materials, many more repetitions are given. These repetitions are necessary for the disabled learner. We should remember, however, that no book can be as meaningful as a story based on the child's immediate experiences. Therefore, supplementary readers should not completely replace made-up stories that we find in a class of special education students.

Our special education teachers often ask, "What words should be introduced and made a part of the child's sight vocabulary?" Dolch (1948, Table 4.1) did his research in the 1920s and published his list of the 220 most used basic sight-word vocabulary in the 1930s. This list, although it has been updated, has not changed very much since it was first published. Other sight vocabulary lists have been developed over the years (Hillerich, 1973, Table 4.2). Frye (1957) listed 600 instant words for sight recognition to be used with remedial reading students. We also have the Harrison-Jacobson core words (Harris & Sipay, 1975, p. 382) and is a list of 58 preprimer words, 63 primer words, and 220 first reader words.

## Sight Word Knowledge

Sometimes sight vocabulary refers to overall sight word knowledge. This is proper and involves instant recognition words, but not the meaning of words. The difference between sight words and basic sight words are not to be used interchangeably. Sight words refer to all words that a reader can recognize instantly while basic sight words refer to a designated list of words which is usually of high utility. These words generally appear on someone's list. Any word if read enough times can become a sight word, and thus each of us possesses a different sight vocabulary depending on such factors as, occupation, reading interests, ability to remember, etc.

Because of the difference in meaning of the terms sight word vocabulary and basic sight word vocabulary, techniques for diagnosis for each will be discussed separately. In testing for sight word knowledge, we usually use a sampling of words referred to as a graded sight-word list.

A number of researchers and writers have studied the utility of various words (Curtis, 1938; Hockett, 1938; Stone, 1939, 1941). Although these studies don't generally agree exactly, they are very close in the percentage of total running words that are accounted for by a certain number of words. Table 4.2 is a general summary of the results of these studies. The importance of learning to read and spell high utility words is emphasized by Richard Madden (1959) in a study of low- and high-utility words. Madden pointed out that there is very little value in attempting to teach students to spell words of lower utility unless they have mastered the words of high-utility. To illustrate how futile this is, Madden states that a child in grade two with only 5 percent misspellings in a random sample of the first 200 words in frequency will make more errors in writing than if the child misspells all 400 words in the commonly designated list for grade two. The same concept is true for reading.

William Derr (1973) studied the high frequency words in popular juvenile trade books. He found that in the 80 books studied, 10 words were of such high frequency that a young reader could expect to meet one in nearly every four words read. Derr further stated that the 188 high frequency words which he put into his list made up only 6 percent

Table 4.1. 220 Basic Word Sight Vocabulary.

| Preprimer | Primer | First | Second | Third |
|---|---|---|---|---|
| 1. the | 45. when | 89. many | 133. know | 177. don't |
| 2. of | 46. who | 90. before | 134. while | 178. does |
| 3. and | 47. will | 91. must | 135. last | 179. got |
| 4. to | 48. more | 92. through | 136. might | 180. united |
| 5. a | 49. no | 93. back | 137. us | 181. left |
| 6. in | 50. if | 94. years | 138. great | 182. number |
| 7. that | 51. out | 95. where | 139. old | 183. course |
| 8. is | 52. so | 96. much | 140. year | 184. war |
| 9. was | 53. said | 97. your | 141. off | 185. until |
| 10. he | 54. what | 98. may | 142. come | 186. always |
| 11. for | 55. up | 99. well | 143. since | 187. away |
| 12. it | 56. its | 100. down | 144. against | 188. something |
| 13. with | 57. about | 101. should | 145. go | 189. fact |
| 14. as | 58. into | 102. because | 146. came | 190. through |
| 15. his | 59. than | 103. each | 147. right | 191. water |
| 16. on | 60. them | 104. just | 148. used | 192. less |
| 17. be | 61. can | 105. those | 149. take | 193. public |
| 18. at | 62. only | 106. people | 150. three | 194. put |
| 19. by | 63. other | 107. Mr. | 151. states | 195. thing |
| 20. I | 64. new | 108. how | 152. himself | 196. almost |
| 21. this | 65. some | 109. too | 153. few | 197. hand |
| 22. had | 66. could | 110. little | 154. house | 198. enough |
| 23. not | 67. time | 111. state | 155. use | 199. far |
| 24. are | 68. these | 112. good | 156. during | 200. took |
| 25. but | 69. two | 113. very | 157. without | 201. head |
| 26. from | 70. may | 114. make | 158. again | 202. yet |
| 27. or | 71. then | 115. would | 159. place | 203. government |
| 28. have | 72. do | 116. still | 160. American | 204. system |
| 29. an | 73. first | 117. own | 161. around | 205. better |
| 30. they | 74. any | 118. see | 162. however | 206. set |
| 31. which | 75. my | 119. men | 163. home | 207. told |
| 32. one | 76. now | 120. work | 164. small | 208. nothing |
| 33. you | 77. such | 121. long | 165. found | 209. night |
| 34. were | 78. like | 122. get | 166. Mrs. | 210. end |
| 35. her | 79. our | 123. here | 167. thought | 211. why |
| 36. all | 80. over | 124. between | 168. went | 212. called |
| 37. she | 81. man | 125. both | 169. say | 213. didn't |
| 38. there | 82. me | 126. life | 170. part | 214. eyes |
| 39. would | 83. even | 127. being | 171. once | 215. find |
| 40. their | 84. most | 128. under | 172. general | 216. going |
| 41. we | 85. made | 129. never | 173. high | 217. look |
| 42. him | 86. after | 130. day | 174. upon | 218. asked |
| 43. been | 87. also | 131. same | 175. school | 219. later |
| 44. has | 88. did | 132. another | 176. every | 220. knew |

*Source:* Dale D. Johnson, "The Dolch List Reexamined," *The Reading Teacher 24* (February, 1971), pp. 455–456. The 220 most frequent words in the Kucera-Francis corpus.

**Table 4.2. The 190 Starter Words in Order of Frequency of Use (4 original lists).**

Midyear Norms, based on individual recognition testing in three school districts:
+ = Grade 1 (N = 186)—eighty-nine words were known by 50 percent or more of pupils.
  Grade 2 (N = 208)—all words were known by 50 percent except *through* (47 percent).
  Grade 3 (N = 208)—all known by 75 percent, except *through* (71 percent), *every* (61 percent), *were* (50 percent).

| | | | | |
|---|---|---|---|---|
| + the | from | + down | only | last |
| + and | + up | back | much | away |
| + a | + will | just | + us | each |
| + to | + do | year | + take | never |
| + of | + said | + little | name | while |
| + in | + then | + make | + here | + took |
| + it | what | who | say | men |
| + is | + like | after | got | next |
| + was | her | people | around | may |
| + I | + go | \| come | any | + Mr. |
| + he | + them | + no | use | give |
| + you | time | because | place | show |
| + that | + if | first | put | once |
| + for | + some | more | + boy | something |
| + on | about | many | water | + room |
| they | + by | know | also | must |
| + with | + him | made | before | didn't |
| + have | + or | thing | + off | always |
| + are | + can | went | through | + car |
| + had | + me | + man | right | told |
| + we | + your | want | ask | why |
| + be | + an | way | most | small |
| + one | + day | + work | should | children |
| + but | their | which | don't | still |
| + at | other | + good | than | head |
| + when | very | well | three | left |
| + all | could | came | found | white |
| + this | + has | new | these | let |
| + she | + look | + school | saw | world |
| + there | + get | + too | find | under |
| + not | + now | been | tell | same |
| + his | + see | think | + help | kind |
| as | our | + home | every | + keep |
| were | + two | + house | again | + am |
| would | + into | + play | another | best |
| + so | + did | + old | + big | better |
| + my | over | long | night | soon |
| + out | + how | + where | thought | four |

*Source:* "Starter Words" © 1973, Robert L. Hillerich.

of all the different words found, then made up nearly 70 percent of the running words in print in the 80 books that he studied.

These studies illustrate the importance of learning certain core or basic sight words so that no word analysis skills are required when the student encounters them in print. It should be further stated that many of these high-utility words are not phonetically regular and do not lend themself to phonic word attack. Glen Gagon (1966) in quoting Arthur Heilman stated that approximately 35 percent of the usual primary reading vocabulary is phonetically regular. This author has analyzed other basic sight-word lists and found them to be 30–40 percent phonetically regular depending upon the number of phonetic rules applied.

When testing for knowledge of basic sight words, one must first appear so elementary that almost anyone would be likely to find this an easy task. During the past several years, however, this author has researched several different methods and the results differ considerably one from the other. There also has been considerable controversy over whether basic sight words should be tested in or out of context.

Many people assume that children know more basic sight words or service words when they are using context than when they are not. However, this author has found little evidence to support this. In one study in 1963, H. Allen Robinson found that only about one-seventh of 1 percent of the words he studied were identified by students through context clues alone. Even when context, configuration, and phonetical structural elements are used together, students only scored 3.93 correct out of 22 possible responses.

This author has also heard reading specialists say that it is not fair to the child to test a word out of context. First of all, this author will say "What is fair and what is not fair?" Even if context were a valuable aid, some of the time you would not want a child not to know the same word at another time. The child should know the word whether in context or not.

The common mistake by beginning reading teachers is to think that they can use a group test to assess children's knowledge of basic sight words. A group test is often used for this purpose and it is the Dolch Basic Sight Word Test. In using this, the teacher gives each student a sheet of paper that has numbers down the left-hand column of the page. Opposite each number are four words. The teacher calls out one of the four words and each child is expected to mark the word called out by the teacher. The main problem with this type of test is that even if a child does not know any of the words he or she would be likely to get one-fourth of them right by guessing. The teacher should give each child an individual test to determine the child's knowledge of basic sight words.

## Independent Activities for the Beginning Stages of Reading

Slow and disabled learners sometimes learn to read mechanically and without much comprehension. The teacher should constantly help these children understand what they are reading.

Table 4.3. The Percentage of Total Running Words in
Reading Materials Accounted for by Various Numbers of Words.

| Number of Words | Percentage of Total Running Words |
|---|---|
| 3 | 8 –12 |
| 10 | 20 –25 |
| 100 | 60 –65 |
| 200 | 66 –70 |
| 500 | 75 –80 |
| 1000 | 83 –85 |
| 1500 | 87 –88 |
| 2000 | 89 –90 |
| 3000 | 91 –92 |
| 5000 | 92.5–93.5 |

One good method for assuring adequate comprehension which will offset any emphasis on mechanics of reading is to provide seat work activities that direct the child to read for understanding.

Not all reading performance can be accomplished by direct instruction and incidental learning. The child must develop some independence in reading and at the same time engage in purposeful activities while the other children are receiving instruction from the teacher. However, in some of the resource rooms in special education, the teacher will have only two or three children at one time. This way, a child can be engaged in a purposeful activity while the teacher is only working with one or two other children. In this type of special education resource room set-up, the other children will not be a disturbing factor. Some methods for seat work, though, are presented here:

1. Stories may be made up and traced on charts for moving picture reading. The moving picture method presents reading materials in a novel and interesting fashion. To use this method, a large box should be constructed by the teacher. This box is about the size of the other reading charts except it has a roller at each end. The roll of reading material may be placed on one roller and at the end attached to the second roller. A crank is attached to the second roller and the teacher or the child can turn the crank until the story appears. When the story appears, the children can read the story and turn the crank and then read the next story. This presentation is highly motivating because it has the appearance of a picture show. The teacher can also have one child read the story from the moving picture show and as the child reads it, she will write it on the board, then have the other children read it aloud. This also is a motivating factor.

2. There must be a way of developing word recognition and one such way is to duplicate pictures and words and instruct the child to draw a line from the picture to the correct word. You can have a picture of a dog, boy, ball, horse, etc. and the printed word and the child draws a line from the word to the picture.

3. Another method similar to the one just described is to write short sentences under pictures and instruct the children to circle the sentence that describes the picture.

4. Picture cards with a word and picture on one side can be used and will prove helpful as a supplementary means for developing word recognition. The teacher will call out the name of the word and the child can look at the picture and the word and hold up the word with the picture, of course, on the back side of the card.

5. The teacher can get the children to engage in pasting and cutting. The children will cut words from magazines and pictures from magazines and paste the words into a sentence and paste the picture above the sentence.

6. The children can engage in what is known as the sentence completion method. The teacher will write several words on a ditto and make copies for the children. There will be a sentence, but at the

end of the sentence, there will be a blank. The children are to fill in the blank.

7. Lastly, free reading time must be provided for the children. The children can select a book of their choice or magazine of their choice and must be given time to read for pleasure.

## MAINSTREAMING THE CHILDREN INTO THE REGULAR CLASSROOM

Special education teachers will not have a disabled learner for more than three hours a day. There will be times when the special education teacher will only have the child 30 minutes a day and that will be for instruction in reading. A special education teacher must work with the regular classroom teacher in what is taking place in the special education resource room and the regular classroom. The federal laws encourage mainstreaming as a least restrictive alternative. The regular class teacher must know that there are nine- and ten-year-old special education children who barely know the alphabet and a few preprimer and primer words. A fourth grade teacher in the regular classroom must understand that the child cannot come from the special education resource room and start reading material at the regular fourth grade level. This is absolutely an impossibility and the special education teacher and regular class teacher and all other professionals concerned must be aware of this problem. The author will further state if the environment of the regular classroom requires reading ability as it does in the third, fourth, and fifth grades and the special education child is unable to read at all, the stage has been set for a behavior problem.

## REFERENCES

Curtis, H. M. (1938). Wide reading for beginners. *Journal of Educational Research, 38,* 255–262.

Dolch, E. W. (1931, 1951). *The Psychology and Teaching of Reading.* Boston: Ginn and Co.

Dolch, E. W. (1942). *Basic Sight Word Test.* Champaign, IL: Garrard Press.

Durr, W. K. (1973). Computer study of high frequency words in popular trade juveniles. *Reading Teacher, 27,* 37–42.

Gagon, C. (1966). Modern research and word perception. *Education, 86,* 464–472.

Harris, A., & Sipay, E. (1975). *How to Increase Reading Ability* (6th ed.). New York: David McKay Co.

Hillerich, R. L. (January 1974). Word Lists—Getting It All Together. *The Reading Teacher, 27,* 353–360.

Hockett, J. A. (1938). Comparative analysis of the vocabularies of twenty-nine second grade readers. *Journal of Educational Research, 31,* 665–671.

Johnson, D. D. (February, 1971). The Dolch list reexamined. *The Reading Teacher, 24,* 455–456.

Madden, R. (1959). *Language Arts Notes—Number 11.* New York: World Book.

Robinson, H. A. (1963). A study of the techniques of word identification. *Reading Teacher, 16,* 238–242.

# Chapter 5

# ADAPTATIONS OF METHODS AND MATERIALS FOR ATYPICAL LEARNERS: ADVANCED STAGES OF READING

The teacher has already had several weeks and even years to instruct the child in the beginning stages of reading. This chapter focuses on methods of increasing reading efficiency beyond the beginning stages.

## METHODS OF WORD RECOGNITION

If children are to read independently, they must be taught a method in which to recognize new words. Normal children usually can learn a method of word recognition without prolonged instruction. Children who are mentally retarded, slow learners, as well as specific learning disabled, or even devient learners, require guidance and instruction in learning to recognize new words. In many cases, it takes several weeks to teach a child a method of recognizing only the simplest of words. The atypical learner can use the same method of word recognition as normal children. The teacher, however, must modify the ways in which the material is taught as well as the rate that it is presented.

### Incidental Methods of Recognizing Words

We have already discussed in Chapter 4 incidental learning. Children learn to recognize words incidentally during the first stages of learning to read. They begin to pick up many sight words if these words are repeated often enough in various contexts. The child becomes familiar with words as they appear among pictures or in certain stories and this is known as an incidental method of recognizing words. Reading the same story repeatedly does not help the child to learn to read the words efficiently. The same words must be presented in different settings in order for the child to always recognize the word immediately.

73

## Recognizing Words By Clues

All children use different methods to recognize words. While slow learners and the atypical learner generally use the same method, it takes them longer to recognize words when using the same clues. A child may depend on some characteristics of the words, such as the configuration, shape of the *t,* dot over the *i,* or the total word in its form or shape in order to recognize it. Other methods include analyzing the word, breaking it into visual parts, and sometimes spelling the parts.

It may do the teacher a world of good to evaluate the methods of word recognition as they apply to the mentally retarded, slow learning child, or learning disabled children. The teacher should encourage children to use a variety of methods of word recognition. We do not want them to use a method which teaches them to engage in guess work. It is more difficult for the teacher to correct errors than to teach new words properly; therefore, the child should be taught the best methods for recognizing words. Each child may have a different method for recognizing words. Some children use a visual method, some children use an auditory method, and many children use a combination of the auditory and visual methods. The spelling method is seldom used with atypical or average children. Nevertheless some children may prefer to use the spelling method along with other methods.

## Recognizing Words Through Context Clues

When the child reads the whole sentence, he is capable of guessing an unknown word. The following general techniques will assist students in using context clues to decode unknown words:

1. Have the student preread material silently before reading it orally. Discuss the troublesome vocabulary with each child.
2. Set purposes for reading. The teacher should stress accuracy in reading, not speed.
3. The teacher should use short, easy selections. Have the student stop frequently to explain what he or she has read and do it in their own words.
4. The teacher should have the children use high interest material including student authored language experience stories.
5. The teacher should encourage the students to read past unknown

words to the end of the sentence and then come back. Research indicates that words that come after are often more helpful than those that come before unknown words.

6. Have the students scan for important words, have them guess the content and read to see if the guess is accurate.

7. The teacher should encourage practice in the act of reading. There is no better technique for all students to learn to read for meaning. Provide time and appropriate materials, the proper setting, and encouragement for a long period of silent reading.

## Other Ideas and Exercises Are Listed Below:

1. The tape recorder can be a very valuable tool for making students aware of context clues and oral exercises. The children should read aloud a story and leave out the unknown word. When listening to the stories, the children should use contextual clues to guess the correct word. Next, the teacher can read the story aloud. For example, "I am going to read a short story. Every now and then I am going to leave out a word. When that word is left out, you put the correct word in." Another example follows: The teacher reads into a tape recorder and states, "I am going to read a short story and every now and then I am going to leave a word out. I am going to say 'beep' when I leave a word out. I want you to fill in that beep with the correct word."

2. Give students sentences with words left out. For example, leave every sixth or eighth word out in a paragraph and let the students put the correct word in by using contextual clues.

3. Give the students the same sentences such as those listed in number two, but leave the first letter of the missing word out.

4. Give students sentences such as those listed in number two, but do not give any clues except the beginning and ending letters.

5. Use cloze passages where you leave every fifth, eighth, and tenth word completely out. Ask the students to complete the sentences. An example of a cloze passage follows: *Jim was going to visit _____ and Grandma. He _____ going to go on a bus. His father _____ him to buy his ticket. The clerk _____ the desk asked Jim _____ he wanted to. . . . , etc.*

## A Word Attack Strategy

This strategy consists of four simple steps. When you come to a word you don't know:

1. Say the beginning sound.
2. Read the rest of the sentence and think.
3. Say the parts that you know. Then guess.
4. Ask someone to help, or skip it and go on to the next word or sentence.

## Efficiency Skills

Some students master decoding skills, but fail to read efficiently. These students may possess faulty reading habits, such as inappropriate reading rate, inaccurate reading, improper phrasing or expression, inability to recognize punctuation, lip movements, finger pointing, or head movements. The next general suggestions will be how to remediate these difficulties.

### General Suggestions

1. Make sure that decoding skills of basic sight vocabulary, phonics, structural analysis, and contextual clues analysis have been mastered. If not, provide remediation instruction in these areas.
2. The teacher should always take time to discuss with students the specific nature of their efficiency skill problems and make general suggestions for solving them. It is often helpful to tape record the student while he or she is reading orally, then play back the recording so the student can become aware of specific problems.
3. Do not expect the students to read materials above their meaning-vocabulary level. The teacher should use easy materials which will encourage the students to read in great quantity.
4. The teacher should encourage wide reading from a variety of materials.

## ORAL READING

Oral reading is most effective if it is done in a one-to-one fashion or with very small groups so the students participate as much as possible. In using these methods, it is important for the teacher to stress to students that oral reading is only one way of reading and that this practice will ultimately lead the student to greater ability in silent reading.

Several authors have described different oral techniques and reviewed the evidence to support their use (Anderson, 1981; Ashby-Davis, 1981; and Harris, 1981). These techniques are (1) the Neurological Impress Method, (2) Echol Reading or Imitative Reading, and (3) Repeated Reading.

The Neurological Impress Method (NIM) was developed by R. G. Heckelman, who first described it in 1966. This method, which has some variations, generally consists of having the student and teacher read the same material out loud at the same time. The instructor reads slightly louder and a little faster than the student. The instructor also gets his mouth close to or directs his voice into the student's ear. Sentences of passages may be reread to achieve fluency. In this way the student is reinforcing his reading by his voice and he is being doubly reinforced by the instructor's voice. Advocates of NIM recommend that it be used for up to 15 minutes daily for a total time of eight to twelve hours. Generally students will show progress after only a few sessions. This method should be discontinued after four hours if the student fails to respond positively.

Elizabeth McAllister (1989) presented a paper at the annual meeting of the Eastern Educational Research Association in Savannah, Georgia entitled "A Study of Peer Tutors Using the Neurological Impress Method." The following is a synopsis of the research quoted by McAllister (1989).

A study investigated the efficacy of using the neurological impress method in peer tutoring during reading instruction, which is a unison reading procedure in which the student and teacher or tutor read aloud simultaneously and quickly, with the student placed slightly in front of the teacher so that the teacher's voice is directed into the student's right ear at close range. Ten fourth-grade students received treatment for 12 consecutive weeks, resulting in total contact time of 15 hours. The tutors received training in the impress method from a reading specialist. Library books chosen by the students were used as reading. *The Peabody Picture Vocabulary Test* was used to determine a mental age and I.Q. based on functioning vocabulary. From the I.Q. measure, each child's reading expectancy level could be computed and used to determine how much growth might be expected. Prior to treatment, *The Silvaroli Informal Reading Inventory*, Form A, was administered to each child to obtain oral reading levels in word recognition and comprehension. Form B was used as a posttest after treatment. *The Houghton Mifflin Silent Reading Placement Test* was used to determine each student's silent reading level. Results indicated that each fourth-grade student showed reading improvement of at least one-half year in the 12 weeks. The highest gain was three years in oral word recognition and two years in oral comprehension and silent reading.

## ECHO READING

In echo reading, the teacher reads first and the student repeats what the teacher has read. The material can be read in either phrases or sentences, and finger pointing is used in this method. The common variation uses a tape recorder and the teacher records the texts. The student first listens straight through while following the written text, then reads along with the recording. One advantage of this method is that an instructor need not be present. On the other hand, this variation lacks the immediacy and psychological force of a teacher's presence. At the present time, there are a number of high interest, low vocabulary read-along materials available in different formats with accompanying records, tapes, or slides. Children seem to enjoy these, and if used properly, they are beneficial.

## THE TEACH PERIOD

The teacher must be sure that students can read the material well and that they stay on the task and do read when they are supposed to.

## REPEATED READINGS

Repeating readings is a method that has been suggested by S. J. Samuels (1970), Lopardo & Sadow (1982), and Cunningham (1979). The students are given selections that consist of approximately 50 to 200 words. The children are instructed to practice the selections and then they are timed after each reading and the number of errors are recorded on a chart. While the teacher is checking other students, the children reread the material along with a recording of the text. The rereading may be done over and over. When the children feel ready, another test is given. Then when the student achieves a rate of 85 words per minute, another selection is provided. Comprehension checks must take place and the graphing of the students' results serves as a positive motivator for continuing progress.

## PRECISION READING

Precision reading (Ekwall & Shanker, 1988) has been used successfully at the Hayward Reading Clinic of the California State University. This adaptation emphasizes first accuracy, then speed. While the children read, the teacher records the students' accuracy sentence by sentence. A form is prepared to record the children's reading efficiency. The form has spaces to indicate the beginning and ending page numbers of the material read, the total number of sentences read, and the number of sentences read perfectly. The number of sentences read with one or more errors is also marked. At the beginning, the student is given relatively easy material and reads a set number of sentences such as 20 or 25. The teacher records the student's accuracy on each sentence so that on completion a fraction of correct sentences out of the total is derived. For example, the student may read 20 sentences perfectly and then make one or more errors on five of the sentences and his fraction would be 20/25. The fraction is then changed to percentage and in this case, it would be 80 percent accuracy. This is put on a graph and serves as a powerful motivator for children because they like to see their work placed on a graph. It is important to select material where the child is unlikely to drop below 75 percent. When the student improves and begins to read consistently at 100 percent accuracy, the teacher will want to provide more difficult material.

## ORAL READING FOR MEANING

Oral reading for meaning has been suggested by Barbara M. Taylor and Linda Nosbush (1985) as a technique for improving children's word identification skills. These two suggest a four-step procedure. First, the teacher works with a student for 10 to 15 minutes. During this time, the child is asked to read 100 to 300 words and the teacher records any miscue. The child should be interrupted as little as possible. In the second step, the child is given praise for positive aspects of his or her oral reading. The two people mentioned, Taylor and Nosbush, note that the child should be especially praised for any self-corrected errors. The third step is a discussion between the teacher and the child of the various miscues made by the student. The fourth step is an on-the-spot instruction for specific word attach deficiencies. For example, a child who read *no* for *now* might be given instructions on the two most common sounds which are represented by *ow.* The audio tape recorder may also serve as an excellent device for children to practice oral reading. The teacher could set up a "recording studio" in the classroom. In addition to the tape recorder, the teacher will naturally need a microphone and cassette tapes for the children. The following activities may also be provided:

1. The student reads orally into a tape recorder and plays back the tape and listens to the recording while taking notes. The student could read along silently or read along orally with the recording.
2. The teacher reads a selection into the tape recorder and the student plays it back. The student can read along with it silently or orally. The teacher may make errors on purpose or exhibit poor reading skills to see if the student catches it, if the student evaluates the teacher's performance and tries to apply this to his or her own reading.
3. Two or more students can read into a tape recorder together and use the above technique while listening to both voices.
4. The student can use the language master or equivalent machine to practice phrase or sentence reading.

## CONFIGURATION CLUES

Although the use of configuration clues is an important skill in word analysis, there is little concrete information on effective ways of teaching students to become more aware of this skill. Most research shows that traditional methods are not of much value. For example, many textbooks on reading have suggested that lines be drawn around words printed in lower case to show contrast in shapes. However, research by Gabrielle, Marchbanks, and Levin (1965) has shown that in practice this technique has little value. It does have some value, though, for a student ·who constantly confuses two somewhat similar words. This author knows that words printed in lower case tend to be easier to read than words printed in upper case. Thus, it seems that using the lower case alphabet in beginning reading would be more effective. However, research does not show this to be true.

Occasionally, though, a student will have considerable difficulty with words such as *thought, through,* and *though.* In this case, the teacher should point out the differences such as the *t* sound and the *t* letter at the end of the word and the *r* in through. The teacher can also improve the student's ability to note configurations in teaching word families—phonograms—such as *all* and *ate*. Generally though, unless a student is confusing two similar words, such as *county* and *country*, you should probably spend your time on more effective methods of word attack and configuration clues.

## DICTIONARY SKILLS

This author would like to emphasize that children do not become seriously disabled readers from a lack of knowledge of dictionary skills. This is not to belittle the importance of a child learning about the use of the dictionary. However, from the standpoint of economy of time, the special education teacher probably spends most of his or her time in remediating problems that have a more immediate effect on the student's reading. There are numerous film strips, workbooks, etc. that effectively cover the teaching of dictionary skills. A dictionary should always be present in the resource room and the teacher should teach the student how to look up words and encourage the student to always use the dictionary.

## RECOGNIZING WORDS THROUGH PHONETIC ANALYSIS

The phonics method has been widely used in the United States to teach independence in the recognition of known words and new words. Since the value of phonics has been debated for a number of years, it might do well to evaluate the method and consider its usefulness for the atypical learner.

Phonics refers to the method of recognizing new words by relating a sound (phoneme) with the equivalent of the written symbol (grapheme). This is often referred to as the grapheme-phoneme relationship. When the alphabet method of teaching reading was discarded many years ago, the phonics method replaced it. Later, however, it was discovered that children could learn words and sentences without the use of phonics. Today, however, most all programs in the teaching of reading have an admixture of phonics along with other aspects of teaching reading and we do not need special phonics materials for a special way of teaching phonics. There are some programs, though, such as METRA, Phono Hooked on Phonics, which emphasize phonics more than the others. If the atypical learner learns primarily through the auditory method, he can use these three methods and others effectively to learn new words.

## PHONIC ELEMENTS

The term phonic elements is often used to define various letter combinations and the sounds they represent. There are many methods of teaching the phonic elements. One typical procedure:

1. Developing awareness of hearing the sound:
    1.1. Say, "Listen to these words. Each of them begins with the *bl* sound. Circle the *bl* on each word on your paper as you hear the sound. *Blast, blow, bleed, blue, etc.*"
2. Developing awareness of seeing the sound:
    2.1. The teacher tells the students to circle all of the words in a passage that begins with *bl.*
3. Providing practice in saying words with the *bl* sound:
    3.1. The teacher has the student pronounce each word after she has pronounced it. *Block, black, blur, blow, blue.*
4. Providing practice in blending the *bl* sound with common word families or phonograms:
    4.1. The teacher tells the children to put the *bl* in one column and the phonogram in the second column and the two combined in a third column as follows:
        bl - - - ock - - - block
        bl - - - ack - - - black
        bl - - - ur - - - blur
        bl - - - eed - - - bleed
        bl - - - under - - - blunder
    4.2. Another exercise that the teacher can do is tell the children to place the letters and words as follows:
        bl - - - fl - - - flock - - - block
        bl - - - lack - - - la - - - black
        bl - - - fur - - - blur
5. The teacher can ask the students to make a list of some words that begin with *bl.*
6. The teacher provides practice in reading *bl* words.

Some other types of exercises for practicing phonics skills follow:

1. Omit letters from certain words used in context.
   1.1. Dick and Sue liked to go ——ishing.
       (g, f, b, h)
   1.2. Bob forgot his ——ooks at school.
       (d, p, b, q)
2. Give each student an envelope with several cards in it. On the front and back of each card print one letter. For example, each student might have five or six cards: *c, f, g, h,* and *d.* As you say the words, have students hold up the cards that has a letter representing the sound they hear at the beginning, middle, and end of the various words.

### A Specific Method for Teaching Phonics

The method of teaching phonics that has been proposed in another chapter is the Hegge-Kirk-Kirk Remedial Method (1936) applied to reading disability cases. This method was developed by these three people to be used with mentally retarded children. Although it was developed a long time ago, it is still a good method. The teacher must remember that the English language does not have consistent sound-symbols spelling patterns, and many words will have to be taught as sight words. If children have also learned context clues, they will be able to recognize many new words in reading, partly through phonic analysis, partly through context clues, and partly through structural analysis.

During the reading period, a teacher should not ask the children to sound out a word they have not been taught to sound. For example, if the child has learned the sound of the consonants and the sound of the short vowel *a,* is confronted with the word *hit,* the teacher should say "hit" when the child hesitates over the word so that he or she will not be confused.

After the child has learned the sounds of most of the consonants and the sound of the short vowel *a,* the sound of the short vowels *o, u, i,* and *e* should be taught singly. These should be presented very gradually in connection with sounds and words the child has previously learned.

## ADAPTATIONS OF STANDARD READING METHODS

Often a technique designed for teaching reading in the regular classroom can be modified for use with severely disabled readers in the resource room or self-contained special education classroom. When using standard methods, some cautions should be observed by the teacher. A student may be confused if several approaches are used at the same time. Therefore, avoid exposing the special education student to one method in the classroom, another method in the resource room, and yet a third instructional method after school. Severely disabled readers need to have a consistent method for acquiring reading skills. Thus, the teacher should select a method which is consistent with both the student's aptitudes for learning and the classroom demands. This method should be used consistently for a period of time. For example, six weeks.

It is very important to anticipate the slow pace with which handicapped readers may acquire reading skills. This is particularly true for the beginning phases of instruction. However, we have already talked about the beginning phases and now we're talking about later phases, and it should be pointed out that this is also true in the later phases of reading. One boy in a resource room spent ten weeks acquiring eight new sight words. This appears to be slow and would seem to be very slow to the regular classroom teacher, but often it is not slow for the mildly retarded or the child with specific learning disabilities.

Standard reading methods can be readily adapted for use with handicapped readers. This part of this chapter describes some useful adaptations in (1) the sight word approach, (2) the synthetic phonics approach, and (3) analytic phonics or linquistic approach. Adaptations of standard methods are relatively easy to use; they require few specialized materials and allow much flexibility in the teacher's preparation. If after a trial period, though, these approaches have not proven to be affective the teacher should consider using another special remedial method.

## SELECTING A METHOD

There are three ways to determine the best method for an individual child: (1) determine his learning strength; (2) determine his learning preferences; and (3) consider other instructional programs.

The teacher should see if the student exhibits a distinct strength in learning through either whole word approach or a phonics approach. A whole word approach, such as sight words or language experience, initially favors visual skills. A phonics approach, such as synthetic or analytic phonics, initially favors auditory skills. The teacher should try matching the initial instruction method to the strength of each child. Eventually, of course, the child will need to learn both approaches.

If a method which utilizes a stronger learning area is chosen, the child may also be given activities to build the weaker one.

A diagnostic word learning task can be given to determine the child's comparative abilities in learning through (1) a sight word or language experience method and (2) a phonics method. The student is given the task of learning two sets of words: six words are presented as sight words and six words are presented as phonics words. The teacher then compares the performance on these two tasks and makes a judgment about the student's learning strengths. Directions for a word learning task are presented in Table 5.1.

Another important factor in choosing a reading method is a student's personal preferences for learning. There will be students who prefer to sound out words and there will be students who simply have an aversion to this activity. Sometimes disabled readers associate certain activities as being unpleasant. The teacher would want to avoid that particular approach.

A third factor that the teacher must consider when choosing a method for instruction is a student's other current instructional programs. The teacher should try to harmonize the remedial program in special education with the student's existing classroom program in the regular classroom. For example, if a student is using materials with a special alphabet, for example, reading mastery: DISTAR in the classroom and books with a regular alphabet in the reading clinic, the student could very well be confused. Therefore, learning would be impeded.

## THE SIGHT WORD METHOD

The sight word method involves teaching children to recognize the visual form of words instantly, and without further analysis. Although the teaching of sight words is mentioned in other chapters, special adaptations for the handicapped reader are presented here.

Words to be taught should be selected carefully. In general, long words are harder to learn than short words, although an occasional long word serves to add interest for the child. Research has shown that concrete words are easier to learn than abstract words. An example of this would be parts of the body are easy to learn because the child is not only interested in this, but these are concrete words. Other concrete

**Table 5.1. Diagnostic Word Learning Task**

1. *Sight word task:* Words are "house," "children," "boy," "farm," "wagon."
   a. Print the words carefully on cards.
   b. Go through each word. Read it to the student, use it in a sentence, point out out visual features of the word ("children" is long; "boy" is short, etc.).
   c. Mix up cards. Present five trials of the word, with the words mixed after each trial.
      (1) for the first three trials, pronounce incorrect words for the student and use them in a sentence.
      (2) For the last two trials, do not correct incorrect responses.
   d. Mark results of all trials on the form below.
2. *Phonics word task:* Words are "at," "bat," "cat," "rat," "fat."
   a. Print the words carefully on cards.
   b. Present the "at" card first; pronounce this word for the student.
      Present the other words by showing the "at" within the words and then blending the first letter ("at," "f-at," "fat"). Use each word in a sentence
   c. Mix up cards. Present five trials of the word, with words mixed after each trial.
      (1) For the first three trials, pronounce incorrect words by blending parts together.
      (2) For the last two trials, do not correct incorrect responses.
   d. Mark all results on the form below.
3. *Response form:* Mark correct or incorrect.

| | Sight Word Task Trial | | | | | | Phonics Task Trial | | | | |
|---|---|---|---|---|---|---|---|---|---|---|---|
| | 1 | 2 | 3 | 4 | 5 | | 1 | 2 | 3 | 4 | 5 |
| house | | | | | | at | | | | | |
| children | | | | | | bat | | | | | |
| boy | | | | | | cat | | | | | |
| farm | | | | | | rat | | | | | |
| wagon | | | | | | fat at | | | | | |

Adapted from Barr, 1970

words are the name of the school, the name of a street, the name of students, etc. Words such as *the, when, whom, to* are difficult to learn.

Words should be reviewed as often as possible so that they can be established firmly in the child's memory. The teacher should be careful to use standard manuscript writing for all hand-made materials. Handicapped readers focus on very small differences and may be confused by a "d with a tail attached."

## THE SYNTHETIC PHONICS APPROACH

In the synthetic method, the student learns to blend letter sounds, or groups of letter sounds, into a whole word. For example, to read the word *rat*, the sounds for the letters *r*, *a*, and *t* are pronounced individually and then blended together by the teacher first and then by the child. The synthetic approach often requires that the student learn certain phonics rules. In special education, this should be made very simple and concrete. The phonics rule, for example, would guide the disabled reader to pronounce *"rat"* and *"rate"* differently.

If the synthetic phonics approach is chosen for handicapped readers, teachers should make sure that students possess an appropriate readiness skill. Skill in auditory blending and knowledge of letter sounds are important prerequisites for this method. Many of the handicapped readers confuse letter names with letter sounds, therefore, this author suggests referring to letters by using their sounds.

The synthetic phonics method is often very difficult for the handicapped reader when it is first presented. Many readiness skills are needed and many task demands are made. However, once basic phonics concepts are mastered, the special education student often gains rapidly in reading performance.

## THE ANALYTIC (OR LINGUISTIC) PHONICS APPROACH

In the analytic method, the student looks at whole words that contain regular phonics patterns. Words are never broken apart, but by presenting the words over and over again in patterns or word families, such as *"at," "bat," "cat," "run," "sun," "fun,"* the child learns their sound regularities. Books using the linguistic approach are based upon patterns of word families resulting in texts such as:

> *Dan hurt his hand.*
> *Can Dan get help for his hurt hand?*
> *The pet is wet.*
> *Why is the pet wet?*

The analytic phonics method often proves to be highly effective for teaching handicapped children who can recognize phonics correspondents, but are not ready for synthetic phonics approach. One important prerequisite skill for learning the analytical linguistic phonics method is the skill of rhyming.

Ten-year-old Hank was a nonreader who was instructed by the analytic phonics method for several months. His initial learning rate was about one word family per week. After four weeks of instruction, his rate of learning increased by two word families per week. Hank's special education teacher controlled the word families carefully so that they would not be too similar. After each word family was learned, it was presented in a story. The words from the word family were at first color coded, with one family being yellow and another red. Hank's independent reading was done with books containing rhyming words such as several of the books by Dr. Suesse.

Many older special education children preferred the analytic approach also. It allows them to be independent and also to have fun. One fifteen-year-old boy learning by this approach decided to create his own book of word families. Under each word family such as -*ight* and "*ag,*" he entered all the words he could find.

## KINESTHETIC APPROACHES

A variety of approaches known as kinesthetic approaches use the sense of movement to reinforce word learning. They include the VAKT and the VAK method and the so called Fernald method. Grace Fernald gets credit, but Maria Montessori first used this approach around 1900.

## THE VAKT METHOD

The VAKT method utilizes visual, auditory, kinesthetic, and tactile senses to reinforce learning. It is reserved generally for the most severe cases of reading disability. The method emphasizes tracing and tactile stimulation to promote learning. It is sometimes referred to as a multi-sensory approach. The student sees the word and listens to the teacher pronounce it, then the student pronounces it and the word is traced as the student says it. The word is generally traced in sand or on a piece of screen. There are many variations of the VAKT approach.

## THE VAK METHOD

The VAK method combines visual and auditory associations with writing. The student sees and says the word while writing it from memory. The VAK uses the following procedure: (1) the child sees the word to be learned and then he says the word, (2) he tries to write it from memory, and (3) he compares the results with the original word. This procedure is repeated over and over again.

## THE FERNALD METHOD

Grace Fernald and Helen Keller (Fernald, 1943, 1988) developed a method for use with severe reading disorders that combines the language experience approach and the VAKT modes of learning. The approach is designed to be used on a one-on-one basis. The Fernald method emphasizes the wholeness of words and does not require the student to learn separate phonic elements. Progress will be very slow and this method generally is only used when all other methods have failed. The Fernald outlines some very specific procedures. There are four stages in the Fernald approach. After the first stage has been mastered, they move to stage two and so on. The four stages of the approach are: (1) tracing and writing from memory individually presented words, (2) writing from memory individually presented words, (3) writing from memory words found in text, and (4) learning by sight words presented in text.

## REFERENCES

Barr, R. Development of a word learning task to predict success and identify methods by which kindergarten children learn to read. Final Report to the U.S. Department of Health, Education, and Welfare, Office of Education, Contract 9E125, 1971.

Ekwall, E. and Shanker, S. (1988). *Diagnosis and Remediation of the Disabled Reader*, 3rd ed., Newton, MA: Allyn and Bacon.

Fernald, G. M. (1988). *Remedial Techniques in Basic School Subjects*. L. Idol (Ed.), Austin, TX: Pro-Ed.

Fernald, G. M. (1943). *Remedial Techniques in Basic School Subjects*. New York: McGraw-Hill.

Kelly, E. M. (July 1934). The improvement of reading in special education classes for mentally retarded children. *Proceedings, American Association Mental Deficiency, 39*, 67–73.

Kirk, S. A. (1936). *Manual of Directions for Use with the Hegge-Kirk-Kirk Remedial Reading Drills.* Ann Arbor, MI: George Wahr.

Lopardo, G. & Sadow, M. W. (1982). Criteria and procedures for the method of repeated readings. *Journal of Reading, 26,* 156–160.

McAllister, E. A. (1989). A study of peer tutors using the Neurological Impress Method. A paper presented at the Annual Meeting of the Eastern Educational Research Association (Savannah, GA, Feb. 23, 1989). p. 14.

Samuels, S. J. (1979). The method of repeated readings. *Reading Teacher, 32,* 403–406.

Taylor, B. M. & Nobush, L. (1985). Oral reading for meaning: A technique for improving word identification skills. *Reading Teacher, 37,* 234–237.

# Chapter 6

# SPECIALIZED REMEDIAL
# READING TECHNIQUES

The methods presented in this chapter are select, highly specialized ways of teaching reading. These methods are not ordinarily used by the regular classroom teacher, nor are they included in the developmental approach. These methods are reported by educators to be effective with many of the handicapped readers.

This chapter presents these special methods and they are different than the developmental methods discussed in other chapters in this book.

## VAKT APPROACH

The VAKT approach to reading makes a concerted effort to encourage the child to use several of the sensory modalities in learning to read. The letters V–A–K–T stand for visual, auditory, kinesthetic and tactile. This is a multisensory approach that was first advocated by Maria Montessori in approximately 1900. It was later mentioned by Grace Fernald, Helen Keller, Samuel Orton, Anna Gillingham, and Bessie Stillman. Most of the modern day approaches to teaching reading use the VAKT approach in one way or another. This approach is based on the assumption that if a child uses all the sensory measures in the learning process, learning will be reinforced. For example, the child is asked to say the word (auditory), see the word (visual), and trace the word (kinesthetic). Later the child is asked to trace the word on sandpaper or in sand (tactile). This tracing not only offers the learner a tactile approach but also the kinesthetic approach which is now available in some of the modern techniques. This multisensory approach has been used successfully to teach many of the learning disabled children to read even after they had been in school for a number of years with little or no success in reading. Some research supports this specialized approach to reading instruction for the atypical learner. Many other educators caution against this approach as the only approach to teach a child who has severe learning disabilities in reading. Most authorities state that this approach should be used along with other approaches in the teaching of reading.

Two specialized methods which are often associated with the early multisensory approaches are the Fernald method and the Gillingham method. Both of these approaches utilize the tracing procedure but they differ in some of the other essential respects. The Gillingham method (Gillingham and Stillman, 1968; Orton, 1966) uses a multisensory approach to beginning reading by teaching the units of sounds or letters of the alphabet. The Fernald Approach uses a tracing procedure as does the Gillingham method, but the Fernald Approach (Fernald, 1943) uses the approach to teach the whole word.

## FERNALD APPROACH

Grace Fernald, a psychologist, developed her method of teaching children to read in an attempt to enable children with "word blindness" to learn to read. Her approach was used in a one-to-one situation with children that had failed to learn to read in conventional settings.

The children in her classroom made up their own stories, dictating them to their teachers, rather than using a reader. The child then learned to read and spell the words used in his story. Words were written in cursive because the child learned the word as a total pattern, tracing the entire word, and thereby strengthening his memory and visualization of the entire word.

The Fernald Approach is a multisensory method of teaching reading, writing, and spelling. The following steps are involved:

1. The child is told he is going to learn words in a new way that has proved to be very successful. The words in the story he has dictated are presented to him one at a time.
2. The teacher writes that word on a piece of paper, 4 inches by 10 inches, as the child watches and as the teacher says the word.
3. The child traces the word with one or two fingers, saying it several times. When he feels that he has mastered the spelling of the word, he writes it with his finger on the table. The next step is to write the word on a separate piece of paper while saying it.
4. The word is then written from memory without looking at the

original copy. If it is incorrect, the tracing and saying steps are repeated. If the word is correct, it is put in a file box. The words in the file box are used in later stories.

5. At later stages this painstaking tracing method for learning words is not needed. Now the child learns a word by **looking** as the teacher writes it, **saying** it, and **writing** it. At a still later stage, the child can learn by only looking at a word in print and writing it, and, finally, by merely looking at it.

## SRA'S CORRECTIVE READING (1989)

Corrective Reading is designed for students who haven't learned in other programs and don't learn on their own—students who misidentify, reverse, or omit words; students who have little recall and limited attention span; students who fail to remember and follow directions; and students who read without understanding.

Teachers work with these students for 30 to 45 minutes each day, giving them direct remediation. Scripted lessons provide carefully sequenced tasks, consistent instructional language, and the structure necessary to produce mastery.

The series uses a two-pronged approach. Depending on their needs, students work in a Decoding Program, or in a Comprehension Program, or in both. Each is a core program—not a set of ancillary materials. All of the necessary instructional materials are included. Placement tests provide multiple entry points that ensure each student is placed at the appropriate instructional level.

Both the Decoding and the Comprehension programs have been revised to incorporate special features teachers have asked for, such as:

### IN DECODING

- New story-reading procedures and student workbooks enhance comprehension
- Daily timed readings improve rate and fluency
- Wordlists in the Student's Book save time for the teacher

### IN COMPREHENSION

- Improved placement procedures ensure student success from the beginning
- Fact games strengthen students grasp of facts and rule applications
- Mastery tests provide solid ongoing assessment information

**DECODING A** is for extremely poor decoders, third grade through high school, who lack systematic word-attack skills. These students read so inaccurately that they are prevented from comprehending what they read.

**COMPREHENSION A** is for students who don't understand the concepts underlying much of the material taught in classrooms and who have trouble understanding information even when it's presented orally. They do not have well-developed recitation skills.

**DECODING LEVELS B1 AND B2** are for students in grades 4 through 12 who misidentify, omit, reverse, and substitute words. Decoding B1 is appropriate for students who have completed Decoding A or whose scores on the Placement Test indicate that they belong in the program. Decoding B2 is for those students who complete Decoding B1 or whose scores on the Placement Test indicate such placement.

**COMPREHENSION B1 AND B2** are for students who have some difficulty with reasoning skills. They have trouble identifying deductions and how things are the same. Their deficiencies in vocabulary skills and their lack of background knowledge make it difficult for them to perform many reading comprehension activities.

**DECODING C** is for students who have fair reading skills but who are not fluent readers and who tend to make word identification errors. These students have mastered many basic reading skills but have trouble with multisyllable words and typical textbook material.

**COMPREHENSION C** is for students who have difficulty, not in core skills, but in comprehending sophisticated text. It is for students who do not learn well from material they have read or who do not have good analytical skills. They have trouble thinking critically. They do not know how to organize information or how to use information to make deductions or to support conclusions.

## REBUS READING PROGRAM

The authors of the Peabody Rebus Reading Program (REBUS) are Richard W. Woodcock, Charlotte R. Clark, and Cornelia Oakes Davies (1969). The REBUS is a unique method for introducing children to reading by having them first learn a vocabulary of rebuses, or pictures, in place of spelled words. Since the rebuses are easy for a pupil to learn and remember he is directing his first learning efforts toward the reading process, rather than a complex abstract code. After learning the basic skills of the reading process, the pupil proceeds through a controlled transition program in which spelled words are substituted for the rebuses and certain structural and phonic analysis skills are taught.

"Rebus" is derived from a Latin word which means "thing." In the linguistic sense, a rebus is a symbol or a "thing" which represents an entire word or a part of a word in contrast to letters which represent sounds. A rebus may be pictorial, geometric, or abstract.

The instructional materials for REBUS include two programmed workbooks at the readiness level, and a third workbook and two readers at the transition level. A pupil learns a reading vocabulary of 122 spelled words by the end of the third workbook. This enables him to move into primer level instruction with relative ease, and in less time than most other programs (six to eight weeks). REBUS is largely self-instructional and self-correcting.

The supplementary Lessons Kit is for use with Book One and Book Two. The Kit includes 17 comprehensive lessons designed to serve two purposes: First, to facilitate group instruction; and second, to provide the younger, more immature, or mentally retarded pupil with a more intensive introduction to the vocabulary and skills of the program.

The Peabody Rebus Reading Program has been designed for use with all children. The readiness level of REBUS provides a valuable end-of-year experience for kindergarten, Head Start, and other preschool programs. Concluding such programs with REBUS provides a stimulating two- to four-week introduction to academic learning activities. The transition level of REBUS is ideally suited for use in kindergarten and preschool programs which include beginning reading in their curriculums.

The nature of REBUS is such that it lends itself to potential use with children having special problems or physical limitations. The materials of Supplementary Lessons Kit have been used by teachers of the deaf and hard of hearing to provide a system of visual language paralleling that available to the child with normal hearing. REBUS also uniquely lends itself to teaching reading to non-English-speaking pupils. Since rebuses are pictorial in nature, it is appropriate to call them by name in the pupils native language and then teach the counterpart name in English.

The two characteristics of REBUS which particularly set it apart from traditional readiness and beginning reading programs are the incorporation of a programmed text format, and the use of REBUS as a link between spoken language and reading. Rebuses are so easy for a child to learn and remember, almost all his learning effort may be directed to acquiring other essential reading skills. Once these skills have been acquired the child proceeds through the Transition Level in which spelled words are gradually phased into the text as Rebuses are phased out.

The first beginning reading program which utilized rebuses extensively was for use in the Peabody-Chicago-Detroit Reading Project. This study compared six different approaches for teaching reading to young mentally retarded children and involved 120 classes in Detroit and Chicago. One of these approaches was a REBUS approach. Out of this experience developed the experimental edition of REBUS. Though REBUS is primarily intended for use with kindergarten and first graders, the program has been developed and tested using many children having marginal learning problems.

## DISTAR READING I

The basic concept of the Distar Reading I Series (Englemann and Bruner, 1988a) is "that virtually all children can learn if taught carefully." The program provides step by step instruction for teachers to follow.

Distar includes prereading exercises, activities associated with beginning decoding, work with symbol identification, rhyming, comprehension activities and so forth.

1. Tasks are made as simple as possible and the vocabulary used by the teacher is reduced.
2. The practice that the children receive is carefully controlled and realistic.
3. The sequence of skills is controlled. This allows children to master all the skills they need for later, more complicated tasks (copy of score and sequence presented).
4. The teacher's behavior is also an important aspect of administering the test. She is provided with exact words to say while testing.

There is a big emphasis on details because they do make a difference. Many times students may get confused with general instruction. General instructions do not give enough direction and frequently do not reach every child. The Distar program prevents this confusion from happening.

The Distar program is appropriate for any child who has not mastered basic decoding and comprehension skills. It can be used on bright children or hard to teach children.

Children may proceed through the program as fast as they are capable. The program can be completed by April if it began in September. An extremely slow child may not complete the program but should get through at least 130 to 160 lessons.

The teacher's kit includes:

1. Three Teacher Presentation Books which specify each activity in each lesson and tell the teacher how to present it.
2. The teacher's guide explains the program and provides the instructions of how to teach it.
3. The spelling book contains spelling lessons.
4. The test book includes a placement test and mastery test.
5. Copies of three storybooks that children use.
6. A teacher's edition of the take home books.
7. A cassette demonstrating pronunciation of sounds and how to present the tasks.
8. An acetate page protector to enable you to write on the pages of the presentation books when necessary.
9. A set of group progress indicators to enable you to keep track of the place each group has reached in the program.

The student's materials include:

1. A set of three storybooks for each child.
2. A set of three take home books for each child.

Lessons should be scheduled on every available school day. The children should be divided into small homogeneous groups for instruction.

It takes approximately 30 or 40 minutes a day for teacher instruction of groups. For children's independent work it takes 20 or 30 minutes a day for each group. Work check takes about 20 minutes and spelling lessons take about 10 minutes a day.

## Overview of Skills Taught

The purpose of Pre-reading Activities is to prepare for reading of simple, regular spelled words. We can figure out what skills should be taught before children are introduced to word reading by analyzing a simple word such as *mat*. The skills needed to "attack" this word are:

1. **Symbol Identification** — The child must be able to recognize the letter symbols and produce the sounds they represent.

2. **Sequencing** — The children need to know the order in which to read symbols.
3. **Blending** — The children need to know that the word can be separated in order to sound it out and put it back together by saying them fast.
4. **Rhyming** — The need of rhyming skills so they can be aware of similarities among words.

Before they get to Lesson 37 they need these prereading skills. The Distar has separate tracks for learning the skills needed. These tracks are:

1. **Sounds** — In the sounds track the children learn to recognize symbols and produce the sounds they stand for.
2. **Symbol Action Game** — Children learn left-to-right sequencing through symbol action games. These appear in the first 24 days of the program. This prepares them for reading words and sentences from left-to-right.
3. **Blending** — The children need to know that the word can be separated in order to sound it out and put it back together by saying them fast.
4. **Say It Fast** — This is an oral blending skill. They learn to put separated sounds together to make a word. This starts on the first day and goes through day 31.
5. **Sound It Out** — This begins at Lesson 26. They do everything to read here except say it fast. This is different from Say the Sounds in two ways:
   A. Children are working from written words rather than orally presented words by the teacher.
   B. They are not asked to say it fast, later when they do say it fast they will be blending.
6. **Rhyming** — This is introduced in Lesson 18, after they know the sounds and experience saying it fast. Rhyming is an additional attack skill. If they understand how it works he can discover the relationship of how a word looks and sounds.

## Reading

The first 36 lessons introduce prereading skills, then the children put these skills together to decode regularly spelled words.

Beginning with lesson 96, children are taught how to identify words without sounding them out. These steps that lead to "reading the fast way" are sequenced so that the child can relate the strategy of sounding our words to the skills of remembering. They do not lose their sounding out ability.

### Story Reading

When the children first begin to read, the lessons are from the Teacher Presentation Book. Most of the load is on reading rate and inflection as the program progresses. They also help with comprehension.

From Lesson 40 to the end of the program every lesson has a story. They increase in length from one word to more than 130 words.

### Written Work

The children begin their work on Take Homes on the first day of the program. The worksheets provide up to 30 minutes a day of independent work that relates to the skills the children are learning. Many of the activities prepare the children for standardized tests.

### Spelling

The spelling lessons start when the children reach lesson 50. The spelling activities begin with the children writing individual sounds from teacher dictation. Spelling words follow the sequence of reading words taught in the program.

Spelling is an optional part of the program. It is a very important skill for children to master. It can be taught to the entire class when the lowest performer reaches lesson 40.

## EDMARK READING PROGRAM

### For the Moderately and Profoundly Handicapped

The Edmark Reading Program is a carefully sequenced, highly repetitive sight word approach. It was developed through research conducted in the 1960s and it became commercially available in 1972. The program has two levels.

Level I of the Edmark Reading Program has proven to be effective with preschool students (aged 3–5), elementary students having difficulty with traditional classroom reading materials, adults, ESL (English as a Second Language) students, and most special education students. It should be considered for anyone who has not been successful in learning to read.

Level II provides the student with an additional two hundred sight words plus a review of Level I words. The student is also introduced to compound words in Level II. A student must complete Level I before beginning Level II.

The Edmark Reading Program eliminates incorrect responding and it leads the student to perceive himself as a "reader" not a "nonreader." The Edmark Reading Program, Level I, provides all the materials you need to introduce and teach 150 basic sight words.

The student prerequisites for Level I and Level II are very minimal. The student must be able to point or respond in some way. They must be able to say or sign back words. And the student must have sufficient receptive language to follow the cues of the teacher.

No special skills or training is required for the teacher. The teacher can be anyone who can speak or write the English language. The most important asset for the teacher to possess is a positive, encouraging attitude toward the student and the patience to work slowly and consistently. The teacher is encouraged to enlist the assistance of grandparents, parents, other students, teacher's aides, and volunteers to work with the student. It is very important to have a good reinforcement system. After each correct response, be certain to praise the student. The teacher needs to be sure not to give too much help too soon.

The Edmark Reading Program, Level I has five types of lessons: Prereading, Word Recognition, Direction Cards, Picture/Phrase Cards, and Storybook. The Prereading consists of the program's first eight lessons. These match to sample lessons familiarize the student with the program and teach visual discrimination. The criterion is no more than four errors. In the Word Recognition lessons, the student learns 150 words plus endings by pairing the spoken words with the printed word. There are thirty nine **Direction Card** lessons. The student learns the meaning of the words by selecting Illustration Cards that correctly depict the words and phrases presented. The criterion is **no errors.** There are thirty nine Picture/Phrase Cards that teach the student a broader understanding of the meanings of the words. In these lessons, word, phrase, and sentence cards are paired with simple illustrations of items, situations, or activities. The criterion is **no errors.** After the first ten words are learned, the words are introduced to the student in a story format. These Storybook lessons provide a bridge from manipulative materials to the type of reading the student will encounter daily. The student completes tests throughout the program. A discrimination test at the end of the Prereading lessons provides us with an overview of the section. A pretest at the beginning of the first ten words taught in Word Recognition and a posttest after each ten words taught in Word Recognition ensure that the student is learning the words.

There is a total of 227 lessons in Level I. One lesson should take the student approximately five to fifteen minutes to complete. The number of lessons taught per day is at the teacher's discretion, but the lessons should be discontinued if the student shows signs of fatigue or is making successive errors. The Edmark Reading Program is set up for sequential progression of lessons. Only the teacher knows best the needs of each student.

The student record book identifies exactly how a student is progressing within a given amount of time. If a student moves to another school, the record book should stay with the student as part of his/her permanent record.

With the addition of Level II, the student's reading vocabulary is greatly increased. When the student completes Level II, his/her reading level will be approximately 2.5 to 3.5.

The Edmark Reading Program, Level II, contains twenty review lessons. The first four of these lessons contain words from Level I and one or more words from Level II that the student has not yet been taught. The criterion is no more than four errors. There are 200 Word Recognition lessons in level II of the Edmark Program. Each lesson teaches a single word. The criterion is no more than four errors. There are two story-books containing the 100 stories in Level II. The stories use only the words the student has learned up to that point in the lesson sequence of the program. The adolescent-age characters, Judy and Scott, are used in the Stories, Word Recognition, and Picture/Phrase lessons. Compound words are introduced in Story Ten. The criterion is 80 percent accuracy. The Comprehension Questions Book provides the questions that should be asked of the student for each story. These questions are read aloud. There are twenty-five Picture/Phrase lessons in Level II. The lessons consist of matching phrases to their corresponding illustrations and phrases, then progress to four, and finally, five. The criterion is no errors.

There is a signing manual included in the Edmark Reading Program for those who wish to use the program with nonverbal students. There is also a software version of the Edmark Program. The software version matches exactly the lessons in the print program. All of the software can be used with the Edmark Reading Program's Touchwindow. This is a low cost, portable touch screen, it can be attached to your computer monitor, allowing the students to touch the screen to interact directly with the Edmark Program. There are many other supplemental materials that are available for you to use.

The Edmark Reading Program is a very complete system. It can be used for a wide variety of people and it is easily administered.

## THE ORTON–GILLINGHAM METHOD

The Orton-Gillingham remediation technique is an alphabetic phonic approach to teaching language skills using the multi-sensory method of eyes (visual), ears (auditory), and muscles (kinesthetic). This is an alphabetic method which concentrates on fusing smaller units into more complex wholes. This method is for students who have been unable to acquire reading, writing, and spelling skills using traditional methods. It has been found to be effective with students who have specific types of reading disabilities.

This method was developed by Anna Gillingham and Bessie Stillman in the 1930s as an instructional treatment for the kinds of children diagnosed by Samuel Orton as language-disordered. Orton's theory stated that reading problems occurred in these children because of an incomplete cerebral hemispheric dominance. When Samuel Orton died, a group of his associates formed the Orton Society to continue his work. Today, The Orton Society is a nonprofit, scientific and educational organization.

This method emphasizes drill and repetition. It requires exclusiveness. No other method of teaching should be used if you are using this method. The authors require that the remedial lessons be held daily for a minimum of two years to be effective. This method was also designed for children identified as dyslexic, described as having normal or superior intelligence but unable to acquire reading skills by ordinary school methods.

The materials included in this method are: a 344-page, hardcover manual describing in detail this method of teaching, each phonic unit is presented on separate Drill Cards, twenty Word Cards with familiar words which can be made from the first ten letters introduced in the drill cards, and graded phonetic stories, exercises on syllable division and practice in the use of a dictionary are additional methods in this remedial approach.

This method has several criticisms. It does not make an accommodation for children with auditory discrimination and auditory perception problems. The procedures are overly rigid, the reading material in this program is not interesting, and the reading of other methods is delayed. Children instructed in this approach have a tendency to develop a labored reading style with much lip movement.

Teachers do not have to follow the program rigidly, but they may use it in an ongoing program. Some experts comment that this approach has been found to be successful when it is used with modifications.

## THE HEGGE-KIRK-KIRK REMEDIAL READING DRILLS

The Hegge-Kirk-Kirk Remedial Reading Drills (1936) were developed at the Wayne County Training School for mentally retarded children. The reading drills are systematically developed, using principles now known as programmed instruction. In its initial stages it is primarily a phonics method that differs from the conventional phonics system in its completeness and in its emphasis on certain principles of learning and retention. It uses the principles of minimal change, one response to one symbol, repetition, and social reinforcement. This method has proved successful with children who had failed to profit from various conventional methods.

The Remedial Reading Drills are divided into four parts:

Part I consists of the most frequent sounds, namely, the sounds of the consonants, the short vowel sounds, and the sounds of ee, sh, oo, ch, tch, ar, ay, ai, or, old, ea, oa, ck, ow, ou, ing, all, ight, th, wh, qu, er, ir, ur, and, and final e.

Part II consists of certain combinations of sounds previously learned in isolation: an, in, un, en, on, ink, ank, unk, ang, ong, ung, ound, est, ill, ell, and consonant combinations.

Part III consists of more advanced and less frequently used sounds presented in word wholes: jaw, Paul, new, took, find, boy, boil, muddy, badly, little, seemed, asked, age, ice, city, fancy, taught, ought, protest, other, return, before, defend, prevent, pension, addition, plantation, solution.

Part IV includes supplementary exercises that teach exceptions to sounds presented in parts I to IV, configurations not previously taught, word building exercises, and exercises on sounds whose letters are frequently confused, such as b, d, p, m, n.

This method is not a general method of teaching reading to all children or to children in the higher grade levels. It is applicable to clinical reading cases, children who have failed to learn to read after a number of years in school. The following general principles should be kept in mind when this method of treatment is used:

1. The method is applicable to children whose reading status is only first-, second-, or third-grade level. It is not a remedial method for retarded readers in the higher grades.
2. The child must have a reading problem; that is, there must be a discrepancy of approximately two or more years between reading grade and the grade consistent with the child's mental age.
3. Any extreme visual or auditory deficiencies must have been corrected.
4. A child must be trainable in sound blending.
5. The child must be willing to learn and must develop cooperation. It should be remembered that at the onset, many children appear uncooperative and uninterested.
6. The child must lack the perceptual-motor abilities developed by the drills and must need to develop skills in recognizing details.
7. It is necessary that the teachers of slow and disabled learners transfer the ability to sound words to a natural reading situation.

## THE PHONOVISUAL APPROACH

### "A Complete Phonics Program"

The primary reason for the development of this program was because of the authors' concern for the vast number of nonreaders and of children reading inadequately.

Lucille Schoolfield and Josephine Timberlake were the authors of the phonovisual method. Ms. Schoolfield was an instructor of speech and Ms. Timberlake was an educator of the hearing impaired.

The wide acceptance of the phonovisual method is partially due to the fact that the authors admit readily that this is not a method of teaching reading by itself. It is a supplementary tool which should be added. The phonovisual method is taught using two charts, the consonent chart and the vowel chart. The consonent chart is implemented first, the reason for that is because 66 percent of this test are made up of consonents.

The sounds on the consonent chart are organized later vertically and horizontally. In the vertical arrangement, the sounds are related in the muscular order in which they are produced.

The phonovisual method develops skills in three fields: Better Reading, Better Spelling, and Better Speech. Average children can master the two charts in the first two years of school. The program has also been proven to be a valuable program with remedial students. The learning disabled student is provided with a multisensory approach to learning letter sounds—auditory, visual, and kinesthetic. Remedial students are given an organized and simple means to learn a basic step in beginning reading.

Upon presenting the phonovisual method there are basic steps and guidelines which must be adheared to. For example, the instructor would say "keep," the student: K____. Second, the instructor "keep," the student: k__p. Third, the instructor "keep," the student: k-e-e-p. There are numerous varieties of support material which can be purchased: workbooks, audio tapes, charts, duplicating masters, and game activities.

In summation, the training and stimulation of the three senses, the auditory, visual, and kinesthetic, result in accuracy in spelling, improvement in speech, and in achieving the main goal—fluency and real joy in reading.

## THE CLOZE PROCEDURE

The Cloze procedure was developed to determine the difficulty level of a selection, to test reading comprehension, and to provide instruction in reading. It is used to help the students use the structure and grammatical patterns of oral language to comprehend written language. The Cloze procedure is a psycholinguistic approach to teaching reading because it forces the child to deal with the syntactic and semantic cue systems of written language.

In the Cloze procedure every nth word is deleted and replaced with a blank line. It is usually good to delete every 5th word. Students are to read the material and fill in the blanks using the correct word according to the proper context of the sentence. Passages may very in length depending on the grade level of the students. For third or fourth grade, a passage of about 250 words should be used. The entire first sentence and the last sentence should be left intact.

Cloze passages may be given like a group standardized reading test, but there is no specific time limit. In scoring the passage only the exact word omitted is counted as correct. Synonyms are not accepted. In scoring, students are not penalized for incorrect spelling as long as there is little or no doubt about which word was meant to be used. A quick way to check the passage is to have a plastic overlay of each cloze passage with the correct answers. When this is laid on the student's copy the answers can readily be checked and converted to percentages. The independent level will be 58 percent to 100 percent. The instructional level will be 44 percent through 57 percent, and the frustration level will be 43 percent or below.

Some of the advantages of the Cloze procedure is that it forces the reader to bridge gaps in both language and thought. It does not take very long to administer and is good for classroom teachers because they do not have to have special training in test administration.

The Cloze procedure can also be used to analyze errors. This will also provide useful information on the reading ability of the student. It gives practical information on the student's ability to read and write. It shows the student's overall comprehension and vocabulary by noting whether substitution are synonyms or out of context. The teacher can tell if the student has been able to remember detail given earlier in the passage.

## OPEN COURT BASAL READING PROGRAM

Open Court is a complete basal reading program that strives to build a strong foundation for a lifetime of learning. Skills and strategies are stressed in this program that leads to early independence in decoding, comprehension, writing, and thinking for **all** children. Slow students, as well as average or gifted students, need the foundation of strategies. Open Court helps **all** children learn not only to get the correct answer, but **how** to get the correct answer.

The Open Court series incorporates reading, reading and writing, and language art skills into a single program. These skills are designed to reinforce and motivate each other. Literature is the core of this program in which the stories keep the interest level of students high in reading and in writing.

Phonics is the basic decoding strategy in the Open Court Program.

The common sound-symbol correspondents are taught from the very beginning with the blending of the sounds shortly following. Phonics is reinforced by two other important strategies: visual memory for irregular words and analysis of word parts. Together these three strategies produce skilled, independent decoders by the end of second grade—and usually by the end of first.

Important writing strategies are also taught in Open Court to help students make effective use of the writing process. Students work on writing in every lesson. Grammar, punctuation, and usage skills are presented as needed during the course of student's editing of their own writing.

The basic components of the Open Court program include the student reader, teacher's guide, teacher's resource book, and reading skills workbook. The student reader included classics in their original version, delightful content to motivate reading, and carefully controlled initial selections to ensure early success. The teacher's guide includes simple 5-step lesson plans, clear structure and labeling, lesson outlines, and complete, integrated lesson plans for reading, writing, and all of the language arts. The teacher's resource book includes blackline masters of activity sheets, bulletin board ideas, comprehension strategy charts, parent letters, overhead transparencies, and instructional charts, and posters. The workbook contains carefully designed practice pages for decoding, comprehension, literature, vocabulary, and study and research skills.

Authors of Open Court are Carl Bereiter, Valerie Anderson, and Jan Hirshberg. These people designed this program with two goals in mind. First, the early stories help children apply newly acquired decoding strategies. As the children become more independent readers, they are given the opportunity to read real literature. Second, the readers are designed to look like trade books so that the children will be motivated to read.

## THE GLASS ANALYSIS METHOD

The Glass Analysis Method for teaching the decoding skills of reading is described by Glass as a method of developing perceptual conditioning for the decoding of letter clusters within words. The student is guided to recognize common letter clusters easily and quickly while looking at the whole word. The Glass Analysis Method concentrates on the decoding of words through intensive auditory and visual training focused on the word being studied.

Decoding is defined as the act of correctly determining the accepted sound connected with the printed word. Decoding precedes reading. Reading cannot occur until the person has developed the ability to decode. If one does not learn to decode efficiently and effectively, one will never be able to read.

The Glass Analysis Method proposes eight points about the teaching of decoding:

1. Decoding is not reading and should be taught separately from reading.
2. Children should learn to decode words whose meanings they already know.
3. Emphasis should be on decoding skills.
4. Syllabication is not useful in teaching decoding and should not be part of the decoding program.
5. Successful decoders do not apply prescribed rules or a conscious reasoning process in decoding.
6. Words are first seen as wholes and then as parts or letter clusters that combine to form the correct sound.
7. The student needs correct visual and auditory clustering perception to learn the decoding process.
8. Correct decoding requires that the child learn the correct mental set and respond to the appropriate letter-sound structures within a word.

The materials needed for this method can be teacher-made. They consist of flash cards about three inches by six inches in size. Commercially-published materials are available. On each card is printed a carefully selected word containing letter clusters. The words selected for study are within the child's meaning vocabulary.

Four steps are required to teach each word:

1. Identify the whole word and the letters and sound of that target cluster.
2. Pronounce the sound or sounds and ask the child for the letter or letters.
3. Give the letter or letters and ask for the sound or sounds.
4. Take away letters and ask for the remaining sound.

This method shapes perception by examining whole words in a way that will help the child when he or she sees other words containing the same letter clusters. The method literally forces the issue of clustering.

## NEUROLOGICAL IMPRESS METHOD

The Neurological Impress Method is a relatively new approach to reading instruction designed for students with severe reading disabilities. It is a system of unison reading in which the student and the instructor read together, the voice of the instructor being directed into the ear of the student at a fairly close range. The student or instructor uses a finger as a locator as each word is read. At times, the instructor may be louder and faster than the student and at other times the instructor may read more softly and slightly slower than the student. The object is simply to cover as many pages of reading as possible within the time available without causing fatigue to the student.

## INITIAL TEACHING ALPHABET

The Initial Teaching Alphabet (i/t/a) Approach is a method for beginning reading instruction. Forty-four characters are employed in the i/t/a orthography, each symbol representing one speech sound in the English language. The i/t/a alphabet includes twenty-four of the familiar letters, dropping q and x. Twenty additional characters are added to achieve greater correspondence between the written and spoken forms of a word. Only lower case letters are used in i/t/a; a larger size or the lower case form indicates capital letters.

In i/t/a, a word is spelled the way it is pronounced. For example, baby is baeby. The initial teaching alphabet is used only in beginning reading instruction. After the child achieves some proficiency in the use of this system, the i/t/a characters are gradually phased out of the reading materials and the child is transferred to traditional orthography, the conventional alphabet and spelling.

The i/t/a system has been used with varying degrees of success with atypical children. The method cannot be modified extensively but can be combined with other methods to make it more appropriate for slow and disabled learners.

# REFERENCES

Edmark Associates (1972). *Edmark Reading Program, Teacher's Guide.* Seattle, WA: Edmark Associates.

Englemann, S., & Bruner, E. C. (1988a). *Reading Mastery I: Distar Reading.* Chicago: Science Research Associates.

Englemann, S., & Bruner, E. C. (1988b). *Reading Mastery II: Distar Reading.* Chicago: Science Research Associates.

Fernald, Grace (1943). *Remedial Techniques in Basic School Subjects.* New York: McGraw Hill.

Gillingham, A. & Stillman, B. (1968). *Remedial Teaching for Children with Specific Disability in Reading, Spelling, and Penmanship.* Cambridge, MA: Educator's Publishing Service.

Glass, G. G. (1973). *Teaching Decoding as Separate from Reading.* Garden City, NY: Adelphi University Press.

Kirk, S. A. (1936). *Manual of Directions for Use with the Hegge-Kirk-Kirk Remedial Reading Drills.* Ann Arbor, MI: George Wahr.

Langford, K., Slade, K., & Barnett, A. (Spring 1974). An explanation of impress techniques in remedial reading. *Academic Therapy, 9,* pp. 309–319.

Lerner, J. W. (1976). *Children with Learning Disabilities.* Boston, MA: Houghton Mifflin.

Orton, S. T. (1937). *Reading, Writing, and Speech Problems in Children.* New York: W. W. Norton & Co.

Parker, D. (1989). *Corrective Reading.* Chicago: Science Research Associates.

Parker, D., & Scallell, G. (1962). *SRA Reading Laboratory I Word Games.* Chicago: Science Research Associates.

Sceats, J. (1967). *i.t.a. and the Teaching of Literacy.* New York: Putman.

Woodcock, R. W., Clark, C. R. & Davies, C. O. (1969). *Peabody Rebus Reading Program.* Circle Pines, MN: American Guidance Service.

# Chapter 7

# FORMAL ASSESSMENT PROCEDURES

## OVERVIEW OF FORMAL READING TESTS

By formal tests, we mean commercially prepared, formally developed instruments. Many of these tests are norm-referenced or standardized tests. By using norm-referenced tests, the scores of a student who is tested can be compared with the scores of a sample of students who were used to standardize the test. This group is known as the "norm sample." Norm-referenced tests have generally been developed carefully using a large number of children who are representative of the general population. In order to assure that a student's score can in fact be compared with a norm sample, it is essential that procedures for test administration, scoring and interpretation be followed strictly. There are also formal tests called criterion-referenced tests, and these are constructed from a different theoretical base. Rather than comparing students with one another, a criterion-referenced test determines whether a student has mastered certain competencies. Criterion-referenced tests are generally used to assess student mastery of specific reading skills. Sometimes a standardized test is used to develop a criterion-referenced evaluation procedure.

Both formal tests and informal measures can offer important information about the child. When trying to diagnose or evaluate a child's reading ability, teachers should use both kinds of measurement in order to learn as much as possible about the child. The information from one type of test can corroborate that of the other.

## THE SURVEY READING TEST

The purpose of the survey test is to give general information about the child's reading level. The survey test usually has two parts: one measuring the pupil's reading vocabulary and the other measuring paragraph comprehension. Some survey tests also have subtests that measure sentence comprehension and rate of reading. Survey tests are usually designed as group tests. The students read silently and then answer multiple choice questions. These tests can also be given to one student at a time. The tests usually have fairly long time limits so that the pupil is stopped by the increasing difficulty of the reading material rather than by being timed. Generally speaking, a survey test is one of the first tests given to assess the reading ability of the child.

## SCORES ON READING TESTS

The raw score on a reading test is simply the total number of items that the child has correctly answered. For interpretation, this must be converted to a more meaningful score, such as the grade level score, the age score, the percentile rank, or stanine or scale score.

### Reading Grade Score

To obtain a reading grade score, the raw score is converted to a grade level score such as 2.5 (fifth month of the second grade), which indicates that the child's reading level is the same as the score of a child in the middle of the second grade. For example, if Johnny scores 5.2 on the ABC Reading Test, he receives the same raw score as a median of the children in the second month of the fifth grade who took this test. Generally, the tests are broken down into 10 months, meaning that a child who scores 6.10 has scored at the tenth month of the sixth grade. There are few tests that break the scoring down into beginning grade, middle grade, and end of the grade. For example, a child who has a 4B score means that he is reading at the beginning fourth grade level. A child who has a 4E score means that he is reading at the end of the fourth grade level.

### Reading Age Score

The reading age is similar to a reading grade score except that norms are based on the age of the children rather than grade placement. A reading grade score of 6.11 means that the child scored the same as the median of the norm population aged six years and 11 months. Reading age scores are reported in terms of years and twelfths, as chronological age is based on a twelve month year. The difference between a person's reading age and reading grade is roughly five years. To convert a reading grade to a reading age, simply add five years. For example, Betty's reading grade is 4.2. Her reading age is, therefore, 9-2.

Reading grade and reading age scores are useful when trying to determine the reading growth of a child over a period of remediation time. For example, Hal scored at the 2.2 level in September and at the 3.3 level in March following six months of remediation. This means that in six months Hal gained one year, one month grades in reading. Grade level scores are easy for parents to understand.

## DECILES, QUARTILES, AND STANINES

**Decile.** A decile is any one of the nine points that divide a distribution into 10 parts, each containing one-tenth of all the scores. The first decile is the tenth percentile, the eighth decile is the eighteenth percentile, etc. (every tenth percentile along a normal curve).

**Quartile.** A quartile is any one of three points that divide the subjects into four equal parts. The middle quartile is the same as the fiftieth percentile (or median). The third quartile sets off the top fourth, or seventh-fifth percentile. The first twenty-fifth percentile defines the lowest one-fourth of the subjects.

**Stanine.** The word stanine was derived from two words, *standard nine*. Therefore, it is defined as any one of the steps in a nine-point scale of standard scores. The stanine has values from one to nine, with a mean of five and a standard deviation of two. Each stanine (except one and nine) is one-half standard deviation in width. The middle stanine (five), extends from one-fourth standard deviation below the mean to one-fourth standard deviation above the mean. Stanines provide a single-digit scoring system with a mean of five and a standard deviation of two. When scores are converted to stanines, the shape of the original distribution is changed into a normal curve.

**Statistical Significance.** Significance levels refer to the risk of error we are willing to take in drawing conclusions from data.

In educational research, it is often necessary to generalize from a particular sample to a larger population. There are statistical procedures for estimating probable fluctuation to expect from sample to sample in the size of correlations, means, standard deviations, and other group measures.

In correlations the question often asked is if the correlation is significantly greater than zero. When we say that a correlation is "significant at the 1 percent (.01) level," it means the chances are no greater than one out of 100 that the population correlation is zero. The variables are related.

Minimum correlations significant at the .01 and .05 levels for groups of different sizes can be found by consulting tables of the significance of correlations in statistics textbooks.

If two means are significant at the .01 level, this indicates that with one chance out of 100 of being wrong, that a difference in the obtained direction would be found if we tested the whole population from which the samples are drawn.

**Standard Error of Measurement.** The standard error of measurement is a statistical procedure for quantifying reliability when reliability data have been gathered. It examines the variability found with repeated measures. Examiners can compute standard deviations to describe variability, if the measurement is repeated a number of times with a single subject and the distribution of the repeated measurements are examined.

Synonymous terms are "standard error," "test error," and "error of measurement." The standard error of measurement of a test indicates the extent that chance errors cause variations in the score obtained by an individual if the same test was administered an infinite number of times. Tests with a relatively small standard error are much more desirable than tests with a relatively large standard error.

**Correlation.** Correlation refers to how two or more characteristics are associated or related and what they have in common. These characteristics are called variables, and can be changed, manipulated, controlled, and/or observed by the person conducting the experiment.

When addressing the term correlation, the terms positive correlation and negative correlation are often referred to. Positive correlation is obtained when a large amount of one variable is associated with a large amount of another variable. Or it may be positively correlated when a small amount of one variable is associated with a small amount of another variable.

> *Example:* Teachers observe that students who have high intelligence quotients tend to receive high scores in mathematics tests; whereas those with low IQs tend to score low.

Negative correlations are obtained when a large amount of one variable is associated with a small amount of the other. As one increases, the other will decrease.

*Example:* As a student's anxiety level concerning taking tests increases, the scores he obtains on tests may tend to decrease.

Actually, the word *correlation* describes a relationship which exists between two variables. The *coefficient of correlation* describes the degree of relationship that exists between characteristics and scores and sets of scores. You may obtain a perfect positive relationship ($+1.0$) or a perfect negative relationship ($-1.0$). Ordinarily, a correlation of $+.75$ or above, or $-.75$ or below is considered a very high correlation.

**Validity.** The validity of a test refers to the extent to which a test measures what it is supposed to measure. The test must be valid for the particular purposes for which it is being used or the results cannot be used with any degree of confidence. There are four types of validity: content validity, criterion-related validity, concurrent validity, and predictive validity.

**Concurrent validity.** Concurrent validity refers to whether the test scores are related to some currently available criterion measure. Concurrent validity should be used with tests to measure existing status but not for predicting future outcomes.

**Population, Sampling, Parameters.** We use the term population to refer to an entire group or the total number from which samples are taken for a particular purpose.

Most methods of sampling are designed to obtain a small sample which represents a much larger population. The population may be tested, observed, surveyed, or whatever is appropriate for that situation.

When we test an entire population and then characterize or describe the population in terms of particular properties, these properties would be called *parameters.*

**Item Analysis.** When one analyzes individual items on a test it is called *item analysis.* There are several ways to analyze individual items and there are several different purposes for analyzing items. The objective generally is to learn of the difficulty of the item. Many times though, the items will be analyzed to determine how well they discriminate between such factors as knowledge, ability, those who are likely to succeed and those who will not. Some item analyses involve a very complex statistical analysis while other procedures are not so strict.

**Examples of Survey Reading Tests**

There are many standardized or norm-referenced survey reading tests on the market. The survey reading tests found at the primary, elementary, and intermediate levels include the following:

*California Reading Test* (California Test Bureau)

*Comprehensive Reading Scales* (Van Wagen Psycho-Educational Laboratories)

*Gates-MacGinitie Reading Tests* (Teachers College Press)

*Iowa Every-Pupil Tests of Basic Skills* (Houghton Mifflin)

*Iowa Silent Reading Tests* (Harcourt Brace Jovanovich)

*Metropolitan Achievement Tests: Reading* (Harcourt Brace Jovanovich)

*New Development Reading Tests* (Lyons and Carnahan)

*SRA Achievement Series: Reading* (Science Research Associates)

*Stanford Achievement Tests: Reading* (Harcourt Brace Jovanovich)

*Wide Range Achievement Test (WRAT)* (Guidance Testing Associates)

Survey tests at the secondary or high school level include:

*California Reading Test* (California Test Bureau)

*Comprehensive Test of Basic Skills* (California Test Bureau)

*Diagnostic Reading Tests* (Committee on Diagnostic Reading Tests)

*Iowa Silent Reading Test* (Harcourt Brace Jovanovich)

*Iowa Tests of Educational Development (ITED)* (Science Research Associates)

*Iowa Tests of Basic Skills* (Houghton Mifflin)

*Gates-MacGinitie Reading Tests* (Teachers College Press)

*Nelson-Denny Reading Test* (Houghton Mifflin)

*Cooperative English Tests: Reading Comprehension* (Educational Testing Service)

*Sequential Tests of Educational Progress (STEP)* (Educational Testing Service)

*Traxler Silent Reading Test* (Bobbs Merrill)

*Davis Reading Test* (Psychological Corporation)

In addition there are several reading tests designed for adult basic education students:

*Tests of Adult Basic Education (TABE)* (California Test Bureau)

*Adult Basic Learning Examination (ABLE)* (Harcourt Brace Jovanovich)

*Basic Reading Inventory (BRI)* (Scholastic Testing)

Several of the most widely used standardized survey tests are described below:

**California Reading Tests.** *Level 1* (grades one to two); *Level 2* (grades two to four); *Level 3* (grades four to six); *Level 4* (grades six to nine); *Level 5* (grades nine to twelve). Each level has subtests on vocabulary and comprehension. Levels 1 and 2 have word attack subtests. There are two or more forms available at each level. Administration time: ranges from 35 minutes at *Level 1* to 80 minutes at *Level 5*. (California Test Bureau)

The three most widely used survey tests are the Wide Range Achievement Test—Revised (WRAT-R), the Peabody Individual Achievement Test—Revised (PIAT-R), and the Woodcock Reading Mastery Test—Revised (WRMT-R). The WRAT-R contains a reading test consisting of a graded list of words for oral reading. A grade placement level is determined by having the student read this list. Although short and convenient to administer, this test does not present a comprehensive assessment of reading abilities. This test also does not break the levels down into grade and months. For example, on the WRAT-R beginning at the third grade level, you would have 3B which means beginning third grade word recognition, 3M which would be middle third grade, and 3E, end of the third grade.

The reading sections of the Peabody Individual Achievement Test—Revised (PIAT-R) measure word recognition and comprehension. Word recognition is measured through oral reading of a list; in the reading comprehension subtest, students choose a picture that describes a reading paragraph. The PIAT-R also measures mathematics, spelling, and general information.

The Woodcock Reading Mastery Test—Revised (WRMT-R) is an individual survey test which contains many diagnostic features. The test measures individuals from a beginning reading level to that of an advanced adult. It is available in two forms, and both forms can be jointly administered. The WRMT-R contains four basic subtests, (1) word identification, (2) word attack, (3) word comprehension, and (4) passage comprehension. These may be combined to obtain a full scale reading performance assessment.

Several of the most widely used standardized reading tests are described below:

**Iowa Tests of Basic Skills.** *Primary Battery* (grades 1.7 to 3.5); *Levels Edition* (grades three to eight). Reading comprehension, vocabulary, word analysis, work-study skills. Two forms at each level. Administration time: 60–85 minutes. (Houghton Mifflin)

**Metropolitan Achievement Tests: Reading.** *Primer* (grades K.7 to 1.4). Listening for sounds, word knowledge, comprehension. Two forms. Administration time: approximately one hour. *Primary I* (grades 1.5 to 2.4); *Primary II* (grades 2.5 to 3.4). Word knowledge, word analysis, comprehension. Three forms. Administration time: approximately one hour. *Elementary* (grades 3.5 to 4.9); *Intermediate* (grades 5 to 6.0); *Advanced* (grades 7 to 9.5). Word knowledge, comprehension. Three forms. Administration time: 43–46 minutes. (Harcourt Brace Jovanovich)

**SRA Achievement Series: Reading.** *Primary I* (grades 1 to 2.5) *Primary II* (grades 2.5 to 3); *Multilevel Blue* (grades 4 to 5); *Multilevel Green* (grades 6 to 7); *Multilevel Red* (grades 8 to 9.5). Vocabulary and comprehension subtests. Two forms. Administration time: approximately one hour. (Science Research Associates).

**Stanford Achievement Tests: Reading.** *Primary I* (grades 1.5 to 2.4); *Primary II* (grades 2.5 to 3.5); *Primary III* (grades 3.5 to 4.4); *Intermediate I* (grades 4.5 to 5.4); *Intermediate II* (grades 5.5 to 6.9). Vocabulary, reading, comprehension, and word study skills. There is also a listening comprehension subtest. *Advanced* (grades 7 to 9.5). Vocabulary and reading comprehension. Two forms at each level. Administration time: 35–95 minutes. (Harcourt Brace Jovanovich)

**The Botel Reading Inventory** (Botel, 1978) contains a Decoding Test, a Spelling Placement Test, a Word Recognition Test, and a Word Opposites Test. The latter two tests have two forms each and are designed for use as reading placement tests. The Decoding Test includes twelve subtests:

1. "Letter Naming"
2. "Beginning Consonant Sound/Letter Awareness"
3. "Rhyme Sound/Letter Pattern Awareness"
4.–12. "Decoding Syllable/Spelling Patterns"

**Brigance Diagnostic Inventory of Basic Skills.** Contains 141 criterion-referenced subtests for reading, readiness, and reference skills as well as for math, handwriting, spelling, and grammar. Used for assessing skill levels between grades Pre-K–6 for remedial students. Subtests include 24 for readiness, 6 for word recognition, 3 for reading (oral reading level, comprehension, and oral reading rate), 19 for word analysis, 5 for vocabulary, and 9 for reference. Contained in easy-to-administer binder with student's copy and examiner's on opposite pages. Yields ratings of satisfactory/needs to improve for given grade level. Subtests coordinated with IEP rating system. Individual test: 15–90 minutes. One form. (Also *Brigance Diagnostic Comprehensive Inventory of Basic Skills* grades pre K–9;

**Inventory of Early Development,** ages 0–7; *Inventory of Essential Skills* grades 6–adult; and *Diagnostic Assessment of Basic Skills, Spanish version,* grades K–9 (Curriculum Associates).

**Doren Diagnostic Reading Test of Word Recognition Skills.** Diagnostic: Specific Area (Grades: 1–4). Measures 12 specific areas for remedial readers. Each skill is arranged from simple to complex. Subtests include letter recognition, beginning sounds, whole word recognition, words within words, speech consonants such as the difference between "ch" and "sh," ending sounds, blending, rhyming, vowels, discriminate guessing, spelling, and sight words. Criterion referenced with overlay correcting form for scoring. Remedial activities presented in manual. Individual skill profiles contain ratings for satisfactory/not satisfactory for each area (American Guidance Service).

**Durrell Analysis of Reading Difficulty.** Diagnostic Battery (with oral reading test) (Grades: 1–6). Contains (1) eight short, progressively harder paragraphs for oral reading from which rate and comprehension (using questions) are determined; (2) eight short paragraphs for silent reading from which reading rate and free recall are determined; (3) six paragraphs to determine listening comprehension; (4) two sets of isolated word lists to analyze instant recognition (tachistoscopic) and word analysis; (5) other subtests including listening vocabulary, visual memory for words, identifying sounds in words, sounds in isolation, phonic spelling of words, prereading phonics abilities, and spelling ability. Subtests administered vary. Yield grade equivalent scores (Psychological Corporation).

**Gates-McKillop-Horowitz Reading Diagnostic Tests.** Tests oral reading, sight knowledge, phonics, spelling, and writing. Contains (1) continuous set of graded short oral reading paragraphs; (2) four reading sentences with regular words; (3) flashwords presented with tachistoscore; (4) untimed word list for sight recognition or analysis; (5) tests of word attack using nonsense words; syllabication, recognizing and blending word parts, reading words, letter sounds, and naming capital and lowercase letters; (6) test of identifying spoken vowel sounds; (7) test of auditory blending vowels, discriminate guessing, spelling, and sight words. Criterion referenced with overlay correcting form for scoring. Remedial activities

presented in manual. Individual skill profiles contain ratings for satis-
factory/not satisfactory for each area (American Guidance Service).

   **Ekwall Reading Inventory.** *Informal Reading Inventory, Grades: 1–9.*
Contains word recognition test (PP–9) and passages for oral and silent
reading from preprimer through grade nine. Comprehension questions
following passages: literal, inference, vocabulary. Oral and silent reading are presented alternately at each level. Testing continues in one
mode if frustration level is reached in the other. Yields independent,
instructional, frustration reading levels. Also contains El Paso Phonics
Survey. Longest passage 202 words. Individual test: 20–30 minutes. Four
forms available in one binder. (Allyn and Bacon).

   **Formal Reading Inventory (FRI).** *Oral Reading Test, Grades: 1–12.*
Measures oral reading, silent reading, and comprehension through thir-
teen graded passages followed by five multiple-choice completion questions for each passage. Forms A and C require silent reading; forms B
and D require oral reading. Silent reading quotient is derived. Scores
are standardized. In addition, forms are provided for an analysis of
miscue types (meaning similarity, function similarity, graphic/phonemic
similarity, use of multiple clues, self correction). Individual test: 20–40
minutes. Four forms in one binder (Pro-Ed).

   **Gates-MacGinitie Reading Tests.** *Diagnostic Battery (with oral reading
tests) Grades 1–8 1978.* This test evaluates grades 1–12 in vocabulary,
comprehension, speed, and accuracy. Each Survey test includes sub-tests
of the four areas mentioned above. All of the tests consist of two or
more forms. Administration time ranges from 45–65 minutes (Riverside
Publishing).

   **Gilmore Oral Reading Test, New Ed. (GORT).** Tests oral reading
using 10 graded paragraphs each followed by 5 comprehension questions.
Yields grade equivalent, stanines, and percentiles for oral reading,
comprehension, and rate (Psychological Corporation).

   **Gray Oral Reading Tests-Revised.** Revision of the classic test by Gray
and Robinson. Measures oral reading through 13 timed, graded passages,
each followed by 5 comprehension questions. Passage score is derived
from the rate and errors in reading. In addition, there are standard
scores for oral reading comprehension and a total reading score. Miscue
analysis form is also provided (Pro-Ed).

   **Love Diagnostic Reading Inventory.** Measures oral reading through 10
graded passages, each followed by five comprehension questions. Passage score is derived from accuracy and comprehension. Miscue analysis

is also provided. This test also has a word recognition sub-test which is graded (Ginn Press).

# INTELLIGENCE TESTS

One kind of standardized test is the intelligence test. Intelligence tests are extremely important in the assessment of reading problems, for they help determine the child's potential for learning, usually in terms of an IQ score and/or mental age. The numerical difference between a child's scores on an intelligence test and a reading test is the discrepancy between potential and achievement. The size of the discrepancy helps the teacher determine if the child has a significant reading problem. Intelligence tests are divided into two types: (1) individually administered intelligence tests and (2) group administered intelligence tests.

## Individual Intelligence Tests

Individual intelligence tests are administered by a trained psychologist or examiner to a single child. Administration can take from 10 minutes to several hours, depending on the test. The individual intelligence test is considered very useful for estimating the general mental capacity of a child. While testing, the examiner has the opportunity to observe the child and to make sure that the child puts forth his or her best effort. The most widely used individual tests are described below:

**Wechsler Intelligence Scale for Children—3rd Ed. (WISC–III).** This is the third edition of the Wechsler Intelligence Scale for Children (WISC; Wechsler, 1949). It is an individually administered clinical instrument for assessing the intellectual ability of children aged 6 years through 16 years, 11 months. This test retains many of the essential features of the WISC and its revision, the Wechsler Intelligence Scale for Children—Revised (WISC–R; Wechsler, 1974), the WISC–III provides current normative data and updated test materials, test content, and administration procedures. As with all Wechsler intelligence scales, the WISC–III consists of several subtests each measuring a different facet of intelligence.

As in the WISC–R, the child's performance on these various measures is summarized in three composite scores, the Verbal, the Performance, and Full Scale IQ, which provide estimates of the individual's intellectual abilities.

Additionally, the WISC–III provides four optional factor-based index scores. In addition to the Verbal, Performance, and Full Scale IQ scores, four factor-based index scores can be calculated. They are: (1) verbal comprehension (VCI), (2) perceptual organization (POI), (3) freedom from distractibility (FDI), and (4) processing speed (PSI). These factor-based scales, like the IQ scales, have a mean of 100 and a standard deviation of 15. Table 7.1 presents the subtest composition of each factor-based scale. Also, Table 7.2 indicates the descriptions of all the WISC–III subtests and Table 7.3 is a copy of the front page of WISC–III Record Booklet.

Table 7.1. Scales Derived from Factor Analyses of the WISC-III Subtests.

| Factor I Verbal Comprehension | Factor II Perceptual Organization | Factor III Freedom from Distractibility | Factor IV Processing Speed |
|---|---|---|---|
| Information | Picture Completion | Arithmetic | Coding |
| Similarities | Picture Arrangement | Digit Span | Symbol Search |
| Vocabulary | Block Design | | |
| Comprehension | Object Assembly | | |

**Wechsler Preschool and Primary Scale of Intelligence — Revised (WPPSI–R).** The WPPSI–R has been published about two years now and although it is similar to its predecessor, there are differences. The age range has been extended from 4–6½ to 3–7¼. Ninety-one new items were added in order to increase the range and the total number of items have been expanded from 182 to 217. The revision contains a new subtest, Object Assembly, which makes it more similar to the WISC–R. Scoring guidelines and administrative procedures have been modified on some of the subtests. The Animal House Subtest was renamed Animal Pegs and made an optional subtest. Also, the Animal House retest has been excluded in the revision. On the Block Design Subtest, speed, coupled with correct performance is awarded additional bonus points in the revision. Finally, the WPPSI–R covers a more extensive I.Q. range, 41–160, instead of the WPPSI's 45–155. Figure 7.1 is a copy of the front page of the WPPSI–R Record Booklet.

**Stanford-Binet Intelligence Scale.** The Stanford-Binet Intelligence Scale 1986 revision is recommended with subjects from two years of age through adulthood. The test is seldom used in school systems for children other than 10 or 12 because of the time involved in administering it. In cases of

**Table 7.2. Descriptions of the WISC–III Subtests.**

| Subtest | Description |
| --- | --- |
| Picture Completion | A set of colorful pictures of common objects and scenes each of which is missing an important part which the child identifies. |
| Information | A series of orally presented questions that tap the child's knowledge about common events, objects, places, and people. |
| Coding | A series of simple shapes (Coding A) or numbers (Coding B), each paired with a simple symbol. The child draws the symbol in its corresponding shape (Coding A) or under its corresponding number (Coding B), according to a key. Coding A and B are included on a single performated sheet in the Record Form. |
| Similarities | A series of orally presented pairs of words for which the child explains the similarity of the common objects or concepts they represent. |
| Picture Arrangement | A set of colorful pictures, presented in mixed-up order, which the child rearranges into a logical story sequence. |
| Arithmetic | A series of arithmetic problems which the child solves mentally and responds to orally. |
| Block Design | A set of modeled or printed two-dimensional geometric patterns which the child replicates using two-color cubes. |
| Vocabulary | A series of orally presented words which the child orally defines. |
| Object Assembly | A set of puzzles of common objects, each presented in a standardized configuration, which the child assembles to form a meaningful whole. |
| Comprehension | A series of orally presented questions that require the child's solving of everyday problems or understanding of social rules and concepts. |
| Symbol Search | A series of paired groups of symbols, each pair consisting of a target group and a search group. The child scans the two groups and indicates whether or not a target symbol appears in the search group. Both levels of the subtest are included in a single response booklet. |
| Digit Span | A series of orally presented number of sequences which the child repeats verbatim for Digits Forward and in reverse order for Digits Backwards. |
| Mazes | A set of increasingly difficult mazes, printed in a response booklet, which the child solves with a pencil. |

children over 10 or 12, the WISC–R or WAIS–R is normally used. The Stanford-Binet contains a series of items, increasing in difficulty, grouped by age level beginning at age two and progressing to adulthood. There are six test items and an alternate item for each age level, with the

**RECORD FORM**

Name _____ Parent's Name _____

Address _____

School _____ Grade _____

Place of Testing _____ Examiner _____

Age _____ Sex _____ Handedness _____

|  | Year | Month | Day |
|---|---|---|---|
| Date Tested |  |  |  |
| Date of Birth |  |  |  |
| Age |  |  |  |

| Performance Tests | Raw Score | Scaled Score |
|---|---|---|
| Object Assembly |  |  |
| Geometric Design |  |  |
| Block Design |  |  |
| Mazes |  |  |
| Picture Completion |  |  |
| (Animal Pegs) | ( ) | ( ) |

Total
Performance Tests [ ]

| Verbal Tests | Raw Score | Scaled Score |
|---|---|---|
| Information |  |  |
| Comprehension |  |  |
| Arithmetic |  |  |
| Vocabulary |  |  |
| Similarities |  |  |
| (Sentences) | ( ) | ( ) |

Total
Verbal Tests [ ]

|  | Scaled Score | IQ |
|---|---|---|
| Performance Score |  |  |
| Verbal Score |  |  |
| Full Scale Score |  |  |

**WPPSI-R PROFILE**

Clinicians who wish to draw a profile should first transfer the child's *scaled scores* to the row of boxes below. Then mark an X on the dot corresponding to the scaled score for each test, and draw a line connecting the X's.*

Performance Tests — Verbal Tests

Object Assembly, Geometric Design, Block Design, Mazes, Picture Completion, (Animal Pegs), Information, Comprehension, Arithmetic, Vocabulary, Similarities, (Sentences)

Scaled Score [ ] [ ] [ ] [ ] [ ] [ ]   Scaled Score [ ] [ ] [ ] [ ] [ ]   Scaled Score

19 · · · · · ·  19  · · · · ·  19
18 · · · · · ·  18  · · · · ·  18
17 · · · · · ·  17  · · · · ·  17
16 · · · · · ·  16  · · · · ·  16
15 · · · · · ·  15  · · · · ·  15
14 · · · · · ·  14  · · · · ·  14
13 · · · · · ·  13  · · · · ·  13
12 · · · · · ·  12  · · · · ·  12
11 · · · · · ·  11  · · · · ·  11
10 · · · · · ·  10  · · · · ·  10
9 · · · · · ·  9  · · · · ·  9
8 · · · · · ·  8  · · · · ·  8
7 · · · · · ·  7  · · · · ·  7
6 · · · · · ·  6  · · · · ·  6
5 · · · · · ·  5  · · · · ·  5
4 · · · · · ·  4  · · · · ·  4
3 · · · · · ·  3  · · · · ·  3
2 · · · · · ·  2  · · · · ·  2
1 · · · · · ·  1  · · · · ·  1

*See the Manual for a discussion of the significance of differences between scores on the tests.

**THE PSYCHOLOGICAL CORPORATION**
**HARCOURT BRACE JOVANOVICH, INC.**

Figure 1.

# WISC-III™
## Wechsler Intelligence Scale for Children – Third Edition

Name _____ Sex _____

School _____ Grade _____

Examiner _____ Handedness _____

| Subtests | Raw Scores | Scaled Scores |
|---|---|---|
| Picture Completion | | |
| Information | | |
| Coding | | |
| Similarities | | |
| Picture Arrangement | | |
| Arithmetic | | |
| Block Design | | |
| Vocabulary | | |
| Object Assembly | | |
| Comprehension | | |
| (Symbol Search) | | ( ) |
| (Digit Span) | ( ) | |
| (Mazes) | | ( ) |
| Sum of Scaled Scores | | |

| | Verbal | Perfor. | VC | PO | FD | PS |
|---|---|---|---|---|---|---|
| | Full Scale Score | | OPTIONAL | | | |

|  | Year | Month | Day |
|---|---|---|---|
| Date Tested | | | |
| Date of Birth | | | |
| Age | | | |

| | Score | IQ/Index | %ile | __% Confidence Interval |
|---|---|---|---|---|
| Verbal | | | | – |
| Performance | | | | – |
| Full Scale | | | | – |
| VC | | | | – |
| PO | | | | – |
| FD | | | | – |
| PS | | | | – |

## Subtest Scores

| | Verbal | | | | | | Performance | | | | | | |
|---|---|---|---|---|---|---|---|---|---|---|---|---|---|
| | Inf | Sim | Ari | Voc | Com | DS | PC | Cd | PA | BD | OA | SS | Mz |

## IQ Scores    Index Scores (Optional)

| VIQ | PIQ | FSIQ | VCI | POI | FDI | PSI |
|---|---|---|---|---|---|---|

Figure 2.

exception of the average adult level, which has eight items and an alternate item. Test items appearing at each age level are shown in Table 7.3 and the table suggests the number of months given toward the subject's mental age (MA). The MA is determined by adding to the basal age the month of credit earned above the basal age. Deviation I.Q.s are computed from standard scores on an assumed mean of 200 and a standard deviation of sixteen.

Table 7.3. Age Levels for Stanford-Binet Test Items.

| Age Level | | Number of Items MA | Months added to |
|---|---|---|---|
| Years | Months | plus alternate (A) | for each item passed |
| 2 | 0 | 6 plus A | Subject must pass all items for the test to be valid |
| 2 | 6 | 6 plus A | 1 month |
| 3 | 0 | 6 plus A | 1 month |
| 3 | 6 | 6 plus A | 1 month |
| 4 | 0 | 6 plus A | 1 month |
| 4 | 6 | 6 plus A | 1 month |
| 5 | | 6 plus A | 2 months |
| 6 | | 6 plus A | 2 months |
| 7 | | 6 plus A | 2 months |
| 8 | | 6 plus A | 2 months |
| 9 | | 6 plus A | 2 months |
| 10 | | 6 plus A | 2 months |
| 11 | | 6 plus A | 2 months |
| 12 | | 6 plus A | 2 months |
| 13 | | 6 plus A | 2 months |
| 14 | | 8 plus A | 2 months |
| Average Adult | | 6 plus A | 2 months |
| Superior Adult I | | 6 plus A | 4 months |
| Superior Adult II | | 6 plus A | 5 months |
| Superior Adult III | | 6 plus A | 6 months |

**Kaufman Assessment Battery for Children (K-ABC).** The authors conclude the five years of intensive research reached culmination in the official publication of the K–ABC on April 4, 1983. The K–ABC is a clinical instrument for the evaluation of preschool and elementary school children. Developed from recent research and theory in neuropsychology and cognitive psychology, the K–ABC assesses the ability to solve problems using simultaneous and sequential mental processes. In addition, the K–ABC has a separate Achievement Scale which measures a child's acquired knowledge, including skills in reading and math. The authors claim that the Achievement Scale provides a frame of reference for evaluating the extent to which children have been able to apply their mental processing skills to a variety of learning situations.

The K–ABC is an individually administered measure of intelligence and achievement for children ages two and a half through twelve and a half years. This instrument is a multisubtest battery yielding scores in Simultaneous Processing, Mental Processing Composite (Sequential plus Simultaneous), and Achievement. There are 16 subtests although a maximum of 13 are administered to any particular child.

American Guidance Service says that the K–ABC is the only major intelligence test to use a norm group stratified using 1980 census data. The norming sample includes representative proportions of Whites, Blacks, Hispanics, Asians, and Native Americans. The publisher also tells us that exceptional children were systematically included in the K–ABC standardization sample in representative proportions.

The authors also conclude the factor analytic investigations demonstrate strong evidence of content validity. About 40 validity studies have been conducted on data testing a wide variety of normal and exceptional populations and show evidence of construct, concurrent, and predictive validity.

Reliability coefficients, using the split-half methods, for the global scales are reported by the authors to be:

Preschool ages     .86–.93
Elementary ages    .89–.97

**Goodenough-Harris Drawing Test.** The Goodenough-Harris Drawing Test is designed to test the intelligence of children between the ages of five through fifteen. It may be used for screening and is fast, non-threatening, a means of gaining a good impression of a child's mental maturity. It is also a nonverbal test and can be used with bilingual and disadvantaged children. The child draws a picture of a man, a woman, and a "self" drawing. In the directions, the child is asked to draw the very best picture he can of a man, a woman, and himself or herself. The test may be administered either as a group or individual test.

The scoring is not based on artistic skills, but on the presence of essential details and their relationship with each other. Credit is given for the inclusion of body parts, clothing details, proportion, and perspective. Scoring items is done on the basis of age differentiation and related to the total score on the test. There are 73 scorable items on the man scale and 71 items on the woman scale.

The author has used this test for many years and has found its best use is for screening young mentally retarded and gifted children.

**Slosson Intelligence Test.** The Slosson Intelligence Test (SIT) is a relatively short screening test which was designed to evaluate mental ability. The test includes many items that appear in the Stanford-Binet Intelligence Scale. The test is designed to be administered by teachers, counselors, principals, psychologists, school nurses and other people who in their professional work need to evaluate an individual's mental ability. Items on this test range from the .5 month level to the 27 year level; however, the author does not report an age range for individuals who may be evaluated with this test. There are directions in the manual about testing infants, those who have reading handicaps or language handicaps, the blind, hard of hearing, those with organic brain damage, the emotionally disturbed and the deprived.

The raw score on the SIT is an age score. An individual earns a specific number of months credit for each item answered correctly. Those items between the basal and the ceiling are the only ones administered. The age score is then transformed into a ratio IQ.

**Peabody Picture Vocabulary Test—Revised.** The Peabody Picture Vocabulary Test—Revised (PPVT–R) is an individually administered test designed to measure verbal intelligence through receptive vocabulary. This test, and all others like it, measures only one aspect of intelligence; receptive vocabulary. The PPVT–R Test is much better standardized than the old Peabody Picture Vocabulary Test and its technical characteristics far surpass those of other picture vocabulary tests. It is a very good screening device and inexperienced individuals may overgeneralize its utility.

**Draw A Person.** The Draw A Person (DAP) intelligence scale by Jack Naglieri (1988) is a revision of the Goodenough-Harris Drawing Test. The DAP was developed to meet the need for a modernized, recently normed, and objective scoring system to be applied to human figure drawings produced by children and adolescents. The same scoring criteria are applied to three drawings (man, woman, self), and the same four scoring categories (Presence, Detail, Proportion, and Bonus) are applied to nearly all of the 14 criteria.

The DAP was developed with the following goals in mind:

- To provide a nonverbal measure of ability which can be administered in a relatively short time and may be used either as part of a test battery or as a screening device
- To provide a scoring system using modern scoring criteria and reducing the influence of current styles of dress, hair, and other characteristics
- To provide a scoring system normed on a large representative sample of students stratified according to recent U.S. Census data
- To increase the precision of the standard scores by providing norms for half- and quarter-year age intervals
- To provide a scoring system that is as objective and efficient as possible in order to reduce subjectivity and thereby increase interrater reliability
- To provide norms for the Self drawing
- To provide a composite standard score composed of the scores of all three drawings, for greater reliability

## PHONICS SURVEY

**The El Paso Phonics Survey.** This is a survey test which uses nonsense words in testing students' knowledge of sound-symbol or phoneme-grapheme correspondents. However, since the teacher, before giving the test, will have made sure the student knows the word endings this type of test does not pose the difficulties normally associated with using nonsense words in testing phonics knowledge.

In the El Paso Phonics Survey, the student is first asked to give the name of the letter, not the sound it stands for, then pronounce the short stimulus word, then give the nonsense word formed by the two. There are teachers that assume that having students pronounce the name of the letter rather than the letter sound will pose undue difficulty. The fact remains, however, that once the student understands what is expected, he or she will pronounce the letter name and blend the parts of the non-sense word as easy as if the letter sound were first pronounced.

Ekwall and Shanker (1988) state

that for students who have adequate phonic's word attack skills the examiner can save a great deal of time by simply administering a group of long nonsense words such as those in the Quick Survey Word List found in the Ekwall Inventory (Ekwall, 1986). These are words such as *pramminciling* and *twayfrall.* Similar word lists are found in the Botel Reading Inventory and the Gates-

McKillop-Horowitz Reading Diagnostic Test. If the student is able to pronounce these words, there is really no need to test in the areas of phonics mentioned above, or for that matter, in structural analysis. You should keep in mind that the learning of vowel rules, syllable principles, and so on is simply a means to an end. The student who is able to decode new words does not need to be able to tell you the vowel rules or syllable principles. Indeed, in this case there is no need for the student to pronounce vowel or consonant sounds in isolation. Many students in reading methods courses can pronounce almost any word, but they have long since forgotten, or never knew, how they learned to do so. For this reason, we recommend that students above the third grade level, where most of these skills should have been mastered, be given a list of nonsense words at the beginning of the diagnostic procedure to determine whether they know the various phonics word attack skills. If after attempting one or two of these words, it becomes obvious that the student cannot pronounce them, the examiner should put the list aside and conduct further diagnosis to determine the specific phonics skills in which the student is weak."

**The Sipay Word Analysis Test (SWAT)** (Sipay, 1974) are 17 subtests, administered individually, to test students' knowledge of word-analysis skills: "Survey Test," "Letter Names (Lower-Case and Upper-Case)," "Symbol-Sound Association: Single Letters (Sounds and Words)," "Substitution: Single Letters (Initial Consonants, Final Consonants, and Medial Vowels)," "Consonant-Vowel-Consonant Trigrams," "Initial Consonant Blends and Digraphs (Blends, Digraphs and Triple Clusters)," "Final Consonant Blends and Digraphs (Blends and Digraphs)," "Vowel Combinations (Most Common and Consistent Vowel Digraphs, Most Common Consistent Diphthongs, More Common Vowel Combinations that Usually Represent One of Two Sounds, Less Common Vowel Combinations that May Represent One of Two Sounds)," "Open Syllable Generalization," "Final Silent *e* Generalization," "Vowel Versality," "Vowels + *r* (Single Vowel + *r*, Two Vowels + *r*, Single Vowel + *r* + Silent *e*)," "Silent Consonants," "Vowel Sounds of *y,*" "Visual Analysis (Monosyllabic Words, Root Words and Affixes, Syllabication)," "Visual Blending (Component Elements into Syllables, Syllables into Words)," and "Contractions."

**Group Phonics Analysis Test.** Diagnostic: Specific Area, Grades: 1–3. Criterion-referenced test assessing basic phonics skills that are presented in developmental order. Covers number reading, letter reading, consonant sounds, alphabetizing, recognizing long and short vowels, and the use of vowel sound rules. No norms. Group test: 20–30 minutes. One form.

# SUMMARY

This chapter discussed formal assessment procedures in reading as they affect the handicapped reader.

Three kinds of formal reading tests discussed were: (1) standardized or norm-referenced tests, (2) diagnostic reading tests, and (3) criterion-referenced tests. Standardized, norm-referenced tests are standardized on large populations and give standardization data. The meaningful scores include reading grade scores, reading age scores, percentile scores, and stanine scores. Two kinds of norm-referenced standardized tests are the survey reading test and the diagnostic reading test. The survey test gives general information about the person's reading level; the diagnostic test gives more analytical information. Criterion-referenced tests yield a description of reading behavior in terms of a predetermined sequence of reading skills. For example, an author may take a basal reading series and devise a criterion-referenced test from that series.

In general, norm-referenced survey tests determine the reading grade level of the child. They are also used to measure progress over time. Criterion-referenced tests are used to determine the mastery of specific instructional objectives.

The norm-referenced individual intelligence scale was also described in this chapter because we can never know if a child truly has a reading problem if we do not know his ability level. There must be a discrepancy between a child's reading ability and his mental ability of one to two years for a reading problem to really exist.

# REFERENCES

Ekwall, E. E. (1986). *Ekwall Reading Inventory* (2nd ed.). Newton, MA: Allyn and Bacon.

Ekwall, E. E. (1988). *Diagnosis and Remediation of the Disabled Reader* (3rd ed.). Boston, MA: Allyn and Bacon.

Naglieri, J. (1988). *Draw-A-Person: A Quantitative Scoring System.* New York: Psychological Corp., Harcourt Brace Jovanovich.

Sipay, E. R. (1974). A Comparison of Standard Reading Scores and Functional Reading Levels, *Reading Teacher 1974, 17,* 265–268.

Wechsler, D. (1974). *Manual for the Wechsler Intelligence Scale for Children—Revised.* New York: Psychological Corp.

Wechsler, D. (1949). *Manual for the Wechsler Intelligence Scale for Children.* New York: Psychological Corp.

# Chapter 8

# INFORMAL ASSESSMENT PROCEDURES

The first part of this chapter deals with a general description of informal reading inventories and why they are used. Detailed descriptions are given for their administration, scoring, and interpretation. Information on developing your own informal reading inventory is provided as well as information on using informal reading inventories for matching students and instructional material. The cloze procedure is explained along with information and techniques for using the cloze procedure. The author will also identify an analysis of error patterns from oral errors and also describe interviews and check sheets that can be used for informal evaluation.

## THE INFORMAL INVENTORY

Informal Reading Inventories (IRIs) usually consist of a series of graded passages from preprimer to at least the seventh or eighth grade level. In special education, the teacher might want to go only to the sixth grade level because very seldom will a special education child be reading at the seventh or eighth grade level. From the first grade level on, there are usually two passages; one to be read orally and one silently at each grade level. As the student reads orally, word recognition errors are recorded and from these a percentage of word recognition is computed. After the student finishes reading the passages from the silent and oral pages, the student is then asked a series of comprehension questions regarding the material. From these answers, a percentage score for reading comprehension can be derived. For older students, oral reading is sometimes omitted.

In a review of the issues involving IRIs, Michael McKenna (1983) stated, "In the past half century, the informal reading inventory (IRI) has become a foremost weapon in the arsenal of reading and classroom teachers" (p. 70). Dechant (1981) estimated that it is the foremost means of determining reading levels and diagnosing reading behavior. Zintz

(1981) called the IRI "the most accurate test measure that can be provided to evaluate the child's ability to use textbooks for instructional purposes" (p. 99). Johns (1977) stated, "We cannot afford not to use informal reading inventories" (p. 136).

Over the years, there has been a great controversy as to whether IRIs or other means of measurement are more accurate in placing students at their instructional level. Jo Ellen Oliver and Richard D. Arnold (1979) compared the results of a standardized test, teacher judgments, and an informal reading inventory using third grade subjects:

> Based upon previous studies and the data gathered here, it would appear that scores from informal inventories placed students in easier materials for instructional purposes than either standardized test scores or teacher judgment. Further, it would seem that as children proceed through the elementary grades, they are placed in increasingly more difficult and perhaps even frustrating material. The data suggests one-half to one grade level in primary grades... with up to two full years in the fifth and sixth grade.... If this interpretation is accurate, it is understandable why students are frustrated by reading material in many schools and why they have problems in the secondary schools, where reading is prerequisite to learning (p. 58).

This author believes that most teachers will benefit a great deal from the knowledge they gain in administering IRIs. However, the questions which must be answered, is there one best way to measure the student's reading level? It seems best for the teacher to use several measures of reading procedures to determine a student's reading performance.

## OVERVIEW

Emmett Betts (1946) saw many inadequacies in existing formal reading tests. He believed that they did not give enough information for a comprehensive reading diagnosis, and did not permit the teacher to observe pupils reading the types of materials used in classrooms. He suggested using an informal reading inventory.

When an informal reading inventory is given, a student reads actual material from textbooks at different grade levels. This makes it possible for the teacher to see how the student functions with classroom material. This makes it more useful and realistic than the results of a standardized test. It also enables the teacher to answer specific instructional questions efficiently and to understand the nature of the student's reading.

The teacher gives the IRI to one student at a time which gives the teacher an opportunity for observation. The test is extremely helpful on both general and specific phases of diagnosis. The general phase will determine the student's level of reading and how the student functions while reading actual instructional material. Using these materials enables the teacher to determine three levels of reading which are *independent, instructional,* and *frustration.* In addition, the general phase can compare performance in major areas of reading. The students are required to read passages orally and answer comprehension questions. This makes it possible to compare word recognition with the level of comprehension. It requires the student not only to read the story but to listen to it. It also allows the teacher insight into the student's language abilities.

The specific phase provides information about the strategies a student uses for word recognition by analyzing oral reading in depth. Insight on comprehension may be gained through comparing oral and silent reading comprehension, and by seeing how the student responds to different types of questions.

The IRI does have some limitations. Examiners can miss oral reading miscues and a student's performance on a passage may be greatly affected by their interest or background with the subject. Thus, teachers need to prepare carefully for administration of the IRI. They need to use professional observation and judgment to translate results of the test effectively. Remember, the IRI is only a tool for your use in gathering diagnostic information.

## CONSTRUCTION AND ADMINISTERING OF IRI

### Construction of IRI

The important aspects involved in constructing an IRI is to select a basal reading series that is interesting to a cross-section of children. It is important to (1) select twenty-five words for the graded word list, (2) select passages for oral reading and silent reading, and (3) develop comprehension questions for the oral and silent reading passages.

### Word Lists

The word lists contain twenty-five words selected randomly from new words for each difficulty level through grade six. Proper nouns (names, places) are excluded. Use the word lists in the basal reader series or a graded word list.

## Reading Passages

When a teacher constructs the reading passages a number of items need to be present, (1) open with a motivational statement that will focus and draw the attention of the student to the subject of the passage, (2) two reading selections are selected for each level—oral reading and silent reading. The following guidelines for length are suggested: preprimer, 25–35 words; primer, 35–60 words; grade one, 75–100 words; grades two and three, 75–150 words; grades four and five, 160–220 words; grades six, seven and eight, 200–400 words. Some important aspects to keep in mind when selecting the reading passages is (1) students background knowledge, (2) age appropriate subject, (3) selection should be able to stand alone from the passage it was taken from.

## Comprehension Questions

After you have selected the reading passage the teacher must select a series of comprehension questions. The questions should be of various types (vocabulary, sequence, facts). As a general rule, passages from grade's preprimer and primer should contain four or five questions; passages from grades' three to grade six should contain five questions. When choosing the answers for these questions it is best to avoid yes/no answers because the student has a 50-50 chance of guessing correctly. The questions should be asked in a clear and concise manner.

## Advantages and Disadvantages

There are advantages to developing your own IRI; (1) they can be based upon material the students are presently using, and (2) can be inexpensive to produce. One disadvantage is the construction of IRIs can take a great deal of time to produce, require a firm knowledge of the subject matter, and require a fair amount of technical knowledge.

## Administering an IRI

When a teacher administers the IRI, it is important to prepare the student by explaining that they will have to read passages orally and silently, they will be asked questions dealing with the subject material, and that the passages will become more difficult as the test goes on. Usually the IRI will take one-half hour to administer. The teacher may wish to divide the test into two periods to avoid test fatigue but this author does not recommend this. The student reads the passages orally and silently from a copy given him/her. It is also important to use a testing easel or place a scoring pad between the teacher and the student, to reduce the student's apprehension of the coding process. As the student reads orally the teacher grades another copy.

### Administering Reading Passages

The first step in administering the reading passages is to determine what level to start at and can be done in a number of ways: (1) give a word recognition test, (2) use the information from previous achievement test scores, and (3) begin testing at least one or two grade levels below the student's present grade levels.

## LEVELS OF READING AND LISTENING

Reading levels may vary from student to student, depending on how familiar a student is with the subject matter of specific passages. Reading levels are based on performance on the reading passages and do not include scores from word recognition lists. The reading levels are based on the oral reading scores and average comprehension scores (oral and silent). There are three reading levels: (1) the independent reading level, (2) the instructional reading level, and (3) the frustration reading level.

The independent reading level should be used for free or recreational reading. The reader can handle material easily and independently and not need assistance from the teacher. At the independent level, oral reading is 95–100 percent and comprehension average is 90–100 percent.

The instructional reading level should be for work with a teacher. The reader makes some errors and requires instruction to benefit from the reading. The teacher anticipates the difficulties and plans appropriate instruction. At the instructional level, oral reading scores are 90–95 percent and comprehension average is 70–90 percent.

The frustration reading level should be avoided because effective learning cannot occur. The material becomes too difficult for the reader, even with assistance. Oral reading scores are below 90 percent and comprehension averages are below 70 percent for the frustration reading level.

The IRI also enables the teacher to assess the student's listening levels. After the three reading levels have been determined, the teacher reads passages aloud to the student, starting at the frustration level, and then asks comprehension questions. The highest level at which the student gets 70 percent or more of the answers correct is considered the listening level. This listening level provides an estimate of the student's level of understanding receptive language. The listening level gives us an idea of how well the student understands what is read to him/her.

**Table 8.1. Criterial for Three Reading Levels.**

| Reading Level | Oral Reading | | Comprehension |
|---|---|---|---|
| Independent | 95–100% | and | 90–100% |
| Instructional | 90–95% | and | 70–90% |
| Frustration | Less than 90% | or | Less than 70% |

## SCORING AND INTERPRETING

The method of scoring oral reading should take into account the fact that the ultimate goal of reading is meaning. Therefore, miscues that do not affect the measure of the passage should count less heavily than those that do affect meaning. The reputation of the entire phrase is continuous and one-word repetition should not be counted as an error at all. Also, if the same mispronunciation is made over and over, it should only be counted twice. We suggest the following criteria:

| TYPE | MAJOR MISCUES | MINOR MISCUES |
|---|---|---|
| Substations | 1 error | 1/2 error |
| Omissions | 1 error | 1/2 error |
| Additions | 1 error | 1/2 error |
| Reversals | 1 error | 1/2 error |
| Repetitions | 1 error | 1/2 error |
| Aid by Examiner | 1 error | 1/2 error |

Some miscues should never be counted as errors. These include mispronunciations which are due to dialect differences, speaking English as a second language, immature speech patterns, or speech impediments. There are other types of miscues that should not be counted. These include spontaneous corrections, repetitions of only a single word, and disregard for punctuation and insertions. However, all three types of miscues should be noted for the diagnostic analysis.

After the child reads each passage, the teacher gives the child questions to check comprehension. If the answer is incorrect, the teacher writes the exact student response. A percentage correct score is obtained for both oral and silent reading. For example, if the student answers four of five comprehension questions correct, the comprehension score would be 80 percent on that selection. The oral and silent comprehension scores may be averaged to compute the average comprehension score at each level. The testing continues until the child reaches a frustration level.

## COMMERCIAL AND READING INVENTORIES

There are several commercial reading inventories available on the market today. These may be published separately or may accompany a basal reading series. There are several features to consider when the teacher is selecting a commercial inventory. First, since the literary quality of the passages is the heart of the inventory, be sure to read the passages and decide if they are well written and if they fit your classroom students. The teacher should always try to find informational as well as narrative passages for the middle and upper grades. The passages should also require information that students in a particular area would reasonably be expected to know. And finally, the passages should be long enough for some meaningful comprehension to develop. It is also helpful to have more than one passage at each level. This permits the testing and retesting of both oral and silent reading. Most commercial IRIs provide the directions for administration, and these may vary in some detail from the ones in this book or other books about reading instruction.

## DEVELOPING YOUR OWN
## INFORMAL READING INVENTORY

If the teacher wants to determine the student's instructional frustration and independent reading level, it would probably be easier to use one of the commercial IRIs. It can take years to develop a good inventory and there is little use in duplicating the efforts of experts. Besides the consideration of time, teachers will find it difficult to select proper passages. Fuchs, Fuchs, and Deno (1982) stated, "Investigations have established that extreme variation exists in the readability of basal readers . . . " (p. 8). This author would also point out that the practice of using arbitrarily drawn samples often leads to the inadequate placement of students. One way that a teacher can determine a quick placement of a student is to select passages indiscriminately from a basal reader and have the student read the passages aloud. The teacher can make up comprehension questions and score the student as he reads aloud. This is a crude method, but if the teacher is in a hurry or does not have a commercial reading inventory, this is an acceptable way to find out about the types of errors that the student is making and to place him at the proper reading level in a basal series.

If the teacher would like to order commercial informal reading inventories, the following were published in 1980 or later:

Bader, L. A. (1983). *Bader Reading and Language Inventory.* New York: Macmillan.

Burns, P. C., & Roe, B. D. (1985). *Informal Reading Inventory* (2nd ed.). Chicago, IL: Rand McNally.

De Santi, R. J., Casbergue, R. M., & Sullivan, V. G. (1982) *The De Santi Cloze Reading Inventory.* Newton, MA: Allyn & Bacon.

Ekwall, E. E. (1986). *Ekwall Reading Inventory* (2nd ed.). Newton, MA: Allyn & Bacon.

Johns, J. L. (1985). *Basic Reading Inventory* (3rd ed.). Dubuque, IA: Kendall/Hunt.

Rinsky, L. A., & de Fossard, E. (1980). *The Contemporary Classroom Inventory.* Dubuque, IA: Gorsuch Scarisbrick.

Silvaroli, N. J. (1986). *Classroom Reading Inventory* (5th ed.). Dubuque, IA: Wm. C. Brown.

Woods, M. L., & Moe, A. J. (1985). *Analytical Reading Inventory* (3rd ed.). Columbus, OH: Charles E. Merrill.

The following is an example of the scoring and recording system for the Love Diagnostic Reading Inventory (1985) (Table 8.2).

Also included below is the oral record blank for the fourth grade oral story and five comprehension questions (Table 8.3).

In Table 8.4 the reader will find the word recognition test in the LDRI and in Table 8.5 one will find the grade equivalency table for the word recognition subtest.

## CLOZE PROCEDURES

A second useful technique for placing students, the procedure of deleting every nth word and replacing it with a blank line. The students are to read the material and fill in the blanks using the correct word according to the context of the sentence. The percentages of correct answers are calculated and from these percentages, instructional and frustration reading levels are derived.

Jones and Pikulski (1974) in a report on the cloze procedure pointed out that their study with sixth graders drew these conclusions:

> the data suggested that the cloze test gave a considerably more accurate reading level placement than did the standardized test. If the cloze test can approximate reading levels on an informal reading inventory as much as 70 to 80 percent of the time, its relatively brief administration time recommends its use to the classroom teacher. Not only does cloze procedure appear to provide a reasonably valid determiner of instructional reading level, but its very ease of construction and administration makes it a practical tool for teachers who have had no special training in test administration (p. 437).

For passages in which every fifth word has been deleted, Rankin and Kulhane's percentage scores for the various levels follow (1969):

Independent Level = 58%–100%
Instructional Level = 44%–57%
Frustration Level  = 43% or below

The cloze procedure is an important and versatile informal procedure for use by elementary and secondary classroom teachers in determining students' reading levels and in discovering the possible causes of reading problems. It was developed by William Taylor in 1953 primarily as a tool for measuring comprehension; however, further research indicates that the cloze procedure can also be used as an alternative to the informal reading inventory for determining students' reading level.

In constructing cloze passages you could omit every third, fifth, tenth, etc. word. However, most of the research that has been done is based on the deletion of every fifth word.

An example of a story using the cloze procedure follows:

**Table 8.2. Scoring and Recording System—Love Diagnostic Reading Inventory.**

## ADMINISTERING THE TEST AND RECORDING PUPIL RESPONSES

Most examiners prefer facing the child across a table of suitable height, but other arrangements are permissible. To be valid the test should be done in a quiet, secluded place.

**Recording.** Use the following system for recording errors in the Examiner's Booklet as the child reads:

In order to illustrate the types of errors and the method of recording them, the following paragraph is included:

> The Indians would trade animal skins to the early settlers for glass beads. Many early Americans earned their living by making glass beads and bottles. A man in Sandwich, Massachusetts developed a way of making dishes, lamps, and candlesticks by pressing molten glass into iron molds. The Indian traded for these also, but liked the glass beads better.

If a word is wholly missed circle it as in the case of "settlers." If a portion of the word is mispronounced underline the part of the word mispronounced. For example, in "developed" the middle part of the word was mispronounced, the "s" was omitted in "skins" and the "in" has been omitted from "into." The word "for" was inserted between "trade" and "animal," and the word "made" (in parenthesis) was substituted for earned. The symbol · · should be used when punctuation is disregarded and hesitations should be recorded by a ⌐ . Repetitions should be indicated by placing a · above the word and an X above the word indicates that the word has been omitted. If the examiner pronounced a word for the student ⌐ ⌐ should be placed above the word.

In case you are not sure that an error was made give the student the benefit of the doubt. The marked errors are very important in devising a remedial plan for the child having a reading disorder.

| ERROR RECORD | Number |
|---|---|
| Substitutions | |
| Mispronunciations | |
| Words pronounced by examiner | |
| Disregard of pronunciation | |
| Insertions | |
| Hesitations | |
| Repetitions | |
| Omissions | |
|     Total Errors | |

**Table 8.3. Fourth Grade Oral Story, Five Comprehension Questions, and Oral Record Blank—Love Diagnostic Reading Inventory.**

### GRADE 4 (Form A)

Mother likes to cook outdoors in the summer. The family loves picnics during the warm weather. Father builds the fire for mother. Dick and Jane help Mother cook the delicious meals. The family likes the food cooked in the fresh air. The family next door sometimes eats outside too. The two families often eat together on certain holidays.

Both families hate to see winter come because it is too cold to cook outdoors.

1. When does Mother like to cook outdoors?
2. Who builds the fire for Mother?
3. Who helps Mother cook?
4. When do the two families eat together?
5. What time of the year do the two families hate to see?

| ERROR RECORD | Number |
|---|---|
| Substitutions | |
| Mispronunciations | |
| Words pronounced by examiner | |
| Disregard of pronunciation | |
| Insertions | |
| Hesitations | |
| Repetitions | |
| Omissions | |
| Total Errors | |

That evening they all had dinner together in grandmother's cozy kitchen. Then Hal took Susie _____ to a stone building _____ unbolted its door. Inside _____ seven hound dogs.

"_____ must watch my hounds _____ night," said Hal.

"Susie _____ in, and Hal closed _____ locked the door.

At _____ the hounds began to _____ and bark. They showed _____ teeth at her. But Susie _____ a real sport. She _____ up her courage, instead _____ backing away, she went _____ the dogs. She began _____ speak to them in _____ quiet voice. They stopped _____ and sniffed at her. _____ patted their heads.

"I _____ what it is," she _____. "You are lonely here. _____ will keep you company."

_____ so all night long, _____ sat on the floor _____ talked to the hounds _____ stroked them. They lay _____ to her.

Table 8.4. Word Recognition Test—Love Diagnostic Reading Inventory.

Date _____

Name _____     Age _____

School _____     Grade _____

**Word Recognition Test (Form I)**

| | |
|---|---|
| B A G O S T E H P M Z U Q E N | ( 15) |
| Q E H Z P U A M U Z Q S Y W D | ( 30) |
| me at go an you live how night early about | ( 40) |
| call cold far much first together jump road when town | ( 50) |
| between pretty middle moment several drew straight decided inept | ( 59) |
| exclaimed amazed silent entered realized scanty develop escape grim | ( 68) |
| bridge served splendid abolish trucker apparatus comment commercial | ( 76) |
| gallery bridge amber sundry blight wrest daunted capacious aspen | ( 85) |
| pretext intrigue ascent acrid delusion binocular conscientious galore | ( 96) |
| isolation molecule ritual jaunty zany jerkin nausea linear legality | (105) |
| amnesty rotunda capitalism prevaricate superfluous piebald behaved | (112) |
| appropriation distribution situation federation resolution discrimination | (118) |

## USING INTERVIEWS AND CHECKLISTS AS AN INFORMAL WAY TO DETECT READING PROBLEMS

Interviews can be an important part of the diagnostic remedial process in special education. There are types of information obtained from the interview that is seldom available elsewhere. A special education teacher is not likely to interview the parents or every student or hold a lengthy interview with each person who knows the special education child well. The special education teacher will see the parent of each child approximately two times each year. The parental interview can be important in determining whether parents understand the severity of the child's problem or whether they are pushing the child too hard. If they lack understanding, they will probably fail to provide a proper study environment. The emotional climate of the home is very important in a child's academic success and reading is a part of academics. The teacher will want to know if there are books available in the home and magazines and if not, can she make books and magazines available by having the child take them home. The teacher will also want to find out about the study habits of the child at home. An interview with the parents can provide

Table 8.5. Love's Diagnostic Reading Inventory

Raw Scores and Grade Ratings for the Word Recognition Test.

| Raw Score | Grade | Raw Score | Grade | Raw Score | Grade |
|---|---|---|---|---|---|
| 0 | N.R. | 40 | 2.4 | 80 | 7.1 |
| 1 | N.R. | 41 | 2.5 | 81 | 7.2 |
| 2 | N.R. | 42 | 2.6 | 82 | 7.3 |
| 3 | N.R. | 43 | 2.7 | 83 | 7.4 |
| 4 | N.R. | 44 | 2.8 | 84 | 7.5 |
| 5 | Pre. P. | 45 | 2.9 | 85 | 7.6 |
| 6 | Pre. P. | 46 | 3.0 | 86 | 7.7 |
| 7 | Pre. P. | 47 | 3.1 | 87 | 7.8 |
| 8 | Pri. | 48 | 3.2 | 88 | 7.9 |
| 9 | Pri. | 49 | 3.3 | 89 | 8.0 |
| 10 | Pri. | 50 | 3.4 | 90 | 8.1 |
| 11 | Pri. | 51 | 3.5 | 91 | 8.2 |
| 12 | Pri. | 52 | 3.6 | 92 | 8.3 |
| 13 | Pri. | 53 | 3.7 | 93 | 8.4 |
| 14 | Pri. | 54 | 3.8 | 94 | 8.5 |
| 15 | K | 55 | 3.9 | 95 | 8.6 |
| 16 | K | 56 | 4.0 | 96 | 8.7 |
| 17 | K | 57 | 4.1 | 97 | 8.8 |
| 18 | K | 58 | 4.1 | 98 | 8.9 |
| 19 | K | 59 | 4.2 | 99 | 9.0 |
| 20 | K | 60 | 4.3 | 100 | 9.1 |
| 21 | K | 61 | 4.4 | 101 | 9.2 |
| 22 | K | 62 | 4.5 | 102 | 9.3 |
| 23 | K | 63 | 4.6 | 103 | 9.4 |
| 24 | 1.0 | 64 | 4.7 | 104 | 9.5 |
| 25 | 1.1 | 65 | 4.8 | 105 | 9.6 |
| 26 | 1.2 | 66 | 4.9 | 106 | 9.7 |
| 27 | 1.3 | 67 | 5.0 | 107 | 9.8 |
| 28 | 1.4 | 68 | 5.1 | 108 | 9.9 |
| 29 | 1.5 | 69 | 5.3 | 109 | 10.0 |
| 30 | 1.6 | 70 | 5.4 | 110 | 10.1 |
| 31 | 1.7 | 71 | 5.6 | 111 | 10.2 |
| 32 | 1.8 | 72 | 5.7 | 112 | 10.3 |
| 33 | 1.9 | 73 | 5.8 | 113 | 10.4 |
| 34 | 2.0 | 74 | 6.0 | 114 | 10.5 |
| 35 | 2.0 | 75 | 6.3 | 115 | 10.6 |
| 36 | 2.1 | 76 | 6.5 | 116 | 10.7 |
| 37 | 2.2 | 77 | 6.8 | 117 | 10.8 |
| 38 | 2.3 | 78 | 6.9 | 118 | 10.9 |
| 39 | 2.3 | 79 | 7.0 | | |

excellent information about the child's study habits at home. The teacher can find out in one or two interviews about the parental expectations for the child. Parental expectations vary a great deal and it depends on such factors as their education and socioeconomic level and sometimes even their religious preference. Only through this interview can a special education teacher find out whether parental expectations are realistic. Parents could also tell the special education teacher about the independent work habits of the child and the child's self-concept.

### Student Interviews

Of course, the special education teacher sees each child almost every day. Certainly the special education will see each child three times per week. The teacher can always find out about the child's self-concept by talking to him about things other than school. The teacher might just say, "Tell me about yourself. How do you feel about what you're doing in life?" The teacher can also find out the child's perception of his/her reading problem. It's very difficult to help someone who does not recognize that a problem exists and children can tell the teacher what problems they think they have and what problems they really have. The teacher will find out rather quickly the child's past experiences in reading and the child's attitude about reading. The special education child is not likely to have a good attitude toward reading because he has not had very much success in reading.

The child will be interested in various things and the teacher can find out about the child's interests and direct him to books that he can read which will fulfill questions about his interests. Using the books that the child is interested in, the teacher can develop instructional techniques and materials that the student will use.

## GROUP WORK AND THE CLOZE PROCEDURE

A unique way to use the cloze procedure is to have a group of three children make up a story that is one page long. They will leave out every fifth word and write a list of every word that they leave out. Three other children comprising another group will fill in the words on the cloze procedure. Then one will read it aloud to the group that made up the story. There will be a lot of laughing and discussion and correcting even. The second group then can make up a story and omit every fifth or sixth word. The group that didn't make up the story will fill in the words and write a list of the words which go with the story. These six children can work as a group and eventually compile a booklet that other students can read. They can cut out pictures and make the book's jacket very colorful and even exciting. In this way, all the children involved in the special education classroom can participate in an informal cloze procedure and a way to develop an interest in writing and literature. All the time that this is being done, the teacher can observe and take notes and determine which children are participating and having fun and the words known by the various children and the comprehension that they are developing and in this way this can be an informal reading evaluation technique.

Another way the teacher can get older children to develop stories that they think younger children might be interested in. We are still using the cloze procedure; therefore, they can leave out every fifth or sixth word. The older children can then work one-on-one with younger children and have the younger children read the stories and insert the words. The older children will practice word recognition with the younger children and also make corrections when the younger children don't put the correct words in the passages. In this way, the older children are being used as helpers not only to build interest in making up stories but in developing word recognition and comprehension. The teacher can talk to the older children and also observe the older and the younger children and determine what remedial techniques that she should use on the child who is reading the stories and filling in the words.

## OTHER INFORMAL TESTS

An example of informal testing is illustrated in the case of Johnny, who was a third grade student at the age of eight and also spend two hours each day in the special education resource room. The special education teacher noted that Johnny could not follow the reading lesson and was not participating in the assignment. Mrs. Smith called Johnny to her desk and asked him to read aloud in the basal reader. Johnny was unable to read the first page in the third grade book except for a few words. The teacher then gave him a second grade book and Johnny could not decode very many of the words in the second grade book. In the first grade book, he read the material with difficulty and needed help from the teacher. From these observations, Mrs. Smith estimated Johnny's reading level to be in the middle of the first grade in oral reading. She also noted that Johnny guessed at the words, seemed unable to decode the words he did not know, and made numerous substitutions, repetitions, omissions, and other errors. The next item for Mrs. Smith was to determine Johnny's listening comprehension level. The teacher read the next story aloud to Johnny and this was a story in the first grade reader. Johnny knew the answers. Mrs. Smith then read a story aloud to Johnny in the second grade reader and Johnny understood the material in the second grade reader. She read Johnny a story aloud from the third grade reader and he did not understand the comprehension questions. The teacher assumed that Johnny's listening comprehension was at the second grade level. Then the teacher found a list of the vocabulary words in the back of the first grade reader. She asked Johnny to read these words aloud in isolation and found that Johnny knew only a few of the words. From this Mrs. Smith estimated that Johnny's level of word reading was even lower than middle first grade. While Johnny was reading this aloud, she was able to take notice of his word recognition, word analysis, and made an observation that Johnny had no method of word analysis. When he did not know the word, he did not try to decode it by sounding out. Johnny did not even try to guess at the word if he did not know it.

In order to test Johnny's word discrimination ability, Mrs. Smith covered the words in the back of the first reader except for the first five words and said to Johnny, "Look at these words and find the word *on*. Now find the word *the, boy* and so on." She found that Johnny could recognize and point to two of the words but he could recall only one of these words when he was reading. From this, Mrs. Smith was able to estimate that Johnny's word discrimination ability to be at about the first grade level.

The teacher used only three graded readers and was able to assess Johnny's reading level at first grade with word reading lowest and word discrimination highest but with listening comprehension at the second grade level. The teacher also noted that Johnny had not developed a method of word attack and that he did not use phonics or any other means of word recognition. She did not examine his silent reading ability because Johnny really could not read well enough to have much of a silent reading ability. In this informal way the teacher was able to find out a lot about Johnny's reading errors and inability in just a few minutes. In using an informal appraisal such as Mrs. Smith did, the teacher should always be able to find out (1) the child's level of reading, and (2) the child's reading errors and learning style.

## MODALITY DIAGNOSIS

The most commonly recognized and diagnosed learning modalities are auditory, visual, kinesthetic, tactile, and a combination of all of these. When referred to in the literature, however, they are usually listed as VAKT or visual, auditory, kinesthetic and tactile. One of the best ways to determine a child's method of modality is to devise a list of words representing the primer, first, second, and third grade levels. Each set of words has a word on one side and a picture representing it on the other side. The student is given the list of words to pronounce until the teacher finds 40 words that the student does not know. These 40 words are divided into groups of 10. Each day 10 words are taught in strict accordance with one of the four methods just mentioned. Fifteen minutes is spent on each group of words. The learning method then can be determined by the teacher noting the modality the student uses to a greater extent than the others. This method has been criticized by many educators and special educators. For example, as a part of the visual approach, the student is presented the 10 words picture side up and is told to look at the picture and then at the word. There is a lot of research that questions whether pictures do or do not help children learn sight words. However, it is the opinion of this author that a teacher can notice if a child is using the auditory sense more so than the visual sense in learning sight words. Only a few children will use the kinesthetic and tactile approach sense in learning sight words more so than the auditory or visual sense. It has been the experience of this author that students with specific learning disabilities who have not learned to read by other methods often will respond to the kinesthetic and tactile method of reading. This is a slow and laborious method and one that was used first by Dr. Maria Montessori and later by Grace Fernald and Anna Gillingham.

Walter Barbe, Raymond Swassing, and Michael Milone (1981) argued that modality-based instruction should not be rejected at present because:

1. The fact that something has not been found does not mean it does not exist (p. 263).
2. The failure to discover significant aptitude-treatment interactions between modality strengths and reading instruction may reflect inadequacies of experimental design features rather than the lack of a relationship between the variables of interest (p. 264).
3. Unless the variable of teacher modality strength is controlled, the study of pupil modality strength in reading may be flawed (p. 265).

4. The criteria for determining who is visual, auditory, and kinesthetic in preference is not well established (p. 265).
5. Modality is not a fixed characteristic (p. 265).
6. Ninety-five percent of the teachers of learning-disabled children believe that the research supports this approach.

## SUMMARY

In summary, the author has discussed several informal ways that a regular class teacher or special education teacher can use to determine a child's reading ability and the types of errors that each child makes. In order to determine the child's level of reading and to observe reading errors, the teacher must have the child read in different context. The most common dimensions of reading to observe are: (1) oral reading of passages in a book; (2) reading graded words in isolation; (3) discriminating between words; (4) silent reading, including reading comprehension; and (5) listening comprehension.

All of these have been examined in the area of informal testing in this chapter.

## REFERENCES

Barbe, W. B., Swassing, R. H., & Milone, M. N. (1981). Teaching to modality strengths: Don't give up yet. *Academic Therapy, 16,* 262–266.

Betts, E. A. (1946). *Foundations of Reading Instruction.* New York: American Book Co.

Fuchs, L. S., Fuchs, D., & Deno, S. L. (1982). Reliability and validity of curriculum-based informal reading inventories. *Reading Research Quarterly, 18,* 6–26.

Johns, J. L. (1985). *Basic Reading Inventory* (3rd ed.). Dubuque, IA: Kendall/Hunt.

Jones, M. B., & Pikulski, E. C. (1974). Cloze for the classroom. *Reading Teacher, 17,* 432–438.

Love, H. D. (1985). *Diagnostic Reading Inventory.* Springfield, MA: Ginn & Co.

McKenna, M. C. (1983). Informal reading inventories: A review of the issues. *Reading Teacher, 36,* 670–679.

Oliver, J. E., & Arnold, R. D. (1979). Informal reading inventories: A review of the issues. *Reading Teacher, 15,* 56–59.

Rankin, E. F., & Culhane, J. W. (1969). Comparable cloze and multiple choice comprehension scores. *Journal of Reading, 13,* 193–198.

Zintz, M. V. (1981). *Corrective Reading* (4th ed.). Dubuque, IA: William C. Brown.

# Chapter 9

# READING RESEARCH: DISABLED
# AND HANDICAPPED LEARNERS

The body of research concerned with the teaching of reading is quite extensive. The literature is replete with investigations of the reading process, methods of instruction, appropriate material for teaching, the use of various programmed texts, teaching machines, etc. This chapter will discuss research as it relates to the reading of the handicapped and disabled learner.

Some of the studies that are reviewed in this chapter investigate the reading of children who are diagnosed as mildly retarded or specific learning disabled. Some of the children were also diagnosed as slow learners—those having IQs between 70 and 89. This author will discuss studies about brain injured or children having minimal brain dysfunction.

## THE RELATIONSHIP OF MENTAL AGE
## TO READING ACHIEVEMENT

For many years investigators have tried to determine the potential for reading achievement of slow and disabled learners. A question that seems to keep cropping up is: Do they read above, at, or below their expectancy level as determined by IQ and mental age? The criterion that we ordinarily use to answer these questions is based, of course, on the assumption that reading achievement develops according to mental age. We also assume that an average child develops one year in reading achievement for each chronological age. The reading year is now broken down into 10 months; therefore, a child with average intelligence who is progressing normally in reading would gain 10 months of reading skills for each year. Kirk, Kliebhan, and Lerner (1978) list a table which shows the mental age and reading grade expectancy.

It has been suggested that reading grade expectancy can be determined by subtracting 5-0 from the mental age or chronological age. For example, a child with a mental age or chronological age of seven would have a reading grade expectancy of 7-0 minus 5-0 = grade 2.0.

The earliest study on the relationships between reading achievement and mental age was made by Merrill. The first study which was conducted in the state of Minnesota involved a group of public school special education children and a group of mentally retarded children in a Minnesota residential school (Merrill, 1918). The mental age of the students in both groups ranged between five and eleven. In oral reading the groups reached only 75 percent of expectancy based on their mental age. Merrill found that as the chronological age increased, the percentage of children able to do oral reading up to their reading expectancy level decreased.

The research during the years since Merrill's original search has generally found the same thing. As a child gets older, the discrepancy between reading age and chronological age increases. This leads this author to believe that as a person gets older the mental age concept breaks down. This author believes that mental age denotes a maturational aspect of the child's development and can tell us approximately when a child is ready to begin learning. However, we cannot use the mental age of an 18-year-old child and say that he should be reading at the fourth or fifth grade level, for example. It has long been known that most mildly retarded children will read at the second or third grade level at best. The child with specific learning disabilities, if he is accurately diagnosed, can learn to read at grade level expectancy, and in a few cases, they have been known to read above grade level expectancy. This assumes that the child has been properly diagnosed. Too often, children with IQs is the 70s and 80s are diagnosed as SLD when in reality they should be diagnosed as children who are slow learners. Just because a child is reading below his grade expectancy does not mean that he has a reading problem. Many children are reading up to their ability level when they are in the seventh and eighth grade, yet only reading at the third grade level and they do not actually have a reading problem.

In a second study conducted in California, Merrill (1921) discovered that the majority of 210 special education children were achieving below expectancy when he based it on the mental age criterion. They were most retarded in reading, less so in arithmetic, still less in writing, and these children were least retarded in spelling.

After Merrill's work there was a series of studies to investigate the relationship to reading (Renshaw, 1919, Burt, 1921, Hoyt, 1924 and

Winnie Ann McCafferty, (1930). All of these authors found similar results. Their investigations concluded that the large majority of mentally retarded children read below their mental age.

From this research and research that has continued until 1993, we know that mentally retarded children will read below their mental age expectancy. For some reason, the mental age concept breaks down when we apply it to the mentally retarded child and reading. Once again as the mentally retarded child grows older, there becomes a greater discrepancy between reading ability and mental age expectancy.

Several studies have also been done to determine how far below mental age the mildly retarded children are in their reading achievement. In a survey of about 1,600 retarded children in special classes in New Jersey, Kelly (1934) found that the students have an overall reading retardation of one year below their mental age when they are in elementary school. Furthermore, as they get older, they tend to have two, three, and four years reading ability below their mental age. Kelly also found that approximately 30 percent of the children with a mental age between eight and nine were nonreaders. Most of them did not know the letters of the alphabet. Hill (1939), while studying a group of mildly retarded children who were enrolled in Schenectady, New York special classes, found that they were about one-half year to one year below their mental age expectancy in the elementary schools. Scarborough (1951) and Mullen & Ilken (1952) reported that they found that children who were mildly retarded and in elementary grades were reading between one year and 1.4 years below their mental age expectancy. In the Mullen and Ilken study, very few of the children read at or above expectancy and these were only the young retarded children. Most studies have found that as the children get older there is a huge discrepancy between mental age and reading ability.

George and Evelyn Spache (1977) expressed this viewpoint concerning intelligence and mental age:

> Research studies of school beginners show that intelligence tests results are not highly predictive of early success. If pupils are arranged in the order of their reading test scores after a period of training, the order does not neatly parallel a ranking based on age or intelligence quotient. Only the extreme cases, the very superior and the mentally retarded pupils, tend to agree in their ranks in reading and intelligence. The degree of reading success for most pupils is determined not by their exact level or rank in intelligence but by other more influential factors. (pp. 156–157)

George and Evelyn Spache (1977) are in essence saying that mentally retarded children with low mental ages definitely have a reading problem that can be determined by intelligence test scores and by mental age.

Ekwall and Shanker (1988) state:

> An important point to remember, however, is that many children with low IQs become good readers and many children with medium and high IQs become disabled readers. Therefore, the IQ should only be considered in conjunction with other factors. (p. 17)

It should be pointed out that Ekwall and Shanker said that some children with low IQs become good readers. They did not say that mentally retarded children become good readers. In this author's 35 years experience in special education, he has never seen a mentally retarded person become a good reader.

Helen Robinson (1946), in her book entitled *Why Pupils Failed in Reading,* contributed to the knowledge of research about pupils' failure in reading more so than other research efforts. Robinson, though, did not choose students in her study below the IQ of 90. Helen Robinson wanted to find out why children with average and above IQs failed to learn to read. She knew and indicated that children with below 90 IQs will not achieve up to grade expectancy and would not add very much to her monumental study.

Albert Harris (1972) pointed out:

> The relation between intelligence and reading is low to moderate at the beginning level, but increases as children get older. As the nature of the reading task becomes more one of comprehension and interpretation, intelligence becomes a stronger determining factor. (p. 42)

This author believes that we should not place a great deal of reliance on IQ scores as predictors of potential reading ability if the child has average intelligence or above. However, there is no doubt that the research indicates that mentally retarded children will not be adequate readers at any point in their lives. Children having IQs below 50 should be taught protection words. Children with IQs between 50 and 70 should be taught to read simple words, to fill out forms, try to read the newspaper, and any type of reading that will help them vocationally.

Thomas (1946) stated "Children who do not have a mental age of 6.0 are bound to have difficulty learning to read, while children who have a mental age of 6.6 are likely to achieve success in first grade reading without too much difficulty" (p. 30). The six-year minimum age is still supported in 1993 by a large number of reading authorities.

Schnittjer, Tuten, and Weller (1992) conducted a study concerning the predicting of reading achievement in grades three through ten using the Metropolitan Readiness Test.

This study was designed to determine the degree of correlation between scores on the Metropolitan Readiness Test (MRT), given to entering first grade students, and standardized achievement test scores in math and reading in grades 3, 6, 9, and 10. Educators define readiness differently, but many agree that it is influenced by a supportive home environment, good health care, and parents who read to their children. Factors that negatively influence readiness are hunger and poverty, sensory deprivation, lack of language stimulation, and poor self-image. This study investigates the potential of the MRT by itself and in conjunction with race, gender, IQ, age at school entrance, remediation, and socioeconomic status to predict academic achievement over a 12-year time frame. Subjects were 415 students who entered first grade in 1976 and spent all 12 years of their schooling in one large south Georgia urban school district. IQ ranged from below 90 (111), 90 to 110 (240), and above 110 (64). Results showed that IQ consistently had the highest single correlation with each of the dependent variables. While IQ was a more powerful predictor than the MRT, this study showed that the MRT has long term and stable correlations on performance through grade 10. If IQ is a powerful predictor then, of course, mental age would be too.

Results of investigations concerning the mental age required for beginning reading for the mildly retarded or the specific learning disabled child are not clear-cut or decisive.

Davidson (1931) conducted a study of bright, average, and retarded children whose mental age was four. Each subject was instructed in 10-minute lessons on word recognition each day for six weeks. The three groups of children were able to recognize words at the end of six weeks, but the bright children were found to be vastly superior to the other subjects. The mildly retarded group's performance was the poorest. Moore (1964) taught mildly mentally retarded children with mental ages of three and four to read and write by means of a talking typewriter. Most authorities still believe that these children are not ready to learn to read, but Moore has shown that with somewhat unconventional methods, they can learn to do so. Moore does not say if the children were able to comprehend any of the words or several words together.

In spite of some techniques which are unusual and which teach children with lower than average mental ability to recognize words, the authorities say that it is still best to wait until these children have a mental age between 6.0 and 6.6 to begin formal reading techniques. Very often a mentally retarded child with an IQ of 70 will be nine years old before he has a mental age of 6.0. The schools are not going to wait until the child has a chronological age of 9.0 to begin reading instruction. However, it would be best for the mildly mentally retarded child if we would give him only readiness materials for the first two to three years of his life before we start presenting any formal type of reading.

The authors of DISTAR used culturally deprived, lower socioeconomic level children in their standardization and state that they taught these children with mental ages of 4.0 to read at the beginning level while using the DISTAR program. This author does not doubt the statistics supplied by Engelmann and Bruner (1969), but throughout the experience of this author the children who learn to read words when they had a mental age less than 6.0 really only parroted words and had no reading comprehension.

Many authorities say that no definitive conclusion can be drawn from a review of studies comparing the achievement of the mildly retarded, normal, and superior children of the same mental age. This author believes results strongly indicate that mentally retarded children tend to be poor achievers in reading at all levels of their life. The research further indicates that mildly retarded children tend to be poorer readers than others of the same mental age.

Richek, List and Lerner (1993) tell us that two correlates of reading disability which should be considered in an evaluation are intelligence (the potential or capacity to learn) and language abilities. Both of these factors are critical elements for the initial stages of learning to read and in the ongoing reading process.

There is a strong relationship between intelligence and reading performance. The correlation is somewhat higher with verbal intelligence test scores (.60 to .85) than with nonverbal or performance test scores (.20 to .56) (Harris and Sipay, 1985; Moore and Wielan, 1981). However, the very concept of intelligence and its measurement is subject to many basic questions. These questions relate to the definition of intelligence, how intelligence is measured, and ways of using intelligence test information in the reading diagnosis (Richek, List, and Lerner, 1993).

Sattler (1982) states:

> Reading ability is significantly related to intelligence test scores (Stanovich et al., 1984). The correlations increase with age; typical values are in the .30 to .50 range for early elementary grade children, the .45 to .65 range for middle grade children, and the .60 to .75 range for adults. Median correlations between reading scores and scores on the WISC–R (and WISC) and the Stanford-Binet Intelligence Scale: Form L–M are .44 and .46, respectively (Hammill & McNutt, 1981). The verbal portions of these two intelligence tests tap many subskills critical for reading, such as use of real-world knowledge, inferential skills, memory strategies, and vocabulary. Future reading performance is more accurately predicted by current reading achievement scores than by intelligence test scores, however (Stanovich, 1985).

## REGULAR CLASSES VS. SPECIAL EDUCATION CLASSES

The efficacy of special classes for handicapped children has been repeatedly questioned over the years. The following is a review of research comparing reading achievement of retarded children in special classes with that of retarded children who remained in the regular classroom. Three early studies (Bennett, 1932; Pertsch, 1936; Wassmann, 1933) conducted over 50 years ago indicate that the reading achievement of retarded children who remained in the regular classroom was superior to that of retardates who were placed in special education classes. The first study, by Bennett (1932), compared 50 retarded children who remained in the regular grades with 50 retarded children ages 12 and 13 who were enrolled in special education classes. This author found that the children who were in the special classes achieved less in reading than those enrolled in regular classes. Pertsch (1936) also conducted a study such as this except he used 278 children in the New York schools. He concluded that the children who remained in the regular grades were superior in academic achievement than those who were placed in special education. Cowan (1938) reevaluated Pertsch's study and questioned the selection factor and reversed his conclusions. In 1959, Thurston conducted a large study in North Carolina that concluded that children in special classes were inferior in reading to the retarded children who remained in regular grades. Cassidy and Stanton (1959), Blatt (1958), Elenbogen (1957), and Ainsworth (1959) all compared the reading achievement of mentally retarded children in regular classes with mentally retarded children in special classes and concluded that either there was no difference in reading achievement between the two groups or that those who were enrolled in the regular grades were superior. It should be added by this writer that special education in those days was for the extremely handicapped. We did not have classes then for the mildly retarded. The classes were often in the worse rooms of the school and educational placement was inferior at best. Some of the children had IQs below 50 and some were syndrome-type children, such as Downs.

A study by Goldstein, Moss, and Jordan (1965) investigated all areas of the curriculum, however, only the reading achievement is reported here.

The Goldstein, Moss, and Jordan study found that children with an IQ of 80 or below and those with an IQ of 81 or above responded differently to regular classroom placement. The children having an IQ of 81 and above who remained in the regular grades tended to score only slightly higher than similar children placed in the special education classes. The children having IQs of 80 or less and who were in special education scored slightly higher in reading than the children who remained in the regular grades.

If children who remain in the regular classroom do better in reading, this writer believes that it is due to special class teachers tending to emphasize social adjustment and not academic achievement. Also the expectations of regular classroom teachers for academic achievement could be higher than the expectations of special education teachers. Also it should be pointed out that the discrepancy factor was not included in any of these studies. The discrepancy factor simply means how much lower a person is reading than his mental age. For example, a person in the first or second grade who is reading one year below grade placement could not be expected to gain as much as a child in the seventh grade who is reading three or four years below his grade expectancy. This expectancy criterion was not a factor in any of the studies quoted above. However, there is no doubt that the research indicates that mentally retarded children will not be adequate readers at any point in their lives. Children having IQs below 50 should be taught protection words. Children having IQs between 50 and 70 should be taught to read simple works and to fill out forms and try to read the newspaper and any type of reading that would help them vocationally.

Thomas (1946) stated: "Children who do not have a mental age of 6.0 are bound to have difficulty learning to read, while children having a mental age of 6.6 are likely to achieve success in first grade reading without too much difficulty (p. 30)." The six-year minimum age is still supported in 1993 by a large number of reading authorities.

## INSTRUCTION AFTER THE SIXTH GRADE

Walthall and Walthall (1993) conducted a study in Conway, Arkansas where they compared the scores on the Eighth Edition of the Stanford Achievement Test (SAT) between students enrolled in the regular classroom settings vs. students enrolled in special education resource room settings. These two researchers wanted to find out if there is a significant difference in scores between students placed in different instructional settings. This question was addressed by examining the scores on the SAT of 25 seventh grade students receiving instruction in the regular classroom setting, 25 seventh grade students receiving instruction in the special education resource room setting, 25 eighth grade students receiving instruction in the regular classroom setting, and 25 eighth grade students receiving instruction in the special education resource room setting. This author is concerned with the total reading and total language scores only.

### Summary Statement

1. Among the resource room students there was no change in mean reading scores from the seventh grade to the eighth grade.
2. Among the regular class students there was a negative change in mean reading scores from the seventh grade to the eighth grade.

It was found that the students in the regular classroom setting did not have direct instruction in reading after the sixth grade. Therefore, it can be assumed that this is the reason that their reading level actually went down in the seventh and eighth grades. In the special education resource room, the teachers continued to teach reading to small groups of children after the sixth grade and the reading levels of the special education children increased in grades seven and eight. We can assume by this study that schools should continue to teach reading on a one-to-one basis or in small groups after the sixth grade.

## LATERAL DOMINANCE AND READING ABILITY

Over the years there has been a great deal of research on lateral dominance and reading ability. Cohen and Glass (1968) conducted a study to add empirical evidence which they thought might contribute to a better understanding of the relationship between dominance patterns and reading achievement. The study was conducted in four of the elementary schools of the Levittown, New York Public School System. The sampling included 120 subjects: 30 good readers and 30 poor readers in the fourth grade and there were 30 good readers and 30 poor readers in the first grade. All the subjects were within the IQ range of 91 to 109 as measured by the Alpha Otis Test, Form A. Statistical analysis revealed the following relationships as being significant: knowledge of left and right and reading ability were significant in the first grade. This means that the children who knew the difference between their left and right hands were better readers in the first grade. A child who had established a hand dominance in the first grade turned out to be a better reader also. By the time the children reached the fourth grade, a knowledge of left and right was also significant. However, it should be pointed out that by the time a child reaches fourth grade and he doesn't know his right hand from his left hand, he is probably retarded. By the fourth grade, it was found that hand dominance and mixed dominance had nothing to do with the reading ability.

We have been researching cerebral dominance and laterality as they correlate with reading disabilities for many, many years. Laterality refers to the tendency of individuals to have a preference for using one side of their bodies. For example, a child may show preference for using the right hand, right foot, right eye, and right ear. This child does not have mixed dominance. The child, though, who has a preference for his right hand and right foot and left ear and left eye has mixed dominance. Some authorities believe that mixed laterality or dominance is a cause of reading disability. Dr. Samuel T. Orton in 1937, a professor of neurology at the University of Iowa, was one of the first individuals to study this phenomenon. He noticed that children reversed words and he called this condition *strephosymbolia,* meaning "twisted symbols." He believed that this was caused by a neurological function and that mixed dominance was the culprit. Following Orton's work, there has been hundreds of studies done on handedness, eyedness, mixed laterality, and cerebral dominance as factors that inhibit the child's ability to read. In spite of the lack of evidence from research, many practitioners still believe that mixed dominance is a cause of reading disability. There is no research to back this up. It has been found that when children begin first grade, if they don't know their right hand from their left, they have a tendency to be poor readers. This has to do more with intelligence, this author believes, than mixed dominance.

# LATERALITY, MIXED DOMINANCE, AND DIRECTIONAL CONFUSION

This author would like to define these terms a little more in depth than thus far done. The definitions that follow are those of Alice Cohen and Gerald G. Glass (1968), as derived from Albert Harris (1958).

> **Lateral Dominance** refers to the preference or superiority of one side of the body over the other (hand, eye, or foot) in performing motor tasks. Right lateral dominance would indicate preference for the right hand, eye, and foot.
>
> **Laterality** is another term for lateral dominance.
>
> **Consistent Dominance** refers to the preferential use of one hand, eye, or foot.
>
> **Mixed or Incomplete (hand, eye, or foot) Dominance** exists when the individual does not show a consistent preference for one (eye, hand, or foot).
>
> **Mixed Dominance** without specific reference to hand, eye, or foot concludes both crossed dominance (see below) and mixed dominance.
>
> **Crossed Dominance** exists when the dominant hand and dominant eye are on opposite sides.
>
> **Visual Motor Consistency** occurs when the subject's dominant hand, eye, and foot are on the same side of the body.
>
> **Directional Confusion** refers to knowledge of left and right. "Knowledge of Left and Right" is demonstrated by the subject in response to questions such as, "show me your right hand, left eye," etc. (This is distinguished from actual use of the dominant hand, eye, or foot in performance tasks.) (p. 343)

Studies such as those of E. Shearer (1968), Steven Forness (1968), and R. J. Capobianco (1967) are in general agreement with the findings of Cohen and Glass (1968).

Similar findings were reported by Albert Harris (1979) in a review of research on this topic. Robinson (1946) and her researchers administered tests for lateral dominance but did not feel that they knew how to interpret their findings. Her researchers were simply being conservative in their beliefs. Very little more is known today regarding the accurate interpretation of findings such as those reported by Cohen and Glass. Until more is known regarding effective remedial procedures for these areas that will improve children's reading ability, a diagnosis for laterality, mixed dominance, and directional confusion seems to be of little value.

## RESEARCH ON EDUCATIONAL FACTORS

Robinson (1946) mentioned a number of school factors or conditions that she and others believed influenced or were conducive to reading failure. Among these factors were teachers' personalities, methods of teaching reading, school policy on promotion, materials available, and class size. Ekwall and Shanker (1988) said this about Robinson's study:

> In her final analysis Robinson believed that school methods were a probable contributing casual factor in 18.1% of the cases she studied. She admitted, however, that there are so many factors involved in assessing educational factors that any definite conclusion is nearly impossible.

> It is our opinion that Robinson's figure in this case is not representative of the total percentage of reading failures caused by educational factors. If one views educational factors contributing to reading disability strictly those so bad that many children within any classroom failed to learn, then perhaps Robinson's figure is representative of the situation in general. However, many experts agree with John Manning (1969), in a speech given at the University of Kansas who expressed the viewpoint that more than 90% of our reading failure could or should be blamed on poor teaching. Since only 2% of our students experience learning disabilities so severe as to require the services of a specialist, it seems logical that near-perfect teaching would result in a failure rate no more than this 2%.

S. Jay Samuels (1970) expresses an opinion about instruction in reading:

> It is this author's contention that the assumption of adequate instruction is probably false in numerous instances because at the present time the complete analysis of the skills which must be mastered in the process of learning to read has not been made. Without a complete analysis of each of the subskills and concepts which must be mastered in the process of learning to read, it is difficult to understand how any instruction can be considered adequate. In the absence of a complete analysis of skills necessary for reading, there is a danger that the teacher may omit teaching important skills because she does not realize they are essential; or falsely assuming that certain skills have already been mastered, she may not teach them; or she may teach nonessential skills believing they are important. (p. 267)

Gerald Duffy and Lonnie McIntyre (1981) found that even the highest rated first and second grade teachers do not necessarily provide good quality instruction. The teachers studied were rated by peers and supervisors as "excellent teachers," yet the researchers in the study found that they almost never provided structured lessons or direct assistance to children during reading instruction.

Richard L. Allington (1983 & 1984) has concluded that the amount and type of actual reading students do in school may account for some of the achievement differences between the good and the poor readers. Allington further reports that at every grade level good readers complete more contextual reading than poor readers and that students in the highest reading groups tend to read material silently more and orally less than their less able peers.

Christopher Clark (1979) identified five approaches to research designed to answer the question, what makes a good teacher? Jere Brophy (1979) reviewed much of the research in this area and summarized some of the major findings:

1. Staff Characteristics. Higher-achieving schools had principals who were more effective and involved, used aides significantly more for noninstructional tasks, and had central office administration that was rated higher by teachers in instructional leadership and allocation of material resources.
2. Measures of Contact Between Students and Staff. Teachers at higher-achieving schools did not report spending more instructional time on reading and language development.
3. Instructional and Organizational Characteristics. Students in higher-achieving schools "were perceived to be happier, more engaged in their work, and less disruptive, restless, or bored. (p. 8)

Teachers at higher-achieving schools place more emphasis on student's academic performance, divided their classes into several groups (rather than providing "individualized" instruction), and participated in a reading program that was more stable or less subject to change.

Margaret Powell (1979) reported on a six-year, beginning teacher evaluation study which was conducted in California. Some of the findings:

1. The greater the proportion of time that students are engaged in their work (on task), the more they learn.
2. Some teachers were more effective than others in keeping their students on task.
3. Some teachers were more effective than others in providing their students with instructional tasks that lead to a high success rate.
4. The more total time spent in reading instruction, the more stu-

dents learn in that area. (This finding contradicts those of the school effectiveness study.)

5. Some teachers place greater emphasis than others on "academics" and had higher expectations for students. The teachers with the high standards produced students with higher achievement.
6. In higher achieving classrooms, teachers and students demonstrate greater respect for each other and work in a more cooperative atmosphere.

Jere Brophy (1979b) concluded:

1. Teachers make a difference. Some teachers produce more learning in their students than others.
2. Teacher expectations for student learning are an important factor.
3. Effective teachers possess the skills needed to organize successfully and conduct instruction. They are good classroom managers.
4. Effective teachers provide a maximum amount of instruction on critical skills, with minimal time wasted.
5. Students who receive a great deal of direct instruction in a structured curriculum have the highest achievement.

James F. Baumann (1984) summarized the research on teacher and school effectiveness:

1. If you are a principal, reading specialist, reading coordinator, be an instructional leader. Guide your faculty in the development of your school reading program.
2. Take responsibility for teaching and learning, have confidence in your ability to instruct. Assume your students are capable of learning, and expect them to learn.
3. Have objectives for every lesson you teach, know what they are, communicate them to your students.
4. Allocate enough time for reading instruction.
5. Keep nonengaged and transition time to a minute; that is, keep your students on task.
6. Establish high success rates; success does breed success.
7. Be an effective classroom manager—be organized and prevent misbehavior.
8. Monitor student learning, provide feedback, and reteach when necessary.

9. Administer direct instruction; that is, you teach the lessons. Do not expect textbooks, workbooks, games, or media to teach.
10. Use traditional reading groups, but individualize within and between groups.
11. Strive for a warm, nonthreatening, convivial classroom atmosphere; students will learn better when they are in a structured but secure environment. (p. 112)

There is research to support some basic principles of teaching that are consistent with the philosophy that poor teaching does make a difference in the student's learning. Everything will fail if the teacher does not set high expectations for the learner and maintain the student's task attention and provide direct instruction in a well managed way. The teacher is the most important ingredient in any classroom.

## THE MEANING FOR SOME COMMON TERMS FOR INTERPRETING RESEARCH

### Levels of Significance

When one examines the literature that pertains to research in reading as well as other fields, you will often encounter levels of significance, which are used in a number of statistical procedures to determine whether the results that are gotten are likely to have happened by chance. For example, when you give a reading test to two groups of fourth grade students taught by different reading methods, you might find that one group had a mean grade-level achievement of 4.6 and the other, 4.9. This does not tell whether the higher scoring group happened to do so by chance or if the method of instruction was the reason. If it were superior teaching, these results could be expected nearly every year. To make comparisons between or among scores, we use the level of significance, or the level of confidence.

When we apply the proper statistical procedure to the scores of the two groups of fourth grade students, you can determine whether a mean grade-level achievement of 4.9 is significantly better than 4.6. If it is significantly better than 4.6 at the .05 level of confidence, the reader may conclude that these differences occur by chance only five times out of a hundred. It would be better though if we had a .01 level of confidence because then we could conclude that these differences happen by chance only one time out of a hundred. In significance or confidence levels, you will see .05, .01, or occasionally .001 levels reported:

.05 —The probability of that event's occurring is less than 5 in 100.

.01 —the probability of that event's occurring is less than 1 in 100.

.001 —the probability of that event's occurring is less than 1 in 1000.

Sometimes a researcher reports levels of significance as computed, e.g., the .02 level, and the .10 level. Some statisticians believe that when this is done, researchers are likely to claim that a level of .10 of .15 is significant and therefore draw erroneous conclusions from their data.

## Correlations

The term correlation is often used to indicate that a relationship exists or two things have something in common. However, when used in statistical research, the term refers to the coefficient of correlation (r) between two sets of variables. The most commonly used method of computing is the Pearson Product Moment Correlation.

A correlation is a measure of rank order and distance from the mean of two sets of data or scores. Correlations may be highly positive or highly negative. A perfect positive correlation is shown as 1.00 and a perfect negative correlation is shown as −1.00. It should be pointed out though that in "the real world" there is never a perfect positive or negative correlation of 1.00. If a correlation is less than .20 we say that it is slight and that there is almost a negligible relationship. Between .20 and .40 we say that there is a low correlation. Between .40 and .70 there is a moderate correlation or substantial relationship. Between .70 and .90 there is a high correlation or a marked relationship. From .90 to 1.00 there is a very, very high correlation.

## t Test and f Test

In researching problems in reading, it is often necessary to determine if the test performance of one group is significantly different from that of another group. Sometimes it is necessary to determine whether the test performance of a group is significantly different from the norm. When researchers want to make decisions of this nature, the t test or f test is used. With either t or f tests, you are concerned with whether differences between the means of two or more groups are significantly different from that of another group. If we may, let's assume that a reading achievement test was given to two eighth grade groups and the results showed a level of 7.9 for one group and 8.4 for the other group. Whether this difference occurred by chance depends on such factors as number of students in each group and the standard deviations of the scores. If the t or f test is used and the researcher reports significant differences between the means at high confidence levels (.05, .01, or .001) you can conclude that the higher score indicates superior relationship.

## Chi Square

The chi square test is used to establish the distribution or ratio or frequency of a sample against another hypothetical or known distribution, ratio, or frequency. It tests the difference between expected and observed ratio distributions or frequencies. One can also use the chi square as a test of relationship.

Another use of the chi square test in reading is that on certain tests in previous research found that the expected distribution of mean scores was boys 70, girls 80. In a later testing, the distribution of mean scores was boys 80 and girls 71. We want to find out if this is observed ratio difference from the expected distribution and is it significant? If not significant, it could easily have happened by chance. If the significance is at the .05 level of confidence it would not happen by chance more than five times out of 100.

There are some other things that we should look at when we are discussing reading research. One thing that is very important is how large is the sample and how long were the reading sessions. For example, if we have 100 fourth grade boys and 100 fourth grade girls and they were given two different reading procedures for a period as long as four to six months, we would say that the groups were large enough and the reading periods were long enough. However, if we were comparing only a group of eight boys with eight girls for a period of one month, we could say that the groups were not large enough to draw conclusions from and that the period of the reading instruction was not long enough to draw inferences from. Also something we should look closely at is when we use the intelligence quotient of children in relationship to reading. For example, some researchers will use the Peabody Picture Vocabulary Test—Revised to get an IQ and this is not an intelligence test. We should only use the three Wechsler tests or the Stanford-Binet Intelligence Test if we're going to use IQ as one of the variables. Another thing we should watch for, which reading test did we use to compare the children? For example, the Wide Range Achievement Test—Revised should not be used to draw concrete observations or to make statements about the findings. This particular test should be used as a screening device and not one in research.

## SUMMARY

The author has summarized much of the reading research in some of the areas but there are thousands of research studies that are being done every year which we cannot use in this chapter. If we summarized all the research in reading done during the last 20 years, we would have a volume that would be so heavy we could not get it inside the library. The author has attempted to relate some of the pertinent research and also give to the reader some pertinent things in analyzing the research.

## REFERENCES

Ainsworth, S. H. (1959). *An Exploratory Study of Educational, Social, and Emotional Factors in the Education of Mentally Retarded Children in Georgia Public Schools.* U.S. Office of Education Research Program, Project No. 171. Athens, GA: University of Georgia.

Allington, R. L. (1984). Content coverage and contextual reading in reading groups. *Journal of Reading Behavior, 16,* 85–97.

Allington, R. L. (1983). The reading instruction provided readers of differing reading abilities. *Elementary School Journal, 83,* 548–559.

Baumann, J. F. (1984). Implications for reading instruction from the research on teacher and school effectiveness. *Journal of Reading, 28,* 109–115.

Bennett, A. (1932). *A Comparative Study of Subnormal Children in the Elementary Grades.* New York: Teachers College, Columbia University, Bureau of Publications.

Blatt, B. (1958). The physical, personality, and academic status of children who are mentally retarded attending regular classes. *American Journal of Mental Deficiency, 62,* 810–818.

Brophy, J. E. (1979b). *Advances in Teacher Effectiveness Research.* East Lansing, MI: Institute for Research on Teaching.

Brophy, J. E. (1979a). *Teacher Behavior and Its Effects.* East Lansing, MI: Institute for Research on Teaching.

Burt, C. (1921). *Mental and Scholastic Tests.* London: King.

Capobianco, R. J. (1967). Ocular-manual laterality and reading achievement in children with special learning disabilities. *American Educational Research Journal, 4,* 133–138.

Cassidy, V. M., & Stanton, J. E. (1959). *An Investigation of Factors Involved in the*

*Educational Placement of Mentally Retarded Children: A Study of Differences Between Children in Special and Regular Classes in Ohio.* U.S. Office of Education Cooperative Research Project, No. 032. Syracuse, NY: Syracuse University Institute.

Clark, C. (1979). *Five Faces of Research on Teaching.* East Lansing, MI: The Institute for Research on Teaching.

Cohen, A., & Glass, G. G. (1968). Lateral dominance and reading ability. *Reading Teacher, 21,* 343–348.

Cowen, P. A. (1938). Special Classes vs. Grade Group for Subnormal Pupils. *School and Society, 48,* 27–28.

Davidson, H. P. (1931). An experimental study of bright, average, and dull children at the four-year mental level. *Genetic Psychology Monograph, 9,* 119–290.

Dolch, E. (1951, 1931). *The Psychology and Teaching of Reading.* Boston: Ginn and Co.

Duffy, G., & McIntyre, L. (1981). *A Qualitative Analysis of How Various Primary Grade Teachers Employ the Structured Learning Component of the Direct Instructional Model When Teaching Reading.* East Lansing, MI: Institute for Research on Teaching.

Ekwall, E. D., & Shanker, J. L. (1988). *Diagnosis and Remediation of the Disabled Reader* (3rd ed.). Boston: Allyn and Bacon.

Elenbogen, M. L. (1957). A comparative study of some aspects of academic and social adjustment of two groups of mentally retarded children in special classes and in regular grades. *Dissertation Abstracts, 17,* 2497.

Engelmann, S., & Bruner, E. C. (1969). *Distar Reading: An Instructional System.* Chicago: Science Research Associates.

Forness, S. R. (1968). Lateral Dominance in Retarded Readers with Signs of Brain Dysfunction. Doctoral dissertation, University of California, Los Angeles.

Goldstein, H., Moss, J. W., & Jordan, L. J. (1965). *The Efficacy of Special Class Training on the Development of Mentally Retarded Children.* U.S. Office of Education Cooperative Research Project No. 619. Urbana, IL: University of Illinois.

Hammill, D. D., & McNutt, G. (1981). *Correlates of Reading.* Austin, TX: Pro-Ed.

Harris, A. J. (1979). Lateral dominance and reading disability. *Journal of Learning Disabilities, 12,* 57–63.

Harris, A. J. (1972). *Readings on Reading Instruction* (2nd ed.). Edited by A. J. Harris & E. R. Sipay. New York: David McKay.

Harris, A. J. (1958). *Harris Tests of Lateral Dominance — Manual of Directions* (3rd ed.). New York: Psychological Corporation.

Harris, A. J., & Sipay, E. R. (1985). *How to Increase Reading Ability* (8th ed.). New York: Longman.

Hegge, T., Kirk, S. A., & Kirk, W. (1936). *Remedial Reading Drills.* Ann Arbor, MI: George Wahr.

Hillerich, R. L. (Jan. 1974). Word lists — Getting it all together. *The Reading Teacher, 27,* 353–360.

Hoyt, M. (Dec. 1924). Mental age and school attainment of 1007 retarded children in Massachusetts. *Journal of Educational Psychology, 15,* 297–301.

Kelly, E. M. (July 1934). The improvement of reading in special classes for mentally retarded children. *Proceedings, American Association of Mental Deficiency, 39,* 67–73.

Kirk, S. A. *A Manual of Directions for Use with the Hegge-Kirk-Kirk Remedial Reading Drills.* Ann Arbor, MI: George Wahr.

Lerner, J. W., & List, L. (Fall 1970). The phonics knowledge of prospective teachers, experienced teachers, and elementary pupils. *Illinois School Research, 7,* 39–42.

Lopardo, G., & Sadow, M. W. (1982). Criteria and procedures for the method of repeated readings. *Journal of Reading, 26,* 125–160.

Manning, A. (1964). *Magazines.* Palo Alto: Ardelle Manning Productions.

McCafferty, S. (Feb. 1930). Readiness factors for reading. *Journal of Educational Psychology, 10,* 82–90.

Merrill, M. A. (1921). The relation of intelligence to ability in the three R's in the case of retarded children. *Pediatric Seminars, 28,* 249–274.

Merrill, M. A. (1918). The ability of the special class children in the three R's. *Pediatric Seminars, 25,* 88–96.

Moore, D., & Wielan, O. (1981). WISC–R scatter indexes of children referred for reading diagnosis. *Journal of Learning Disabilities, 14,* 511–514.

Moore, O. K. (1964). Autotelic responsive environments and exceptional children. In J. Hellmuth, Ed. *The Special Child in Century 21,* pp 87–138. Seattle: Special Child Publications.

Mullen, F. A., & Ilken, W. (1952). *The Reading Ability of the Older Ungraded Pupil.* Chicago: Chicago Public Schools.

Pertsch, C. F. (1936). A Comparative Study of the Progress of Subnormal Pupils in the Grades and in Special Classes. Unpublished doctoral dissertation, Columbia University.

Powell, M. (1979). New evidence for old truths. *Educational Leadership, 37,* 49–51.

Renshaw, S. (Feb. 1919). The abilities of pupils in Detroit prevocational classes. *Journal of Educational Psychology, 10,* 83–94.

Richek, M. A., List, L. K., & Lerner, J. W. (1989). *Reading Problems: Assessment and Teaching Strategies* (2nd ed.). Englewood Cliffs, NJ: Prentice-Hall.

Robinson, H. (1946). *Why Pupils Fail in Reading.* Chicago: University of Chicago Press.

Samuels, S. J. (1979). The method of repeated readings. *Reading Teacher, 32,* 403–406.

Samuels, S. J. (1970). Research-reading disability. *Reading Teacher, 24,* 267+.

Sattler, J. M. (1988). *Assessment of Children* (3rd ed.). San Diego: Jerome M. Sattler, Publisher.

Scarborough, W. H. (Fall 1951). The Incidence of Reading Retardation Among 1182 Mentally Handicapped Children. Paper read at American Association for Mental Deficiency Convention.

Schnittjer, C. J., Tuten, B. A., & Weller, L. D. (1992). Predicting achievement in grades three through ten using the Metropolitan Readiness Test. *Journal of Research in Childhood Education, 6,* 121–130.

Shearer, E. (1968). Physical skills and reading backwardness. *Educational Research, 10,* 197–206.

Spache, G. D., & Spache, E. B. (1977). *Reading in the Elementary School* (4th ed.). Boston: Allyn and Bacon.

Stanovich, K. E. (1985). Cognitive determinants of reading in mentally retarded individuals. *International Review of Research in Mental Retardation, 13,* 181–214.

Stanovich, K. E., Cunningham, A. E., & Cramer, B. B. (1984). Assessing phonological awareness in kindergarten children: Issues of task comparability. *Journal of Experimental Child Psychology, 38,* 175–190.

Stanovich, K. E., Cunningham, A. E., & Feeman, D. J. (1984). Intelligence, cognitive skills, and early reading progress. *Reading Research Quarterly, 19,* 278–303.

Thomas, G. I. (Sept. 1946). A study of reading achievement in terms of mental ability. *Elementary School Journal, 47,* 28–33.

Walthall, J. E., & Walthall, C. (Nov. 1993). Paper presented at the Mid South Educational Research Association, New Orleans, LA.

Wassmann, K. (1933). A Comparative Study of Mentally Deficient Children in Regular and in Special Classes. Unpublished master's thesis, George Washington University.

# Chapter 10

# TEACHING READING AND LANGUAGE SKILLS TO THE MILDLY HANDICAPPED

Acommon and well-accepted purpose of special education is to provide mildly handicapped children with remedial training in reading and other basic academic subjects. American schools have been confronted with the demand to develop educational programs for mildly handicapped children who have been commonly labeled as educable mentally retarded (EMR), learning disabled (LD), emotionally disturbed (ED), etc. The provision of services for mildly handicapped children is based on specific federal legislation. It has already been mentioned in this book that the most notable legislation is the Individuals with Disabilities Education Act (IDEA) (PL 101-476), assuring that all handicapped children shall have a free, appropriate public education.

When mildly handicapped children are referred for special service, reading is the subject most frequently mentioned by teachers as causing the learning problems. Poor reading is the number one stumbling block of increasing the learning capacities of a child. There are four essential processes that compose the reading act: sensory, perceptual, linguistic, and cognitive. Breakdowns in these four processes are often the major cause of reading problems found in mildly handicapped children. Reading is a sensory process in which visual and auditory senses are essential. Perception in reading involves the accurate recognition of the sounds and symbols of our language. The perceptual skills related to reading include discriminating, memorizing, sequencing, and synthesizing. Reading requires that the child have the ability to distinguish between different symbols and groups, to correctly associate the appropriate sounds with the symbols, to sequence these sounds into words and then put these words into larger ideas and images. Naturally, reading is a language process. Learning to read involves learning to deal with a language symbol system. One must understand language because it is the key to

A part of this chapter is taken from the book: *Teaching Mildly Handicapped Children* by Harold D. Love, Charles C Thomas Publisher, 1983.

understanding reading. Reading is also a cognitive process. This means that it involves the use of our higher mental processes. Reading demands that we think and form the basic levels of association and symbol relationships through man's highest levels of reasoning and evaluation.

There are various causes for reading problems in mildly handicapped children. For example, experiences of the child are extremely important in the development of reading skills in children. Children who come from poor home conditions are more likely to be behind in their reading skills, because of the lack of good speech models. The parents of these children usually are not likely to read to their children or motivate their children to read. Physical factors are often a cause of reading disability. They may include general health, visual and hearing disorders, speech defects, and motor disturbances. We have always known that intellectual factors have a limiting effect on the child's potential level of reading success.

Since poor reading is a stumbling block to further learning, special and regular teachers need to understand the relevant features of the various reading program that can facilitate learning for the mildly handicapped child. The intent of this chapter is to examine the various elements of teaching reading to mildly handicapped children.

## READING READINESS

Reading is a complex process achieved through an integration of many skills, the foundations of which are developed during the readiness stage. Readiness is the state of maturity and development that allows a person to learn to read. A child's readiness is necessary knowledge for the teacher who is teaching a mildly handicapped child to learn to read. It involves factors relating to age, physical health, intelligence, perceptual abilities, social adjustment, and language skills. Because these factors vary among children, the importance of readiness is stressed. The mildly handicapped child often needs reading readiness instruction for a longer period of time than a normal child.

Savage and Mooney (1979) inform us that the areas of importance to readiness are physical, emotional, intellectual, and linguistic. The physical factors are visual and auditory acuity, eye-hand coordination, large and small muscle development, and good general health. The emotional factors are to achieve personal confidence and security, to maintain attention, to stick with a task until its completion, to work independently, and to adjust well to a learning situation. The intellectual factors are described as perceiving and thinking. Linguistic factors are the learning of sounds and symbols of language. The same authors (Savage and Mooney, 1979) tell us that the reader must be able to understand oral language before being expected to deal with that language in print.

All language and cognitive experiences from birth contribute to the child's readiness for reading. The babbling of an infant includes all the sounds of his verbal language. The child practices these, with intonation and inflection, before he utters his first distinct word. These early stages of language acquisition and the continuing social and language development help children prepare to learn to read. Many studies have supported the correlation between general language ability and reading. Early experiences in using language definitely help develop language skills. Naturally, these would include listening and talking experiences. The child's ability to learn to read is highly dependent upon his spoken language skills. Many studies have shown that there is a relationship between the reading habits of the family, the access to reading materials in the home, and children's success in learning to read.

During the readiness stage, the instructional goal is to help the children develop proper orientation to the reading task. The classroom teacher needs to provide readiness teaching activities for the development of necessary prereading skills in the mildly handicapped. The following readiness skills may be developed in the child by providing readiness teaching activities:

1. Listening Comprehension is the ability to understand and recall what one hears. Read a simple story to the children showing pictures of each of the main characters or events. After the story is completed ask them to name each character or event and tell something that happened in the story.
2. Visual Comprehension is the ability to understand and recall what one sees. Show the children a drawing of an activity being performed by another child. Ask them to tell you what the child in the drawing is doing.
3. Auditory Discrimination is the ability to discriminate likenesses and differences among sounds. Provide the children with the key sound and ask them to clap their hands whenever they hear it. For example, if the sound is "t" they would clap once for table and twice for tattle.
4. Visual Discrimination is the ability to identify printed symbols from each other. Ask the children to match similar shapes and patterns.
5. Auditory Memory is the ability to remember what one hears. After listening to a story involving a series of events, ask the children to tell the proper story sequence.
6. Visual Memory is the ability to remember what one sees. Show the

children a picture of common objects. Remove the stimulus picture and
have them name each of the objects in the picture that they remember.

7. Letter name to letter symbol association is the ability to identify letters by
name. Have children see "a," say "a," and write "a."

8. Visual Tracking is the ability to follow an object or line across space. Ask
the children to complete a single maze by moving a finger along the route.
(Hare and Hare, 1977, p. 42)

Reading readiness is a necessary part of the teacher's instruction of
teaching a mildly handicapped child to learn to read.


## READING SKILLS

The instructional needs of the mildly handicapped child are not
essentially different from those of any other child in the classroom. The
mildly handicapped child needs to master the same basic skills as other
children in the process of learning to read. Teachers must help the child
develop reading skills, adjust his instruction to the child's learning
capacity, and teach according to the child's learning rate. When reading
is emphasized and appropriate methods are used, handicapped children
can learn to read.

Cohen and Plaskon (1980) emphasize that the major classification of
reading skills are word recognition, word analysis, context clues, and
comprehension. Word recognition is the skill that allows the reader to
instantly identify words in print. It is a skill that involves not only being
able to recall and pronounce the word but to know the meaning of the
word as well. Word analysis or word attack is the process of analyzing
unknown words in print. These word attack skills include phonetic
analysis and structural analysis. The process of analyzing unknown
words on the basis of letter-sound relationships in the words is called
phonetic analysis. The process of identifying meaningful units in words
is called structural analysis. Context clues are those clues found in the
surrounding test that aid the reader in determining the pronunciation
and meaning of unknown words. Comprehension is the ability to derive
understanding and meaning from printed language.

The first step in teaching reading to the mildly handicapped is for
them to recognize printed words on sight. The selection of words to be
learned by sight can be drawn from a number of sources such as words
for the parts of the body, number words, and lists of words frequently
used in beginning reading materials like the Dolch Word List.

Savage and Mooney (1979) inform their readers that the mildly handicapped will need many concrete materials in learning to attach meaning to words. The more experience a child has had with an object or activity that a word represents, the greater will be the child's chances of really knowing the word. Knowing a word involves not only recognizing it by sight but also knowing the meaning of the word in the context in which it is used.

After word meaning has been established, the next step is to help the child build a core sight vocabulary, a nucleus of familiar words that the child can use in his initial reading experiences. For example, in presenting the word *tree* as a sight word, the teacher should call attention to the visual shape or form of the word. For the mildly handicapped child, repeated exposure is usually needed before the child instantly responds to words in print as sight words.

Word analysis enables the child to decode the words that he encounters but that are not included in his sight vocabulary. It includes phonetic analysis that allows the child to decode unknown words on the basis of letter-sound relationships. Most basal reading programs include basic phonics training. It is known that children who are able to apply phonics strategies can predict the letter sounds of unknown words. Because of limitations in learning capacity and learning rate, mildly handicapped children require repeated drills in mastering phonics. Some mildly handicapped children have trouble in learning the phonics rules. It is best to simplify the phonics program and to teach it slowly while using the principles of repetition, practice, and generalization. Teacher-made taped phonics exercises are always useful in providing practice in phonics. A synthetic approach in which teachers direct sound-symbol relationships will often be effective. Word analysis also includes structural analysis that refers to the identification of word units such as prefixes, suffixes, and roots. It should be taught in the primary grades and should be closely associated with the child's own vocabulary.

Context clues are very important to the mildly handicapped child in learning to read. Mildly handicapped children often have problems in using context clues. In developing the child's ability to use context clues in reading, cloze exercises may be used. The cloze technique involves systematically deleting certain words from a passage and having a child supply the missing word.

For the mildly handicapped child and all other children, comprehension is a major area of difficulty in learning to read. It includes the skills of locating the main idea, recalling facts, determining causation, drawing conclusions, and evaluating. In discussing the role of language as it relates to reading, Buttery (1979) states that language is an important factor in reading comprehension. Children do not understand the meaning of the words used and the way these words relate to each other in larger sentence structures. For example, Betty was a second grade reader who had a reading comprehension problem. When she read the sentence, "Can you cup a bud with your hands?" Betty could not answer the questions yes or no because she did not understand what she read. When asked the meaning of the word cup, Betty replied, "It's something my mother drinks coffee from." When asked if she knew what a bud was, she responded, "It's a beer." Betty could not comprehend the meaning of the sentence. She was unable to understand the meanings of the words that she translated from print to speech. For mildly handicapped children, practice in identifying the who, what, when, where components of sentences is very important in developing comprehension. Rearranging scrambled words to construct grammatical sentences with similar meanings are good ways for helping children recover meaning from sentences.

The reading problems presented by the mildly handicapped child should be dealt with differently throughout the school years. In the early elementary grades, for example, emphasis should be placed on the development of reading skills aimed at making the child an independent reader. The focus strives toward mastery of both word analysis and comprehension. As the mildly handicapped child proceeds into the intermediate grades, a greater amount of time is devoted to isolated skill development. By concentrating on the deficient skills of the child, it is hoped that the child will be able to acquire the fundamental competencies he needs to develop reading independence. Emphasis on isolated skill acquisition often is associated with repetitive drills and reading practice.

## READING CHARACTERISTICS

According to Buttery (1979) the general learning characteristics often displayed by mildly handicapped children have direct implications for the teaching of reading and should be considered when selecting or modifying a reading approach.

1. Mildly handicapped children are most likely to learn new skills

from concrete materials that have meaning to them and their environment.

2. Generally, mildly handicapped children do not read up to their mental age levels, but come closer when instructed in regular classrooms.

3. When adequate attention is given to reading, we should expect approximately two-thirds of a year's gain in reading achievement for each school year.

4. Reading comprehension tends to be most difficult skill to master. It is even more difficult than reading orally.

5. When compared to normal children who are their equivalents in mental age, the mildly handicapped children are inferior in comprehension, in locating relevant facts, in recognizing main ideas, and in drawing inferences and conclusions.

6. In oral reading, the mildly handicapped children are inferior to normal children who are their mental age equivalents. In word attack skills they make more vowel errors and omissions of sounds. They also tend to be inferior in the use of context clues.

7. Mildly handicapped children approach many learning situations with an expectancy to fail. Structured success in reading activities can be achieved by providing immediate reinforcement, breaking the learning task down into small, attainable units, sequencing learning, and allowing opportunities for the child to experience reading for self-enjoyment.

8. Research has failed to substantiate any one method of teaching mildly handicapped children that is universally superior to another.

9. The teacher seems to be the most important variable in the reading success of mildly handicapped children.

10. Mildly handicapped children may be reading up to their mental capacity, even though they are below grade level. When this condition exists, the children are doing as well as could be expected, and no amount of remedial instruction can bring them up to their chronological achievement level.

## READING APPROACHES

In selecting a reading program for mildly handicapped children, little research tells us which reading program is the best. There is little agreement among authorities as to what approach works best with a particular child or groups of children. Advantages can be cited for different aspects of particular programs for use with the mildly handicapped child. For example, if the child needs a firm foundation in decoding skills, a highly structured code emphasis program such as the SRA Basic Skills Program may be used very effectively. For the mildly handicapped child, it is a good idea to reduce the demands of the reading task by reducing the amount of material to be read. The language experience approach may be especially appropriate in developing comprehension skills, because the reading material is generated from the child's own experiences. Whatever basal readers or programs are used, the placement level and pacing of the child are important in the use of materials. The level of reading materials should be appropriate to the child's reading ability, and therefore, material should be presented at a pace that will assure mastery. In adjusting to the level of the reading ability for the mildly handicapped child, the teacher probably will have to use a book that is a year or more below the grade level of the child. Pacing requires the presentation of material in a manner appropriate to the learning rate of the child. This often means doubling the number of presentations of a sight word and increasing the exposure time for each word.

To match the instructional materials and approaches to the needs of mildly handicapped children is a vital educational process, in which the teacher plays an important role. Because so many new materials and methods are being introduced in the field, it is becoming more important that the teacher have the skills necessary to evaluate materials and approaches. According to Gillespie and Johnson (1974) if the teacher has an adequate knowledge of the needs of his children and criteria for evaluating the effectiveness of materials and methods, he should be more competent in individualizing instruction.

Cohen and Plaskon (1980) inform their readers that the majority of developmental reading programs fall within the following classification: a basal approach, linguistics approach, programmed instruction approach, phonics approach, and language experience approach. The basal approach is a comprehensive approach that provides a series of reading materials extending from preprimer through the eighth grade. The series includes a teacher's manual to guide instruction about skills and suggested activities. Along with the reader, each child has a skills workbook that focuses upon skill development. The majority of reading programs in the United States use a basal approach. This basal approach has several advantages for mildly handicapped children: (1) it provides a carefully graded set of materials with a systematic progression of difficulty in vocabulary and reading skills; (2) it establishes skills that are divided into small units for the systematic teaching of word recognition and comprehension; (3) it establishes a basic vocabulary that is repeated throughout the sequence; (4) it provides diagnostic tools for finding strengths and weaknesses; and (5) it provides the teacher with easily expandable or otherwise adjustable materials to meet with individual needs of mildly handicapped children. While the basal approach has advantages for mildly handicapped children, it also has certain disadvantages for mildly handicapped children: (1) it organizes the teaching of reading for groups for children rather than for individuals, and (2) the material is often too difficult for the children at the lower end of the learning ladder.

The linguistic approach teaches children to decode by seeing differ-ences in letters of word families to understand the difference in word meanings. The children are not directly taught letter sounds but learn them through minimal word differences. It too has advantages: (1) it stresses the transition from spoken to written language by showing the child the relationship between phonemes and graphemes, and (2) it teaches reading by association with the child's natural language. It also has certain disadvantages: (1) it emphasizes auditory memory skills, making this approach extremely difficult for children who have deficits in this area, and (2) it stresses a vocabulary that is too controlled and does not approximate the child's speaking skills; therefore, some children have difficulty relating to it.

The programmed instruction approach is presented in small sequen-tial segments known as frames. For each frame the child is asked to make a response, and immediate feedback is presented to the child while he checks his own work. This provides reinforcement before going on to the next step. The program may have a phonics or linguistics orientation. It has certain advantages for the mildly handicapped: (1) the child is encouraged to proceed at his own pace with reinforcement provided at each learning step, (2) the child learns as an individual child rather than in a group, and (3) the child is instructed during short units made up of many small segments. It also has certain disadvantages: (1) the repetitive material sometimes becomes boring and the child's attention is lost, and (2) the instructional frames sometimes do not lend themselves to interest-ing stories. This approach may hurt the desire of the child to love reading.

The phonics approach is based on letter-sound relationships. Teaching is based either upon the synthetic method (teaches individual letters blended into words) or the analytic method (teaches phonics principles from words the child already knows). It has certain advantages for the mildly handicapped: (1) it emphasizes word recognition that often leads to independent reading, (2) it increases interest in reading because the child discovers new words, and (3) it helps the child associate sounds with the printed letters.

The Phonovisual Method is a systematic phonics method that provides a quick and simple means of teaching all the initial and final consonants and the vowel sounds. It is taught fifteen to thirty minutes per day to the entire class. It helps the child distinguish between letters that are often confused, such as p and q, and b and d. It provides a tool to attack new words and enables the child to read with comprehension and fluency.

In the language experience approach, the child uses his own experiences, and language becomes the vehicle in learning to read with comprehension and fluency.

In the language experience approach, the child uses his own experiences, and language becomes the vehicle in learning to read. The children dictate stories that are then transcribed on experience charts. Children learn to read words that they have used in recounting their own experiences. It has certain advantages: (1) it employs the child's current oral language abilities as the focus of the reading program, (2) it combines speaking, listening, and writing skills into the reading program, and (3) it utilizes direct experiences in order for the child to relate in written form.

Although developmental reading approaches are commonly adapted for individual needs, they have not received complete success with mildly handicapped children. For this reason, other approaches have been designed for the mildly handicapped child.

Marsh and Price (1980) inform their readers that the Gillingham Method uses a multisensory approach to teach sound units or letters for reading, writing, and spelling. This method emphasizes drill and repetition of three phonics-associated levels: (1) association involves learning the name and sound of the letters, (2) association asks the child to name the letter associated with a certain sound, and (3) association includes writing the letter where the child hears a certain sound. Later, letters are blended into consonant-vowel-consonant words, such as hat. A highly specified manual accompanies the materials that include phonics drill cards, phonic words, syllable concept cards, and stories.

The Fernald Method is a visual-auditory-tactual-kinesthetic stimulation in combination with language experiences. It was designed by Grace Fernald and Helen B. Keller to teach reading to word-blind individuals of normal intelligence who could not learn to read through auditory and visual approaches. This method has been used successfully with mildly handicapped children. In the initial stages of the method, the mildly handicapped child is allowed to choose words that he wants to learn to read and write. The word is written for the child. The child traces the word, pronouncing it slowly as he traces. He writes the word and checks his copy with the original. He continues this procedure until he can correctly reproduce the word from memory. The word is added to a story, which is typed for him by the teacher, and he then reads aloud the printed story. After the child has learned a number of words, he is able to generalize and to "attack" new words that are based upon their similarity to known words. For the mildly handicapped child, some modifications may be needed.

The use of language cuts across all areas of the curriculum and includes a wide range of concepts, skills, and attitudes. It is acknowledged that academic difficulties are due to a deficiency in the area of language. It is increasingly recognized by many researchers that "reading problems, spelling problems, writing problems, and math problems frequently are manifest products of an underlying disorder in language comprehension and expression" (Gerber, 1981, p. 81).

A complete language arts program is broad in scope. It encompasses the following subjects: listening, speaking, reading, writing, and spelling. These subjects serve as avenues for communication of ideas, feelings, and appreciations. While specific principles are applicable to each area of the language arts, certain general principles apply to the broad field. Some general principles follow (Evans, 1974): (1) All phases of the language arts program should be developed in relationship with other parts of language arts. Learning in one phase should reinforce learning in other phases of the program. (2) All concepts and skills of the program should be introduced in practical settings. (3) The uniqueness of each child should be recognized and respected. (4) Differences in achievement by the sexes should be expected and accepted. (5) Teachers should involve pupils, parents, community citizens, and professional educators in planning, executing, and evaluating the program. (6) The program should be perceived in its hierarchial position in the academic field.

A look at each area of the language arts and how this affects the mildly handicapped is now given. Each will be considered as a separate entity in the field and presented as a part of a unified whole field of learning. The data presented will give basic principles for these specific areas in the field of techniques of teaching.

## LISTENING

Ability to listen is of utmost importance, because it is the primary source of language. It is the base on which all other language skills develop. Therefore, listening becomes an integral part of all language activities. For example, learning to read is learning to associate the spoken sounds of language with written symbols on a page. Writing is making symbols to represent the words that are heard by the ears or in the mind.

It is often said that more time is spent in listening than in any other language activity. Paul T. Rankin (1928) reveals that of all the time people spend daily in communication, approximately 42 percent is spent in listening, 32 percent in speaking, and 25 percent in reading and writing.

The extent of listening varies in degrees. Ruth Strickland (1969) classifies listening into three types: (1) marginal listening, involving the background of one's consciousness (this is the listening used by the students, young and old, who study with the stereo playing), (2) appreciative listening, occuring when one listens to a concert, a play, a poem, or a story, etc., (3) attentive listening, involving the absorption of directions, participating in discussions, sharing in decision making, etc., and (4) analytical thinking, necessitating the consideration of elements involved, noting their relationship, and evaluating data.

Experts say that listening entails a two-way interaction. When one hears and responds, it is important to realize that the other person may have something important to say that is worth listening to. Listening also involves both passive and active behavior. The type of message conveyed should determine the response.

Mildly handicapped children do not need to listen more, they need to listen better. Lundsteen (1971) points out that children's experience with mass media involves passive listening. Watching television does not permit children to talk back or react to what they hear. This activity forms poor listening habits and cuts down on more productive learning experiences. Mildly handicapped children desperately need help in learning to think about and react to what they hear. They need listening lessons that cause them to question, to sort, to organize, to evaluate, and to choose.

Teachers should realize that they are the models of listening behavior. The teacher is the center of much attention in the classroom, while also acting as the leader, organizer, arbiter, and instructor. It can be said that the skills and attitudes exhibited by the teacher become the way for measuring the importance to listening habits. The teacher should always listen attentively to children when they express themselves.

There are definite standards that should be developed for listening, some of which follow:

1. Look at the speaker.
2. Keep hands free of objects.
3. Keep hands and feet as quiet as possible.
4. Listen until the speaker is finished.
5. Think about what is being said.
6. Ask important questions.
7. Follow oral directions. (McDonald, 1978, p. 131)

Instructors must first develop listening readiness by relating material that is heard to previous experience and by introducing new words. The teacher must then state the purposes of listening. Teachers must also emphasize listening as an integral part of the entire curriculum. Children should be asked to listen attentively in order to be able to follow directions.

Praise is extremely important. All children are able to recognize appropriate and inappropriate listening behavior through praise. Teachers should praise students who do not request a repetition of statements made. Teachers should also praise students who listen courteously to conversations, lectures, and other presentations.

Educators should point out the many advantages to listening. Listening helps to determine the reason "why," to get additional information on a topic, and to follow the sequences of ideas in reporting. Listening also helps to reproduce what is heard creatively and to learn solutions to problems. Listening helps us to identify words and phrases that sound alike, to note good speech habits, and to be able to analyze, compare, and evaluate data.

Children will vary in their listening ability. A good listening program should involve children in identifying their individual strengths, weaknesses, and needs. It should also help them set appropriate objectives. Through class discussions, self-evaluations, and individual conferences, they can become better listeners.

Media can be utilized in developing listening skills. Teachers should make recordings of children's voices while speaking and reading. The teacher should ask students to listen, compare, and contrast the different voices. Videotape machines can also be used in the same manner. Have students interpret commercials heard on the radio or television. In using the media, instructors have motivating tools that develop not only listening skills but also the desire to listen.

A listening center provides individualized instruction for all students. It should contain materials for children to practice skills. These might include tape-recorded stories, puzzles, exercises, and recorded directions for making things. Recorded instructions and stories are very beneficial to the mildly handicapped children. They may use their visual skills together with their listening skills to gather more meaning from materials presented. Working independently in a listening learning center will also develop the student's sense of independence.

Learning activities can be highly motivating. This is especially true if the activities are games, because children are drawn by such activities. They have fun while participating and hardly realize that they are learning. The game *Listen and Tell* builds a story one word at a time and can be an excellent motivator. The teacher says the beginning word and children in turn repeat what has been said plus one more word. *Headlines* is another game where listening skills are involved. The teacher reads newspaper articles to the children, and the children then think of good headlines that contain the main idea of the article. A game using the media that should attract young people is *Sales Pitch.* The teacher records certain radio advertisements. The children listen to them and analyze how the advertisers try to get people to buy their products. *Peer Reports* involve all the children and their surroundings. The teacher should pair the children and have them interview one another about hobbies or special interests. After the interview all students give a report of their partner's hobbies or interests.

Evans (1974) tells us that young mildly handicapped children would benefit from such games as *Name the Animal, What Did I Say?, Sitting Simon,* and *Around the Robin. Name the Animal* consists of one child imitating sounds and the students identifying it. *What Did I Say* is a whisper game. One child is chosen to whisper a message to his neighbor. Each student tells another student what has been told to him and the last student tells the story as he heard it. Interestingly, the finished product seldom has any relationship to the original message. A student leader is selected in the game *Sitting Simon.* This leader directs the students to follow Simon's directions. *Around the Robin* is an effective listening game where one student utters a word and the next student says that word and adds an appropriate word in order to make a story at the end of the game.

Being a good listener involves the use of many skills. Instruction in listening helps children to become aware of these skills and to evaluate their own listening habits. It also provides opportunities to develop and practice skills in meaningful situations. Because listening is a part of the entire school day, it may be taught within the context of various subject areas. Listening can be exercised inconspicuously as well as directly. Whichever is the case, teachers must be aware that listening is a significant part of the language arts and should be developed for all children although it may be more important for the mildly handicapped child.

## LANGUAGE

Oral language is essential to all other language arts learnings. The close relationship between language and learning has often been recognized as extremely important by such greats as Freud, Piaget, and Skinner. Some children with language problems are handicapped in understanding and using the spoken word, consequently many of them have difficulties in acquiring basic academic skills.

Language is a symbol system. It consists of many symbols that are rule governed. Children learn speech with certain rules, instead of randomly. Language is a generative system. It is generative in that it contains many linguistic rules that can be used to make an infinite number of sentences. Disick (1975) says that language is a social code. Children learn particular symbols to represent their knowledge of the world. All languages have socially agreed-upon functions, that is, the communication functions. The rules for communication require the learning of gestures, facial expressions, and rules of politeness. Speech is not the primary mode of communication, but the foundation for other modes.

There are three types of language: (1) inner language, (2) receptive language, and (3) expressive language. Inner language is the language that one uses to communicate with oneself. Inner language development is dependent upon a child's ability to establish verbal imagery for sounds, words, and concepts and to use complex skills needed in a logical thinking process. Receptive language is the ability to understand the spoken language of others. Children with difficulties in this area hear what is said but cannot comprehend it. Expressive language is the spoken language children use in communicating with others. Deficits in spoken language can be very complex. Many children require specialized remediation by highly trained language clinicians. The development of oral language skills must, nevertheless, be recognized as an important goal of the special education teachers.

The major concern of teachers should be to develop children's maximum language ability within their biological limits. In doing this, teachers must start when mildly handicapped children are young. Karnes (1975) has developed early language activities for children as young as one and one-half to three years of age. In addition to activities, she presents some excellent techniques for stimulating language development. The following techniques are presented.

1. Demonstrate what you want the children to do.
2. Tell the children what they are doing.
3. Encourage the children to talk.
4. Give the children something to talk about.
5. Pay attention to the children when they talk.
6. Reflect back what the children say.
7. Note the activities the children enjoy most and repeat them.
8. Give the children a chance to talk.
9. Don't correct the children every time they make verbal errors.
10. Physically get down on the children's level.
11. Let the children know you enjoy their company.
12. Be flexible. (p. 79)

One must have an appropriate model to develop correct speech. Teachers with friendly attitudes and interesting experiences often have a great deal of success in teaching speech habits.

Conversation leads all other types of oral language activities. Learning to be a good conversationalist is an important lifetime skill. Conversation activities ought to encourage the children to participate, to listen, to make worthwhile contributions, to take turns, and to be polite and considerate of others.

Some students hesitate to participate in conversation because they cannot think of anything to say or because they are self-conscious about talking. Other children take large amounts of time and say very little. Discussion of possible and relevant topics is one way to ease the problem. Teachers should have the students brainstorm on subjects for conversation and the compiling of suggestions. Point out that children can have a conversation about many things and present the list for the children to analyze the suggestions.

Another concept to develop is listening, as well as speaking, conversation. Children should realize that a good conversation is not one-sided, but the interaction takes place when listening and speaking are weighed equally. Children must learn to listen to others, to keep up with the conversation, and to show consideration for other people.

Learning to participate in small discussions is another area of importance. Discussions are similar to conversations but more structured. There is a definite goal and usually preplanned ideas of meeting that goal. The first step is to identify the purpose of the discussion. Then the children must learn to take turns. DeHaven (1979) tells of a technique to encourage more equal participation called the "talking stick." A stick or other object is held while one child is speaking. When he finishes, the object is passed on to another child, and the discussion is continued. Gearheart (1980) mentions another technique to encourage participation and calls it an "inner circle" arrangement. Half of the class forms an inner circle, and the rest of the class is seated around them in an outer circle. Only the inner circle is allowed to talk. At the end of a given period of time, the two groups exchange places, and the discussion proceeds from where it left off.

The children ought to have both large and small group discussion experiences. Large-group permits the teacher to model discussion behaviors. For learning and practicing discussion skills, it is probably best to break the class into smaller groups so that each child has a greater opportunity to participate.

Evaluation following discussion sessions is an important learning tool. Children need to become aware of productive and unproductive behaviors and to understand how their actions affect the outcome of a discussion.

Evaluation identifies effective techniques and builds models that enable children to set meaningful discussion skill goals. Many other activities contribute to the development of oral language skills that are both interesting and educational.

Interviewing is one method of developing skills. The interviewer's primary goal is to inquire, and this activity develops responsibility and confidence in speech. Announcements and directions are other methods of acquiring appropriate language skills. Announcements and directions must be clear and concise. This activity makes children aware of their grammar and speech.

Children involved in story telling must first have a background of story experiences. Preparing to retell favorite stories of the class is an excellent way to develop an awareness of the plot and characterization. When children understand a story well, they can concentrate on using their voices expressively and enunciating clearly. Cooperative stories may be exercised by using a round-robin form where children take turns telling part of a story, or it may involve supplying parts of a story told by the teacher.

Reporting begins the first year of school. A simple form of reporting is *Show and Tell.* This can be very valuable to oral language development. More formal oral reporting may present information from the social studies or other content area to the class. When several children work together on the same topic, they may make a group presentation.

Evaluation is, again, a great learning tool. After a report has been given, teachers might provide pertinent questions to help the children identify strengths and weaknesses.

Learning, for young mildly handicapped children, is highly dependent on concrete experiences. As teachers help these children to verbalize their experiences, they provide a meaning base for language and facilitate growth. A range of structured and creative language experiences may be used to stimulate the development of language competence in mildly handicapped children.

## READING

Reading is a lifetime task, beginning with the experiences and perceptions of infancy and extending through adult life. It involves a process of deriving meaning from symbols. To derive meaning adequately, a reader must translate the written symbol into sound symbols of language and use his knowledge to reconstruct the written message (DeHaven, 1979). A child's first language experience involves listening and speaking. Later experiences in reading are extensions of oral language. The alphabet provides a visual representation of the spoken language.

Reading as a communicative process requires readers to reconstruct encoded messages in order to hear in their minds what the writer is saying. Reading involves complex skills and abilities that work together to recreate a flow of meaningful language. Reading ability involves a continual interplay of the reader's knowledge of such things as phonics, word structure, syntax, intonation, and semantics. Each child's background of language provides the basis on which he is able to recognize and use significant reading clues and reconstruct meaningful communication.

Studies in biology and psychology indicate that general process of human development follows three stages, namely, (1) mass action, (2) differentiation, and (3) integration. Kirk (1978) applied the theories and stages of development to the process of reading. He stated that a reading instruction method is successful only insofar as it takes into account and provides for the developmental steps in the reading process. These developmental stages are (1) reading wholes, (2) learning details, and (3) reading without awareness of details.

Difficulties in learning to read have been cited as a single most important cause of school failure. It is natural that many children with reading difficulties also have academic problems in other areas of the curriculum. It is important that teachers be made aware of specific skills with which an individual child is experiencing difficulty. The following list includes general reading problems with which the teacher must be concerned: (1) auditory skills, (2) visual skills, and (3) comprehension skills.

Reading readiness is the development of prerequisite skills for any task of the development of a reading program. The development of language is an important background skill for reading. Language readiness activities should be practiced to develop a readiness for reading.

Auditory discrimination is developed through many different activities. In developing auditory skills, the teacher should realize that children must learn to discriminate among sounds, discriminate initial and final letter sounds, synthesize letter sounds into words, and remember the sounds of letters and words. By listening to the sounds of our language and learning to identify similarities and differences, children are preparing for phonic skills. Discriminating activities include repeating words accurately, listening to a sequence of words to find one that is pronounced twice, hearing or suggesting words that begin with the same sound, picking out rhyming words, and listening to specific words in a story.

Mildly handicapped children with visual skill deficiencies must learn to discriminate sizes and shapes, specific letters, and directionality of letters. Like all children, the mildly handicapped must also remember letter names and words, remember particular words learned mainly by sight, and recognize structural parts of words. Visual discrimination activities include recognizing letters that are the same and different, and the activities must include recognizing words that outline shapes.

Most children have developed some sort of sight vocabulary before they start school. Children have been exposed to television, labels, books, magazines, etc. They usually learn sight words more rapidly when the words have an unusual or interesting shape. The ability to recognize words on sight allows children to concentrate on the meaning of the words. Teachers should give special attention in the meaning of the words. Teachers should give special attention in helping children to acquire a basic sight vocabulary. Once a word has been mastered, word games, puzzles, flash cards, and other activities may be used for additional practice.

Phonics is widely used in learning to read. In teaching phonics, teachers should instruct children to associate sounds of language with letters of the alphabet. The purpose of phonics is to help children develop the ability to figure out the pronunciation of printed words that they do not already know as sight words.

Wide experiences with letter-sound correspondences will help children formulate generalizations they can apply to unknown words. Activities such as listing words that begin alike, comparing the spelling of rhyming words, and analyzing the sounds that single consonant blends, diagraphs, and diphthongs signal when found in different environments strengthen children's phonics knowledge in meaningful ways.

It is a known fact that unfamiliar words often contain known parts. The teacher, when using analysis techniques, helps the child in recognition and identification of whole words. Many longer words contain a familiar base word that is surrounded by suffixes or prefixes. Calling children's attention to groups of letters that form suffixes and prefixes, thus creating new words from known parts and discovering base words that have been combined with prefixes and suffixes, are all ways to help children acquire the skill of using structural and morphemic analysis as a word-identification tool. Learning to recognize word parts leads to more efficient reading.

Contextual clues can help children decide the pronunciation of words that are unknown. Children may not be able to explain why the words seem right in a sentence, but when they are meaningfully engaged in reading, their knowledge of language facilitates their use of contextual clues to identify unknown words. The children must have the knowledge of the meanings of words, word order, and grammatical structures to use context clues.

The use of the dictionary is very helpful in the pronunciation of words and word meanings. To be able to use a dictionary, children must acquire the knowledge of alphabetical order and phonic spellings. Learning to use the dictionary to decode unknown words ought to include attention to the structures and meanings of words, as well as pronunciations. The students should also read definitions carefully and apply the definitions to learning contexts.

Naturally, reading is much more than decoding printed symbols. Comprehension of what is read is of utmost importance. Comprehension of reading requires an understanding of the meanings of words; however, words may have different meanings, and that is where contextual meanings are used. The children must be able to combine the meanings of all the words in a sentence. They must be able to relate the parts to the larger unit. The child must be able to analyze and synthesize a story as a total work. Smith and Barrett (1974) indicate that the skills of comprehension that should be taught most frequently are understanding the meanings, getting the main idea, noting details, following directions, seeing relationships, making inferences, predicting outcomes, and distinguishing between fact and opinion.

The teaching of reading may be approached in several ways. One of the most frequently used techniques is the basal reader approach. In the basal reader approach, the initial emphasis is on development of a basic sight vocabulary. Contexts and picture clues are relied upon, with comprehension of meaning being a major goal. It utilizes a set of reading books and supplementary materials designed to teach children all of the important skills of reading. It is a complete program that provides a developmental sequence of skills and has controlled vocabulary in order that reading is learned in small steps. Mastery of each step must be present before moving on from one unit to the next. In order for mildly handicapped children to learn to read at the maximum potential, teachers must continually practice diagnostic teaching (teach, test, reteach).

The individualized reading method according to Hammill (1975) allows children to select their reading material and to progress at their own pace. Emphasis is on comprehending the meaning of words in sentences. This approach must only be used with mildly handicapped children who have mastered the fundamentals of reading and have a great awareness of what they read.

Evans (1974) relates that the language-experience approach utilizes children's experiences and vocabulary. Since words that are familiar to the children are used, it becomes meaningful and therefore facilitates learning. In the language-experience approach, the children's first reading materials are chart stories dictated by the students about their own experiences. In this system there is no predetermined control over vocabulary, syntax, or content, and the teacher uses the matter that children compose to develop reading skills. The emphasis is on reading material that grows out of the students' experiences, written in the children's natural language.

According to Kirk (1978) the phonics methods teach children to associate speech sounds with letters or groups of letters to help them pronounce unfamiliar words. Phonic systems range from complete reading programs such as the *Open Court Reading Series* or Lippincott's *Basic Reading Program* to supplementary programs of Hay-Wingo Road to Reading, the Heggi-Kirk-Kirk Remedial Drills, and Distar. Phonics must be structured and, if used correctly, can be a very beneficial tool of reading for the mildly handicapped.

The linguistic approach emphasizes breaking the written language code. In linguistic reading materials, words are read as wholes, beginning with words that have a regular spelling pattern. This approach assumes that children are able to discover the relationship between sounds and letters. In dealing with the mildly handicapped, the teacher must teach the child how to use the linguistic approach.

Disick (1975) says that the initial teaching alphabet (ita) approach is a method of beginning reading with forty-four symbols representing one speech sound in the English language. In (ita), the word is spelled the way it is pronounced. The initial teaching alphabet is used only in beginning teaching. When children have mastered the (ita) letters, they are exposed to traditional reading materials.

Regardless of the major approach used to teach reading to mildly handicapped children, procedures must be such that they benefit each child. Maximum growth requires continual assessment and planning on an individual basis.

## HANDWRITING

Many years ago Johnson and Myklebust (1967) said that written language grew out of drawing and progressed through many stages of development to the present alphabetic system. It is one of the highest forms of language and essentially the last to be learned. Its major purpose is communication. It is not enough to encode a message; the message must be readable. Legible handwriting most obviously shows its importance through examples such as mail that may not be delivered when an address is illegible or illegible orders that are filled incorrectly. For several years, many children have been receiving little direct instruction in handwriting. Naturally, the result has been trial and error learning as children develop incorrect responses that frequently lead to illegible handwriting. Teachers have become aware of the need for more handwriting instruction as they see children struggling with written work. Children who have handwriting problems basically have difficulties in executing the motor patterns required for writing letters, words, and numbers. Many children have problems spelling words correctly or properly translating thoughts into written communication. A good handwriting program, Evans (1974) reveals, teaches skills and reinforces them through practices. The most effective way to learn to write is through direct instruction. Handwriting instruction should not be limited to a set period of the day, but rather continually throughout all academics. Letter formation, spacing, alignment, size, and slant are factors that should be emphasized while teaching handwriting. Legibility is the most important criterion for evaluating handwriting produced by these factors.

At the age of six, most children are ready to write, but children must be instructed in the proper ways to acquire writing skills. Children must develop readiness skills such as the conceptual aspects of writing, perceptual competency, visual and kinesthetic memory, and hand/eye coordination (DeHaven, 1979). In developing these skills, some readiness activities include (1) practicing how to hold pencils and crayons; (2) tracing circles, slants, and other shapes on the chalkboard; (3) arranging pictures in left-to-right and top-to-bottom sequence; (4) dot-to-dot games, scribbling, drawing, cutting, and pasting; and (5) tracing letters out of sandpaper.

The first thing children should learn to write is their names. Every new writing skill should be introduced on the chalkboard. This enables the teacher to observe writing techniques, and it also enables children to be free with their movements while they are learning. Children should be provided manuscript paper to help control the size and alignment of letters. Verbalizing the starting point, directing movement, and shaping letters as they are made help children form concepts and gain control of writing movements. The lower case letters should be taught first so that children can write many words as soon as possible. Only one or two letters should be taught at one time. Learning to write well takes practice, therefore, time should be set aside for teacher-directed handwriting practice and instruction.

The switch from manuscript to cursive has often been traumatic for many children. There are two well-known programs of handwriting that attempt to simplify that step: D'Nealian handwriting and Italic handwriting. The D'Nealian letters in manuscript are more oval than round as in the conventional manuscript alphabets, but D'Nealian cursive letters are similar to conventional letters. Italic handwriting is a system based on calligraphy. It is designed to teach a beginning form of letters to be used throughout life.

Helping children overcome problems in handwriting is a matter of helping them replace good habits for bad ones. Remediation begins with an analysis of their writing in terms of a standard model. After problems are identified, the next step is to eliminate them. Some require specific reteaching lessons while others do not. Children with the same problems may be grouped together for direct instruction. Close supervision of children's practice is essential so that errors can be caught and corrected promptly. Most letter formation problems, says DeHaven (1979), stem from visual discrimination or poor memory of letter forms. One of the most common of the letter formation problems is reversals. Children should practice awareness of these letters and the directions that they face to overcome this problem.

Techniques for practicing can be fun and beneficial. Making a class scrapbook containing one sheet for each person can display serious efforts of correct handwriting. Sending homemade greeting cards is another fun opportunity to practice correct handwriting skills. Many more activities can be thought of by the teacher and students to cause the class to become aware of the importance of legible handwriting.

A program to improve children's writing begins with the awareness of need. The teacher and the children must realize the need for legibility. Diagnosis of errors is necessary to progress, and it is most effective when children are involved in the process.

## SPELLING

Spelling is often a difficult and controversial aspect of language instruction. Apparently, inconsistencies in the way words are spelled challenge organized and meaningful mastery. Yet the ability to spell continues to be important both in and out of school. Spelling often influences judgment about a person's educational level and general ability. Spelling errors stand out in writing. They are more obvious than poorly organized paragraphs or unreasonable statements. Frequent mis-spellings suggest carelessness and create a negative attitude toward one that could otherwise be good. Naturally, this can limit opportunities and chances for advancement.

Correlation studies, according to DeHaven (1979), consistently indicate the interrelationship of spelling ability and the other language arts. Children who are good readers tend to be good spellers. Correlations between speech and spelling ability show that incorrect pronunciation and careless articulation reduces the number of oral cues children have to aid them in translating spoken language into written symbols. Correlations are also found between handwriting and spelling. Letters that are illegibly formed cannot be considered to be spelled correctly. Also, slow writing may detract from concentration on the spelling of a word before the child has finished writing it. Aural and oral uses of language, wide reading, writing, and an understanding of the sound and structure of English words provide an important background for spelling. Many children with spelling difficulties come to dislike the idea of written communication and either come up with an elaborate mental plot to compensate for their deficits or simply avoid all written activities.

Spelling is believed to be a more difficult task than reading because, as Wallace (1978) points out, the opportunity to draw upon peripheral clues is greatly reduced. Teachers should be aware that in spelling, children must remember the form of letters and remember the letter sequences and rules for particular words.

Most teachers use a teach-study-test procedure and use repetition as a remedial method for instructing mildly handicapped children to spell. Many methods are available to educators and are most effective in teaching spelling. However, teachers must first determine individual spelling needs to decide which procedures to introduce.

Simon and Simon (1973) described four different procedures that spellers may use. The first is memory or direct recall and involves the spelling of words that are associated with long-term memory with pronunciation and meaning. The second method is called direct phonetic spelling. This procedure is based on stored sound-symbol associations and their rules. The third method is the generate and test process. Stored sound-symbol associations are combined recognitions of trial spelling. This is used in sounding out and for the whole word. The fourth procedure entails each of the proceding processes modified by morphemic information. This method uses rules. While no method can produce accurate spelling, reaching attention to various combinations directed toward individual needs might make great differences in mastery.

In teaching spelling, instructors must develop the areas of basic spelling skills. One of those skills is visual discrimination. Children must learn to look at words and notice the letters and sequence of letters in words. To develop this skill, teachers might give exercises in which the children find words that are the same or different. A domino game using words instead of dots could be used for matching similar words. Visual memory is another basic skill to be developed. Children need to form a visual image of words and be able to remember how words look. One exercise for developing this skill is to help up a word on a flash card and have the children concentrate on it for a few seconds. Then remove the card and ask the children to write the word. Auditory discrimination is a third skill that must be developed. Children must be able to distinguish both individual sounds in words and the correct sequence of the sounds in order to use phonic cues to help them spell words. Identifying words that are alike or different, rhyme, begin the same, or end with the same letter may be used. Saying words slowly helps children hear the particular sounds that make up the word. A fourth skill is using phonic generalizations. A basic knowledge of phoneme-grapheme consistencies is an important aid to good spelling. Activities such as cutting out pictures of things that begin alike, writing word lists, and making alphabet books help develop letter-sound association. Using structural and morphemic analysis is the fifth basic spelling skill that must be developed. When learning to recognize and spell words in syllables and writing each syllable as they pronounce it, children learn to listen more closely and accurately. Recognizing suffixes and prefixes of words children already know may be helpful in spelling successfully and building spelling confidence.

Learning to spell a list of words, according to Hammill (1975), is the heart of a spelling program, whether the words are from a published text or from other sources. Many authorities prefer the test-study-test approach. The test prior to study is to determine words the children do and do not know. A spelling test should be given in a three step procedure that provides pronunciation and meaning cues for children and stimulates an actual writing experience: (1) pronounce the word clearly without unnatural emphasis, (2) use the word in a meaningful sentence, (3) pronounce the word again.

To maximize the learning experience, children ought to grade their own papers. Identifying the words that they have misspelled gives immediate feedback and promotes learning. Horn (1967) states that when pupils correct their own papers and the results are properly utilized, the test becomes the most fruitful single learning activity that has yet been devised.

Teaching children to spell involves helping them to associate printed symbols with words. To do this they need to develop a way of studying words. They may use visual memory, structural analysis, phonic analysis, rote memory, or kinesthetic response. The final test over the week's spelling list indicates the children's mastery after study. Words that are misspelled should be added to the list for study during the following weeks.

Because children cannot learn all the words they will ever need to learn, they must develop a way for learning new words on their own. A common learning plan includes visual, auditory, and kinesthetic learning modes. Children's attitudes toward spelling are of utmost importance. To be good spellers, they must not only develop skills but must value the ability to spell and assume a sense of pride and responsibility for their work.

Teaching the language arts is a process that involves helping mildly handicapped children develop knowledge, appreciation, and skillful use of language. Teaching thus requires a specific plan to stimulate language awareness and provides opportunities for children to use language purposefully. Language learning is an active process. What and how much children learn is related to the opportunities provided for them to learn. Guiding children's language growth means involving them in activities with people, things, and ideas to introduce language and easy growth.

# REFERENCES

Buttery, T. (Winter 1979). Reading improvement for mainstreamed children who are mildly mentally handicapped. *Reading Improvement, 40,* 337(2).

Buttery, T. (Summer 1979). Reading for mainstreamed exceptional children in early childhood education. *Reading Improvement, 19,* 63(b).

Cohen, S. B., & Plaskon, S. P. (1980). *Language Arts for the Mildly Handicapped.* Columbus, OH: Merrill.

DeHaven, E. P. (1979). *Teaching and Learning the Language Arts.* Boston: Little, Brown.

Disick, R. S. (1975). *Individualized Language Instruction.* New York: Harcourt, Brace, Jovanovich.

Evans, Z. S. (1974). *Tricks of the Trade for Teachers of Language Arts.* New York: Exposition Press.

Gearheart, B. (1980). *The Handicapped Student in the Regular Classroom.* St. Louis: C. V. Mosby.

Gerber, A. (1981). *Language and Learning Disabilities.* Baltimore: University Park Press.

Gillespie, P. H. (1974). *Teaching Reading to the Mildly Retarded Child.* Columbus, OH: Merrill.

Hammill, D. D. (1975). *Teaching Children with Learning and Behavior Problems.* Boston: Allyn and Bacon.

Hare, B., & Hare, J. A. (1977). *Teaching Young Handicapped Children.* New York: Grune and Stratton.

Horn, E. (1967). *A Basic Writing Vocabulary.* Iowa City: University of Iowa Press.

Johnson, D. J., & Myklebust, H. R. (1967). *Learning Disabilities: Educational Principles and Practices.* New York: Grune and Stratton.

Karnes, M. B. (1975). *The Karnes Early Language Activities.* Champaign, IL: GEM Materials Enterprises.

Kirk, S. A. (1978). *Teaching Reading to Slow and Disabled Learners.* Boston: Houghton Mifflin.

Lundsteen, S. W. (October 1971). Critical listening: An Experiment. *Elementary School Journal.*

Markoff, A. (1976). *Teaching Low-Achieving Children Reading, Spelling, and Handwriting.* Springfield, IL: Charles C Thomas.

Marsh, G. E., & Price, B. J. (1980). *Methods for Teaching the Mildly Handicapped Adolescent.* New York: C. V. Mosby.

McDonald, B. (1978). *Methods That Teach.* Dubuque: William C. Brown.

Rankin, P. T. (October 1928). The importance of listening ability. *English Journal.*

Savage, J. F., & Mooney, J. F. (1979). *Teaching Reading to Children with Special Needs.* Boston: Allyn and Bacon.

Simon, D. R., & Simon, H. A. (1973). *Revised Educational Research.*

Smith, R. J., & Barrett, T. C. (1974). *Teaching Reading in the Middle Grades.* Reading, MA: Addison-Wesley.

Strickland, R. (1969). *The Language Arts in Elementary School.* Lexington, MA: D.C. Heath.

Wallace, G. (1978). *Teaching Children with Learning Problems.* Columbus, OH: Merrill.

# APPENDIX A

# NAMES AND ADDRESSES OF COMPANIES
# THAT PUBLISH MATERIALS IN READING

ABINGDON PRESS
201 8th Avenue South
Nashville, TN 37202

ABRAHAMS MAGAZINE SERVICE
56 East 13th Street
New York, NY 10003

ACADEMIC PRESS
111 Fifth Avenue
New York, NY 10003

ACADEMIC THERAPY
  PUBLICATIONS
20 Commercial Blvd.
Novato, CA 94947

ACROPOLIS BOOKS LTD.
2400 17th Street N.W.
Washington, DC 20009

ADDISON-WESLEY PUBLISHING
  CO., INC.
Jacob Way
Reading, MA 01867

ADDISON-WESLEY TESTING
  SERVICES
2725 San Hill Road
Menlo Park, CA 94025

ALLIED EDUCATIONAL PRESS
P.O. Box 337
Niles, MI 49120

ALLIED SCHOOL & OFFICE
  PRODUCTS
P.O. Box 25147
4900 Menaul N.E.
Albuquerque, NM 87125

ALLYN AND BACON, INC.
470 Atlantic Ave.
Boston, MA 02210

AMERICAN COUNCIL ON EDUC.
One Dupont Circle
Washington, DC 20036

AMERICAN GUIDANCE SERVICE
Publisher's Building
Circle Pines, MN 55014

AMERICAN LIBRARY ASSOCIATION
50 East Huron Street
Chicago, IL 60611

AMERICAN ORTHOPSYCHIATRIC
  ASSOCIATION
1775 Broadway
New York, NY 10019

AMERICAN PRINTING HOUSE
  FOR THE BLIND
P.O. Box 6085
Louisville, KY 40206

Adapted from Ekwall, Eldon and Shanker, James; *Diagnosis and Remediation of the Disabled Reader,* 1988, 3rd edition. Allyn and Bacon, Inc.

AMSCO SCHOOL PUBLICATIONS,
    INC.
315 Hudson Street
New York, NY 10013

APPLE COMPUTER
20525 Miriana Ave.
Cupertino, CA 94015

ANN ARBOR PUBLISHERS, INC.
P.O. Box 7249
Naples, FL 33940

ARISTA CORPORATION
2 Park Ave.
New York, NY 10016

ARO PUBLISHING INC.
P.O. Box 193
Provo, UT 84601

ASSOCIATION FOR CHILDHOOD
    EDUCATION INTERNATIONAL
3615 Wisconsin Avenue N.W.
Washington, DC 20016

ATHENEUM PUBLISHERS (Subs. of
    Scribner Book Cos, Inc.)
115 Fifth Avenue
New York, NY 10003

A–V CONCEPTS CORPORATION
30 Montauk Boulevard
Oakdale, NY 11769

AVON BOOKS
1790 Broadway
New York, NY 10019

BAKER AND TAYLOR CO.
1515 Broadway
New York, NY 10036

BAKER STREET PUBLICATIONS
    LTD.
502 Range St.
Box 3610
Mankato, MN 56084

BALLANTINE/DEL REY FAWCETT
    BOOKS
201 E. 50th St.
New York, NY 10022

BANTAM BOOKS, INC.
School and College
Marketing Division
666 Fifth Avenue
New York, NY 10019

BARNELL LOFT, LTD.
958 Church Street
Baldwin, NY 11510

BARNES/SALE & NOBLE ANNEX
126 Fifth Ave.
New York, NY 10011

CLARENCE L. BARNHART, INC.
Box 250–1 Stone Place
Bronxville, NY 10708

BASIC SKILLS PROGRAM
Office of Basic Skills Improvement
400 Maryland Avenue, S.W.
Room 1167–Donohoe Building
Washington, DC 20202

BAUSCH AND LOMB OPTICAL CO.
Rochester, NY 14602

BELL AND HOWELL
Audio-Visual Products Div.
7100 N. McCormick Road
Chicago, IL 60645

BENEFIT PRESS
1250 Sixth Avenue
San Diego, CA 92101

BERRENT EDUCATIONAL PRESS
444 Community Dr.
Manhasset, NY 11030

BOBBS–MERRILL EDUCATIONAL
    PUBLISHING
4300 West 62nd Street
P.O. Box 7080
Indianapolis, IN 46206

BORG–WARNER EDUCATIONAL
    SYSTEMS
600 West University Drive
Arlington Heights, IL 60004

R. R. BOWKER CO.
1180 Avenue of the Americas
New York, NY 10036

BOWMAR NOBLE PUBLISHERS
INC.
4563 Colorado Blvd.
Los Angeles, CA 90039

BOYNTON/COOK PUBLISHERS,
INC.
Forge Lane
Box 598
Lakeville, CT 06039

BURGLESS PUBLISHING CO.
7108 Ohms Lane
Minneapolis, MN 55435

CARLSON–DELLOSA PUBLISHING
1946 S. Arlington Road
Akron, OH 44306

C B H PUBLISHING INC.
Box 236
Glencol, IL 60022

C.C. PUBLICATIONS, INC.
P.O. Box 23699
Tigaro, OR 97223

CENTER FOR APPLIED RESEARCH
IN EDUCATION, INC.
P.O. Box 130
West Nyack, NY 10995

CENTURION INDUSTRIES, INC.
167 Constitution Drive
Menlo Park, CA 94025

CHAPMAN BROOK & KENT
1215 Del la Vina Street, Suite F
P.O. Box 21008
Santa Barbara, CA 93121

CHICAGO TRIBUNE
435 North Michigan Avenue
Chicago, IL 60611

THE CHILDREN'S BOOK COUNCIL
67 Irving Place
New York, NY 10003

CHILDREN'S PRESS
1224 West Van Buren Street
Chicago, IL 60607

CLARION BOOKS
52 Vanderbilt Ave.
New York, NY 10017

CLIFF'S NOTES
1701 P Street
Lincoln, NE 68508

COBBLESTONE PUBLISHING, INC.
20 Grove St.
Peterborough, NH 03458

COLLEGE BOARD
45 Columbus Ave.
New York, NY 10023

COLLEGE SKILLS CENTER
Department 865052
320 West 29th Street
Baltimore, MD 21211

CONFERENCE BOOK SERVICE, INC.
80 South Early St.
Alexandria, VA 22304

COMMUNACAD
Box 541
Wilton, CT 06897

COMPRESS
A Division of Wadsworth, Inc.
P.O. Box 102
Wentworth, NH 03282

CONSULTING PSYCHOLOGISTS
PRESS, INC.
577 College Ave.
Palo Alto, CA 94306

CONTEMPORARY BOOKS INC.
180 North Michigan Avenue
Chicago, IL 60601

CONTINENTAL PRESS INC.
520 East Bainbridge St.
Elizabeth Town, PA 17022

CORONADO PUBLISHERS, INC.
1250 Sixth Avenue
San Diego, CA 92101

CORONET
65 East South Water Street
Chicago, IL 60601

COUNCIL FOR EXCEPTIONAL
  CHILDREN
1920 Association Drive
Reston, VA 22091

C.P.S.
Box 83
Larchmont, NY 10538

CRANE PUBLISHING CO.
PO Box 3713
Trenton, NJ 08629

CREATIVE CLASSROOM
Macmillan Book Clubs
866 Third Street
New York, NY 10022

CREATIVE CURRICULUM, INC.
15681 Commerce Lane
Huntington Beach, CA 92649

CREATIVE PUBLICATIONS
P.O. Box 10328
Palo Alto, CA 94303

CRESTWOOD HOUSE
Box 3427
Mankato, MN 58001

CROWN PUBLISHERS, INC.
One Park Avenue
New York, NY 10016

CTB/McGraw-Hill
Del Monte Research Park
Monterey, CA 93940

CURRICULUM ASSOCIATES, INC.
6620 Robin Willow Ct.
Dallas, TX 75248

CURRICULUM ASSOCIATES, INC.
Sound Start
5 Esquire Road
North Billerica, MA 01862

CURRICULUM INNOVATIONS, INC.
3500 Western Avenue
Highland Park, IL 60035

CURRICULUM REVIEW
517 S. Jefferson St.
Chicago, IL 60607

CUSHMAN–FOWLER LEARNING
  ASSOCIATES
P.O. Box 6196
Olympia, WA 98502

C. LUCAS DALTON
5720 Caruth Haven
Suite 130
Dallas, TX 75206

DELACORTE PRESS
c/o Montville Warehousing Co., Inc.
Changebridge Road
Pine Brook, NJ 07058

DELL PUBLISHING CO.
Education Dept.
245 East 47th St.
New York, NY 10017

DEPARTMENT OF DEFENSE
Office of Dependent Schools
2461 Eisenhower Avenue
Alexandria, VA 22331

D.C. HEATH
125 Spring St.
Lexington, MA 02173

DES EDUCATIONAL PUBLICATIONS
25 South Fifth Ave
P.O. Box 1291
Highland Park, NJ 08904

DEVELOPMENTAL LEARNING
  MATERIALS
P.O. Box 4000
One DLM Park
Allen, TX 75002

A B DICK CO.
5700 Touhy Avenue
Chicago, IL 60648

DIAL BOOKS FOR YOUNG
  READERS (Div. of E.P. Dutton)
2 Park Ave.
New York, NY 10016

DOME PRESS, INC.
1169 Logan Ave.
Elgin, IL 60120

DORMAC, INC.
P.O. Box 752 (1983 PO 1699)
Beaverton, OR 97075

DOUBLEDAY & CO., INC.
501 Franklin Ave
Garden City, NY 11530

DREIER EDUCATIONAL SYSTEMS
25 South Fifth Avenue
P.O. Box 1291
Highland Park, NJ 08904

DRP SERVICES
The College Board
45 Columbus Avenue
New York, NY 10023

DURA–CLAD BOOKS
PO Box 82
LaBelle, MO 63447

E.P. DUTTON
2 Park Ave.
New York, NY 10016

DUVALL PUBLISHING
422 W. Appleway
Coer d'Alene, ID 83814

E & R DEVELOPMENT CO.
Vandalia Road
Jacksonville, FL 62650

EARLY YEARS/K–8
PO Box 3330
Westport, CT 06880

EARLIER–TO–LEARN
Box 329
Garden City, NY 11530

EBSCO CURRICULUM MATERIALS
Box 11521
Birmingham, AL 35202

ECONOCLAD BOOKS
2101 N. Topeka Blvd.
P.O. Box 1777
Topeka, KS 66601

THE ECONOMY COMPANY
Box 25308
1901 North Walnut Street
Oklahoma City, OK 73125

EDITS
P.O. Box 7234
San Diego, CA 92107

EDL DIVISION
Artista Corporation
2440 Estandway
P.O. Box 6146
Concord, CA 94524

EDL/McGraw-Hill
1221 Avenue of the Americas
New York, NY 10020

EDUCATIONAL PERFORMANCE
   ASSOCIATES, INC.
600 Broad Ave.
Ridgefield, NJ 07657

EDUCAT PUBLISHERS, INC.
P.O. Box 2158
Berkeley, CA 94702

THE EDUCATION CENTER
1411 Mill Street
P.O. Box 9753
Greensboro, NC 27408

EDUCATIONAL ACTIVITIES
P.O. Box 392
Freeport, NY 11520

EDUCATIONAL ACTIVITIES, INC.
1937 Grand Ave.
Baldwin, NY 11510

EDUCATIONAL BOOK DIVISION
Prentice-Hall
Englewood Cliffs, NJ 07632

EDUCATIONAL DEVELOPMENT
   CORP
8141 East 44th
P.O. Box 45663
Tulsa, OK 74145

EDUCATIONAL PROGRAMS AND
  PROMOTIONS
2227-A Michigan Ave.
Arlington, TX 76013

EDUCATIONAL DEVELOPMENT
  CORP
P.O. Box 45663
Tulsa, OK 74145

EDUCATIONAL SERVICES, INC.
P.O. Box 219
Stevensville, MI 49127

EDUCATIONAL TEACHING AIDS
  DIVISION
555 West Adams Street
Chicago, IL 60606

EDUCATIONAL TESTING SERVICE
Mail Stop 50-D
Rosedale Rd.
Princeton, NJ 08541

EDUCATIONAL TESTING SERVICE
Box 999
Princeton, NJ 08540

EDUCATORS PUBLISHING SERVICE
75 Moulton Street
Cambridge, MA 02238

EDUCULTURE
1 Dubuque Plaza
Suite 150
Dubuque, IA 52001

ELSEVIER–DUTTON PUBLISHING
  CO., INC.
2 Park Avenue
New York, NY 10016

EMC PUBLISHING
300 York Avenue
St. Paul, MN 55101

ENCYCLOPEDIA BRITANNICA
  EDUCATIONAL CORP.
425 North Michigan Ave.
Chicago, IL 60601

ERIC CLEARINGHOUSE ON
  READING AND
  COMMUNICATION SKILLS
1111 Kenyon Rd.
Urbana, IL 61801

ESP, INC.
1201 E. Johnson Ave.
P.O. Drawer 5037
Jonesboro, AR 72401

ESSAY PRESS, INC.
P.O. Box 2323
La Jolla, CA 92037

ETA (Educational Teaching Aids)
159 West Kinzie St.
Chicago, IL 60610

GALLAUDET COLLEGE PRESS
800 Florida Avenue N.E.
Washington, DC 20002

GAMCO INDUSTRIES, INC.
Box 1911
Big Springs, TX 79720

GARRARD PUBLISHING CO.
1607 North Market Street
Champaign, IL 61820

GESSLER EDUCATIONAL
  SOFTWARE
900 Broadway
New York, NY 10003

GINN & COMPANY PUBLISHERS
9888 Monroe Drive
Dallas, TX 75220

GLOBE BOOK CO.
50 West 23rd Street
New York, NY 10010

GLOBAL COMPUTER SUPPLIES
9135 Hemlock Drive
Hempstead, NY 11550

GOLDENCRAFT
1224 West Van Buren St.
Chicago, IL 60607

GOOD APPLE, INC.
Box 299
Carthage, IL 62321

GRALAN DISTRIBUTORS, INC.
PO Box 45134
Baton Rouge, LA 70895

GREENHAVEN PRESS, INC.
577 Shoreview Park Road
St. Paul, MN 55112

GROSSET & DUNLAP, INC.
Education Division
51 Madison Avenue
New York, NY 10010

GROVE PRESS, INC.
196 West Houston Street
New York, NY 10014

E. M. HALE AND COMPANY
Harvey House Publishers
128 West River Street
Chippewa Falls, WI 54729

HAMMOND, INC.
515 Valley Street
Maplewood, NJ 07040

HAMPDEN PUBLICATIONS, INC.
P.O. Box 4873
Baltimore, MD 21211

HARPER & ROW, INC.
10 East 53rd Street
New York, NY 10022

HARTLEY COURSEWARE, INC.
133 Bridge Street
Dimondale, MI 48821

HAWTHORN BOOKS INC.
260 Madison Avenue
New York, NY 10016

HAYDEN BOOK COMPANY, INC.
50 Essex Street
Rochelle Park, NJ 07662

HAYES SCHOOL PUBLISHING CO.,
INC.
321 Pennwood Avenue
Wilkinsburg, PA 15221

D. C. HEATH AND COMPANY
125 Spring St.
Lexington, MA 02173

HEINEMANN
70 Court Street
Portsmouth, NH 03801

HERTZBERG–NEW METHOD INC.
Vandalia Road
Jacksonville, IL 62650

HIGH NOON BOOKS
20 Commercial Blvd.
Novata, CA 94947

HIGHLIGHTS FOR CHILDREN
2300 West Fifth Avenue
P.O. Box 269
Columbus, OH 43216

THE HIGHSMITH CO., INC.
P.O. Box 800 B
Highway 106 East
Fort Atkinson, WI 53538

HISKEY–NEBRASKA CO.
5640 Baldwin
Lincoln, NE 68507

HOLIDAY HOUSE, INC.
18 East 53rd St.
New York, NY 10022

HOLT, RINEHART AND WINSTON
CBS Inc.
383 Madison Avenue
New York, NY 10017

HUMANICS LIMITED
P.O. Box 7447
Atlanta, GA 30309

HUTCHINSON BOOKS, INC.
Chestnut Street
Lewiston, ME 04240

IDEAL SCHOOL SUPPLY COMPANY
11000 S. Lavergne Ave.
Oak Lawn, IL 60453

I/CT–INSTRUCTIONAL/
   COMMUNICATIONS
   TECHNOLOGY, INC.
10 Stepar Place
Huntington Station, NY 11746

IDEAL SCHOOL SUPPLY CO.
11000 South Lavergne Avenue
Oak Lawn, IL 60453

IMPERIAL INTERNATIONAL
   LEARNING CORPORATION
P.O. Box 548
Kankakee, IL 60901

INCENTIVE PUBLICATIONS
2400 Crestmoor Road
Nashville, TN 37215

INCENTIVES FOR LEARNING INC.
600 West Van Buren Street
Chicago, IL 60607

INNOVATIVE SCIENCES, INC.
300 Broad Street
Stanford, CT 06901

INSTITUTE FOR PERSONALITY
   AND ABILITY TESTING
P.O. Box 188
Champaign, IL 61820-0188

INSTRUCTIONAL FAIR
Box 1650
Grand Rapids, MI 49501

INSTRUCTOR PUBLICATIONS, INC.
545 Fifth Ave.
New York, NY 10017

INSTRUCTOR PUBLICATIONS
7 Bank Street
Dansville, NY 14437

INTERNATIONAL READING
   ASSOCIATION
800 Barksdale Road
Newark, DE 19711

ITA
A Non-Profit Educational Foundation
Hofstra University
Hempstead, NY 11550

JAMESTOWN PUBLISHERS
P.O. Box 6743
Providence, RI 02940

JANUS BOOK PUBLISHERS
2501 Industrial Pkwy. West
Hayward, CA 94545

JOSTENS LEARNING SYSTEMS
800 East Business Center Drive
Mount Prospect, IL 60056

HARCOURT BRACE JOVANOVICH,
   INC.
School Division
6277 Sea Harbor Dr.
Orlando, FL 32887

HARCOURT BRACE JOVANOVICH,
   PUBLISHERS
Trade Children's Books
1250 Sixth Ave.
San Diego, CA 92101

KENWORTHY EDUCATIONAL
   SERVICES, INC.
Box 60
138 Allen Street
Buffalo, NY 14205

KEYSTONE VIEW
Division of Mast Development Co.
2212 East 12th Street
Davenport, IA 52803

KIMBO EDUCATIONAL
P.O. Box 477
Long Branch, NJ 07740

KING FEATURES
235 East 45th Street
New York, NY 10017

THE KINGSBURY CENTER
2138 Bancroft Place, N.W.
Washington, DC 20008

THE KLAMATH PRINTERY
628 Oak Street
Klamath Falls, OR 97601

KNOWLEDGE INDUSTRY
PUBLICATIONS, INC.
701 Westchester Avenue
White Plains, NY 10604

H. P. KOPPLEMANN
140 Van Block Ave.
Hartford, CT 06141

KRAUS–THOMSON
ORGANIZATION LTD.
Millwood, NY 10546

LADYBIRD BOOKS, INC.
Chestnut St.
Lewiston, ME 04240

LAIDLAW EDUCATIONAL
PUBLISHERS
Thatcher & Madison
River Forest, IL 60305

LANDMARK EDITIONS, INC.
1420 Kansas Ave.
Kansas City, MO 64127

LANGUAGE RESEARCH
ASSOCIATES, INC.
P.O. Drawer 2085
Palm Springs, CA 92262

LANSFORD PUBLISHING CO.
1088 Lincoln Avenue
P.O. Box 8711
San Jose, CA 95155

LDM TEACHING RESOURCES
One DLM Park
Allen, TX 75002

LEARNING ARTS
P.O. Box 179
Wichita, KS 67201

LEARNING ASSOCIATES, INC.
P.O. Box 561167
Miami, FL 33156

THE LEARNING LINE
Box 1200
Palo Alto, CA 94302

LEARNING LINKS INC.
11 Wagon Rd.
Roslyn Heights, NY 11577

LEARNING MULTI–SYSTEMS
340 Coyier Lane
Madison, WI 53713

LEARNING PERIODICALS GROUP
19 Darvis Drive
Belmont, CA 94002

LEARNING RESOURCES
CORPORATION
8517 Production Avenue
San Diego, CA 92121

LEARNING SYSTEMS CORP.
60 Conolly Parkway
Hamden, CT 06514

LEARNING TREE PUBLISHING
INC.
7108 South Alton Way
Englewood, CO 80112

LEARNING WELL
200 South Service Road
Roslyn Heights, NY 11577

LERNER
241 First Avenue North
Minneapolis, MN 55401

LESWING PRESS
P.O. Box 3577
San Rafael, CA 94901

LIBRARY OF CONGRESS
National Library Service for the Blind
and Physically Handicapped
1291 Taylor Street N.W.
Washington, DC 20542

LISTENING LIBRARY, INC.
P.O. Box L
1 Park Avenue
Old Greenwich, CT 06870

LITTLE, BROWN AND COMPANY
College Division
34 Beacon Street
Boston, MA 02106

LITTON EDUCATIONAL
  PUBLISHING, INC.
7625 Empire Drive
Florence, KY 41042

LONGMAN INC.
College and Professional Book Division
1560 Broad
New York, NY 10036

LONGMAN INC.
95 Church St.
White Plains, NY 10601

LONGWOOD DIVISION
Allyn & Bacon Inc.
Link Drive
Rockleigh, NJ 07647

LOTHROP, LEE AND SHEPARD CO.
  INC.
105 Madison Ave.
New York, NY 10016

LUMEN PUBLICATIONS
1500 Palisade Ave.
Fort Lee, NJ 07024

MACMILLAN CHILDREN'S BOOK
  GROUP
115 Fifth Ave.
New York, NY 10003

MACMILLAN INSTANT
  ACTIVITIES PROGRAM
6 Commercial Street
Hicksville, NY 11801

MACMILLAN PUBLISHING CO.,
  INC.
866 3rd Avenue
New York, NY 10022

MAFEX ASSOCIATES, INC.
90 Cherry St.
Box 519
Johnstown, PA 15907

MAST DEVELOPMENT CO.
2212 East 12th Street
Davenport, IA 52803

MASTERY EDUCATION CORP.
85 Main Street
Watertown, MA 02172

McCORMICK–MATHERS
  PUBLISHING COMPANY
A Division of Litton Ed. Publishing Inc.
7625 Empire Drive
Florence, KY 41042

McDONALD PUBLISHING CO.
925 Demun Avenue
St. Louis, MO 63105

McDOUGAL, LITTELL & COMPANY
P.O. Box 1667-C
Evanston, IL 60204

McGRAW–HILL BOOK CO.
8171 Redwood Highway
Novato, CA 94947

McGRAW–HILL RYERSON LTD
330 Progress Avenue
Scarbrough, Ontario
Canada, M1P 2Z5

McGRAW–HILL SCHOOL DIVISION
(Webster Division, The Economy
  Company)
Bomar/Noble Publishers
PO Box 25308
Oklahoma City, OK 25308

RAND McNALLY AND CO.
Box 7600
Chicago, IL 60680

MEDIA BASICS
Larchmont Plaza
Larchmont, NY 10538

MEDIA MATERIALS, INC.
Department MDR
2936 Remington Avenue
Baltimore, MD 21211

MEDIA–PAK/82
Box 541
Wilton, CT 06897

MELODY HOUSE PUBLISHING CO.
819 N.W. 92nd Street
Oklahoma City, OK 73114

CHARLES E. MERRILL
  PUBLISHING CO.
A Bell & Howell Company
1300 Alum Creek Dr.
Columbus, OH 43216

G & C MERRIAM COMPANY
Publishers of Merriam-Webster Reference
  Books
47 Federal Street
Springfield, MA 01101

JULIAN MESSNER
1230 Avenue of the Americas
New York, NY 10020

MICROCOMPUTER WORKSHOPS
  COURSEWARE
225 Westchester Ave.
Port Chester, NY 10573

MIDWEST PUBLICATIONS
P.O. Box 448
Pacific Grove, CA 93950

MILLIKEN PUBLISHING COMPANY
1100 Research Blvd
P.O. Box 21579
St. Louis, MO 63132

MILTON BRADLEY CO.
Springfield, MA 01101

HOUGHTON MIFFLIN
One Beacon Street
Boston, MA 02107

MINDSCAPE, INC.
3444 Dundee Rd.
Northbrook, IL 60062

MODERN CURRICULUM PRESS,
  INC.
13900 Prospect Rd.
Cleveland, OH 44136

THE MORGAN COMPANY
4510 N. Ravenswood Ave.
Chicago, IL 60640

WILLIAM MORROW & COMPANY,
  INC.
105 Madison Ave.
New York, NY 10016

NATIONAL ASSOCIATION FOR
  THE DEAF
814 Thayer Avenue
Silver Springs, MD 20910

NATIONAL COUNCIL OF
  TEACHERS OF ENGLISH
1111 Kenyon Road
Urbana, IL 61801

NATIONAL PUBLIC RADIO
2025 M Street, N.W.
Washington, DC 20036

NATIONAL TEXTBOOK COMPANY
4255 W. Touhy
Lincolnwood, IL 60646

NCS/EDUCATIONAL SYSTEMS
  DIVISION
4402 West 76th Street
Minneapolis, MN 55435

THE NEW AMERICAN LIBRARY,
  INC.
1633 Broadway
New York, NY 10019

NEWSWEEK
444 Madison Ave.
New York, NY 10022

NORTHWESTERN UNIVERSITY
  PRESS
Box 1093X
1735 Benson Ave.
Evanston, IL 60201

NYSTROM
3333 Elston Ave.
Chicago, IL 60618

OCEANA EDUCATIONAL
   COMMUNICATIONS
75 Main Street
Dobbs Ferry, NY 10522

OPEN COURT PUBLISHING
   COMPANY & CRICKET MAGAZINE
315 Fifth St.
Peru, IL 61354

OPPORTUNITIES FOR LEARNING,
   INC.
20417 Nordhoff St.
Dept. EAS
Chatsworth, CA 91311

OPTIMAL CORPORATION
Open Court Publishing Company
LaSalle, IL 61301

ORYX PRESS
2214 N. Central
Phoenix, AZ 85004

RICHARD C. OWEN, PUBLISHERS
P.O. Box 14007
Chicago, IL 60614

RICHARD C. OWEN PUBLISHERS,
   INC.
Rockefeller Center
Box 819
New York, NY 10185

OXFORD UNIVERSITY PRESS
200 Madison Avenue
New York, NY 10016

THE A. N. PALMER COMPANY
1720 West Irving Park Road
Schaumburg, IL 60193

PAPERBACK SALES, INC.
425 Michigan Ave.
Chicago, IL 60611

PARACHUTE PRESS
P.O. Box 26186
Tempe, AZ 85282

PENDULUM PRESS, INC.
The Academic Building
237 Saw Mill Rd.
West Haven, CT 06516

PENGUIN BOOKS
299 Murry Hill Parkway
East Rutherford, NJ 07073

VIKING PENGUIN, INC.
625 Madison Avenue
New York, NY 10022

PERFECTION FORM COMPANY
1000 North Second Avenue
Logan, IA 51546

PHONOVISUAL PRODUCTS, INC.
12216 Parklawn Drive
P.O. Box 2007
Rockville, MD 20852

PIRT
c/o Tact
P.O. Box 1052
Daylestown, PA 18901

PITMAN LEARNING, INC.
(formerly Fearon Pitman Publishers,
   Inc.)
19 Davis Drive
Belmont, CA 94002

PLAYS, INC.
8 Arlington Street
Boston, MA 02116

PLAYS INC.
120 Boylston Street
Boston, MA 02116

PLEASANTVILLE MEDIA
Suite E-61
P.O. Box 415
Pleasantville, NY 10570

POCKET BOOKS
1230 Avenue of the Americas
New York, NY 10020

POLAROID CORPORATION
575 Technology Square
Cambridge, MA 02139

PRENTICE–HALL
Englewood Cliffs, NJ 07632

PRO–ED
5341 Industrial Oaks Blvd.
Austin, TX 78735

PROGRAMS FOR ACHIEVEMENT
IN READING, INC.
Abbott Park Place
Providence, RI 02903

PRUETT PUBLISHING COMPANY
3235 Prairie Avenue
Boulder, CO 80301

THE PSYCHOLOGICAL
CORPORATION
555 Academic Court
San Antonio, TX 78204

PSYCHOLOGICAL TEST
SPECIALISTS
Box 9229
Missoula, MT 59807

PUBLISHERS TEST SERVICE
2500 Garden Road
Monterey, CA 93940

THE PUTNAM PUBLISHING
GROUP
51 Madison Ave.
New York, NY 10010

RADIO SHACK
Publicity Department
300 One Tandy Center
Fort Worth, TX 76102

RAINTREE PUBLISHERS, INC.
310 W. Wisconsin Ave.
Milwaukee, WI 53203

RANDOM HOUSE/KNOPF/
PANTHEON/VILLARD/TIMES
BOOKS
201 East 50th St.
New York, NY 10022

READER'S DIGEST SERVICES, INC.
Educational Division
Pleasantville, NY 10570

READERS THEATRE SCRIPT
SERVICE
P.O. Box 178333
San Diego, CA 92117

THE READING LABORATORY
P.O. Box 681
South Norwalk, CT 06854

REFLECTIONS & IMAGES
6607 Northridge Drive
San Jose, CA 95120

REGENTS PUBLISHING CO., INC.
Two Park Avenue
New York, NY 10016

REMEDIA PUBLICATIONS
PO Box 1174
Scottsdale, AZ 85252

RESOURCES
Instructional Communication
Technology, Inc.
Huntington Station, NY 11746

RESOURCES FOR THE GIFTED
P.O. Box 15050
Phoenix, AZ 85060

FRANK E. RICHARDS PUBLISHING
CO., INC.
P.O. Box 66
Phoenix, NY 13135

RIVERSIDE PUBLISHING CO.
8420 Bryn Mawr Ave.
Chicago, IL 60631

ROURKE PUBLISHING GROUP
P.O. Box 711
Windermere, FL 32786

SANTILLANA PUBLISHING CO.
575 Lexington Avenue
New York, NY 10022

SCARECROW PRESS, INC.
52 Liberty Street
Box 656
Metuchen, NJ 08840

FRANK SCHAFFER PUBLICATIONS
1028 Via Mirabel, Dept. 34
Palos Verdes Estates, CA 90274

SCHOLASTIC, INC.
730 Broadway
New York, NY 10003

SCHOLASTIC INC.
2931 E. McCarty St.
Jefferson City, MO 65102

SCHOLASTIC BOOK SERVICE
904 Sylvan Avenue
Englewood Cliffs, NJ 07632

SCHOOL DAYS MAGAZINE
19711 Magellan Dr.
Torrance, CA 90502

SCHOOLHOUSE PRESS
191 Spring St.
Lexington, MA 02173

SRA
Science Research Assoc., Inc.
155 North Wacker Dr.
Chicago, IL 60606

SCIENCE RESEARCH ASSOCIATES,
  INC.
College Division
1540 Page Mill Road
P.O. Box 10021
Palo Alto, CA 94303

SCOTT, FORESMAN AND COMPANY
1900 East Lake Ave.
Glenview, IL 60025

SCOTT, FORESMAN AND COMPANY
11310 Gemini Lane
Dallas, TX 75229

SCRIBNER EDUCATIONAL
  PUBLISHERS
866 Third Ave.
New York, NY 10022

DALE SEYMOUR PUBLICATIONS
P.O. Box 10888
Palo Alto, CA 94303

SILVER BURDETT & GINN
191 Spring Street
Lexington, MA 02173

SIMON & SCHUSTER BUILDING
1230 Avenue of the Americas
New York, NY 10020

SIMON & SCHUSTER/POCKET
  BOOKS
1230 Avenue of the Americas
New York, NY 10020

SIRS
P.O. Box 2507
Boca Raton, FL 33432

SKILLCORP PUBLISHERS, INC.
P.O. Box 712
Columbus, OH 43216

SLOSSON EDUCATIONAL
  PUBLICATIONS
P.O. Box 280
East Aurora, NY 14052

SMITHSONIAN INSTITUTION
475 L'Enfant Plaza
Suite 4800
Washington, DC 20560

SOUTHWESTERN PUBLISHING CO.
5101 Madison Road
Cincinnati, OH 45227

SPECIAL LEARNING CORPORATION
42 Boston Post Rd.
P.O. Box 306
Guilford, CT 06437

SPECTRUM EDUCATIONAL MEDIA,
  INC.
P.O. Box 611
Mattoon, IL 61938

SPORTS ILLUSTRATED
Educational Program
10 North Main St.
Yardley, PA 19067

STECK–VAUGHN CO.
Box 2028
807 Brazos St.
Austin, TX 78767

STEMMER HOUSE
2627 Caves Road
Owings Mills, NY 21117

STEP INC.
P.O. Box 887
Mukilteo, WA 98275

STERLING SWIFT PUBLISHING CO.
7901 South IH-35
Austin, TX 78744

STOELTING CO.
1350 So. Kostner Avenue
Chicago, IL 60623

STORY HOUSE CORP.
Bindery Lane
Charlettsville, NY 12036

STRINE PUBLISHING CO.
P.O. Box 149
York, PA 17405

SUNDANCE PUBLISHERS &
  DISTRIBUTORS
Newtown Road
Littleton, MA 01460

SUNBURST COMMUNICATIONS
Room D 57
39 Washington Avenue
Pleasantville, NY 10570

SVE
Society for Visual Education
A Business Corporation
Dept. LX
1345 Diversey Parkway
Chicago, IL 60614

SVE TEACHER'S CHOICE
2750 North Wayne Avenue
Chicago, IL 60614

SWAN BOOKS
PO Box 332
Fair Oaks, CA 95628

TAYLOR & FRANCIS INC.
114 East 32nd Street
New York, NY 10016

TAYLOR & FRANCIS INC.
242 Cherry Street
Philadelphia, PA 19106

TEACHERS & WRITERS
  COLLABORATIVE
5 Union Square West
New York, NY 10003

TEACHERS COLLEGE PRESS
1234 Amsterdam Ave.
New York, NY 10027

TEACHING AND COMPUTERS
Scholastic, Inc.
P.O. Box 645
Lyndhurst, NJ 07071

TEACHING RESOURCES
  CORPORATION
50 Pond Park Road
Hingham, MA 02043

THINKING SKILLS
P.O. Box 448
Pacific Grove, CA 93950

CHARLES C THOMAS PUBLISHER
2600 S. First Street
Springfield, IL 62794

TIME EDUCATION PROGRAM
10 North Main Street
Yardley, PA 19067

TPASSOCIATES/TP PRESS
22181 Wood Island Land
Huntington Beach, CA 92646

TREETOP PUBLISHING
220 Virginia Street
Racine, WI 53405

TREND ENTERPRISES
P.O. Box 64073
St. Paul, MN 55164

TRILLIUM PRESS, INC.
PO Box 209
Monroe, NY 10950

TROLL ASSOCIATES
100 Corporate Drive
Mahwah, NJ 07430

TSC
A Houghton Mifflin Co.
Dept. 70
Box 683
Hanover, NH 03755

TURMAN PUBLISHING
200 West Mercer
Seattle, WA 98119

TURMAN PUBLISHING CO.
809 East Pike Street
Seattle, WA 98122

TUTOR/TAPE
107 France Street
Toms River, NJ 08753

UNITED LEARNING
6633 West Howard Street
Niles, IL 60648

UNIVERSITY OF CHICAGO PRESS
5801 South Ellis Avenue
Chicago, IL 60637
                or
JOURNALS DEPT.
11030 South Langley Avenue
Chicago, IL 60672

UNIVERSITY OF ILLINOIS PRESS
Urbana, IL 61601

UNIVERSITY OF MICHIGAN PRESS
P.O. Box 1104
Ann Arbor, MI 48106

UNIVERSITY OF NEBRASKA PRESS
318 Nebraska Hall
901 North 17th Street
Lincoln, NE 68588

UNIVERSITY PRESS OF AMERICA
4720 Boston Way
Lanham, MD 20706

U.S. GOVERNMENT PRINTING
  OFFICE
Washington, DC 20402

THE VIKING PRESS
Viking Penguin Inc.
625 Madison Avenue
New York, NY 10022

J. WESTON WALCH, PUBLISHER
321 Valley St.
Portland, Maine 04104

JANE WARD CO.
Dept. 4
1642 South Beech St.
Lakewood, CO 80228

FRANKLIN WATTS, INC.
730 Fifth
New York, NY 10019

E.H. WHITE & COMPANY
Suite 710
1025 Vermont Avenue, N.W.
Washington, DC 20005

THE WHITE RABBIT CHILDREN'S
  BOOKS, INC.
7777 Girard Ave.
La Jolla, CA 92037

ALBERT WHITMAN AND
  COMPANY
5747 West Howard Street
Niles, IL 60648

H.W. WILSON COMPANY
950 University Avenue
Bronx, NY 10452

THE WORLD ALMANAC
Education Division
1278 West Ninth Street
Cleveland, OH 44113

WORLD BOOK–CHILDCRAFT
International, Inc.
Merchandise Mart Plaza
Chicago, IL 60654

WORLD BOOK, INC.
Merchandise Mart Plaza
Chicago, IL 60654

THE WRIGHT GROUP/STORY BOX
7620 Miramar Road
Suite 4200
San Diego, CA 92126

XEROX EDUCATION
    PUBLICATIONS
1250 Fairwood Avenue
Columbus, OH 43216

YOUNGHEART RECORDS
P.O. Box 27784
Los Angeles, CA 90027

ZANER–BLOSER
2500 West Fifth Avenue
P. O. Box 16764
Columbus, OH 43216

RICHARD L. ZWEIG ASSOCIATES
20800 Beach Boulevard
Huntington Beach, CA 92648

# Appendix B

# EXAMPLE, INFORMAL READING INVENTORY

## Nature and Purpose

The *Love Diagnostic Reading Inventory* generally takes about twenty minutes to administer and provides teachers with a vehicle to analyze the oral reading ability and word recognition skills of students. This is form A and has ten oral reading paragraphs comprising a story and there are five comprehension questions for each story. Also, there is a word recognition subtest. The child reads the paragraphs aloud and the examiner records his errors on a separate sheet. Also, the child reads the word recognition subtest aloud and the examiner records the errors. The examiner can find the child's reading accuracy, comprehension and word recognition skills and help the child correct specific deficiencies.

## General Discussion

The *Love Diagnostic Reading Inventory* contains two booklets used in administering the test. The booklets consist of the Student's Copy and the Examiner's Copy. The Student's Copy which is reusable contains the materials that are to be read by the child. The Examiner's Copy contains all the materials read by the child, plus it includes the questions to be asked of the child at the end of the reading. The Examiner's Copy also includes the word recognition subtest as does the Student's Copy. All writing done by the examiner should be done in the Examiner's Copy.

Complete directions for test administrations and interpretation of the test scores are contained in this manual. The examiner is urged to read through the entire manual before attempting to use the test. The discussions of the test interpretation appear in a section where they do not distract from the directions for administering the test; therefore, they are available for use when the results are being evaluated.

## Diagnostic Testing

The child's oral reading skills are the subject of the inventory and he or she is individually administered the test. Reading diagnosis aims at discovering causes of reading problems in terms of weaknesses. The inventory proposes to aid the examiner in determining those reading skills which have matured. Also, reading skills which are considered normal or superior can be determined. On the basis of these findings a structured program of instruction can be planned for the student. During careful observation of the child's method of responding to and working the test invaluable information can be provided for the examiner while working with the child's problems.

## Development of the Test

In developing an oral reading test one must maintain a balance among vocabulary level, paragraph length, number of complex sentences, number of polysyllables, and overall readability. The paragraphs become more difficult beginning with grade one and extending through grade ten. Table I gives information about the construction of the test for Forms A and B.

**Vocabulary.** This variable was controlled by several methods. Because pupils mature at different rates and have distinct talents and needs, the number of words in Forms A and B increase in each successive paragraph. A great deal of work was done on the difficulty of the vocabulary used in the paragraphs. The author used three different basal series and selected 100 different words for each grade level. Thorndike and Lorge's *The Teacher's Word Book of 30,000 Words* was used as well as Dolch's *Basic Sight Word Vocabulary*.

The reading paragraphs were written and rewritten according to the comments of field readers. Ten reading teachers, five elementary teachers and five junior high teachers were selected as readers for the paragraphs. They were asked to comment on the appropriateness of the words used in each paragraph, their interest and English usage. After the paragraphs were received from the field readers revisions were made and they were submitted to two English teachers. The English teachers were asked to comment about English usage, sentence structure and readability. The final paragraphs were then drafted.

Table B-1 also provides the reader with information about sentence length, difficulty and the percentage of complex sentences in each story.

The author attempted to challenge all students when organizing the stories, not only for poor readers but gifted ones as well. Some difficult words were put in each story and Table B-2 gives this information.

The author used a core vocabulary taken from materials developed by the Educational Development Laboratory in 1960 to grade the words. This list contains an index of the grades in which the words appear for the first time in a sampling of popular basal readers.

**Comprehension Questions.** The student is asked five questions after reading each paragraph. His reading comprehension is determined by how well he answers these questions.

## Standardization

The standardization program was conducted in 1981–82. Children from the entire state of Arkansas were used as well as twenty-five children from Memphis, Tennessee and twenty-five children from Mississippi. The schools involved ranged from

Table B-1. Vocabulary and Sentence Structure Data for the Test, Forms A and B.

| Paragraph | Length of Paragraph (in words) | | Number of Polysyllable Words | | Mean No. Words Per Sentence | | Percent of Complex Sentences | |
|---|---|---|---|---|---|---|---|---|
| | A | B | A | B | A | B | A | B |
| 1 | 22 | 24 | 3 | 3 | 4.4 | 4.0 | 0 | 0 |
| 2 | 43 | 42 | 4 | 4 | 7.1 | 6.0 | 0 | 0 |
| 3 | 51 | 51 | 5 | 8 | 8.5 | 10.0 | 17 | 25 |
| 4 | 73 | 71 | 24 | 26 | 9.1 | 11.8 | 13 | 25 |
| 5 | 104 | 103 | 35 | 22 | 13.0 | 14.7 | 13 | 33 |
| 6 | 119 | 120 | 50 | 34 | 13.2 | 15.0 | 22 | 38 |
| 7 | 130 | 129 | 48 | 53 | 15.5 | 16.2 | 22 | 25 |
| 8 | 171 | 175 | 37 | 43 | 17.0 | 19.4 | 44 | 31 |
| 9 | 184 | 177 | 87 | 77 | 20.0 | 20.0 | 42 | 37 |
| 10 | 255 | 251 | 101 | 125 | 20.7 | 20.9 | 40 | 39 |

rural and inner city to a college laboratory school and provided cases from a variety of socioeconomic backgrounds. Children were tested in grades one through twelve and at least fifty children were tested at each grade level.

Forms A and B were administered randomly within each grade by teachers, a graduate assistant and the author. The tests were scored by the same people who had been trained by the author.

A total of one hundred children had taken the *SRA Reading Test* and the scores were recorded on the *Love Diagnostic Reading Test* booklet.

## Validity

The author compared the scores of his test with other tests to determine the validity. The *Gilmore Oral Reading Test* and the *Standardized Oral Reading Paragraphs* by Gray were administered to twenty-five children at the same age in grade four. Table B-3 gives the Pearson product-moment correlations obtained from this study.

It has already been mentioned that one hundred pupils were administered the *SRA Reading Test*. Table B-4 presents the Pearson product-moment correlation between the *Love Diagnostic Reading Inventory* and the SRA test.

**Reliability.** To determine if a test will repeatedly measure what it is supposed to measure the author administered Forms A and B to children in grade 3 and a teacher administered Forms A and B to children in grade 5.

The standard error of measurement is also reported in Table B-5 for accuracy and comprehension. One can observe and infer that either Form A or Form B can be administered in the diagnosis of oral reading problems with equal results.

**Table B-2. Distribution of Difficult Words in Terms of Words First Appearing at A Grade Level.**

| Form A | Grade Level | | | | | | | | | |
|---|---|---|---|---|---|---|---|---|---|---|
| Paragraph | 1 | 2 | 3 | 4 | 5 | 6 | 7 | 8 | 9 | 10 |
| 1 | 9 | 2 | | | | | | | | |
| 2 | 12 | 4 | 1 | | | | | | | |
| 3 | — | 3 | 4 | 4 | 1 | | | | | |
| 4 | — | — | 7 | 5 | 1 | 1 | | | | |
| 5 | — | — | — | 5 | 5 | 2 | 1 | | | |
| 6 | — | — | — | — | 5 | 5 | 3 | 1 | | |
| 7 | — | — | — | — | — | 6 | 3 | 4 | 1 | |
| 8 | — | — | — | — | — | — | 6 | 4 | 2 | 1 |
| 9 | — | — | — | — | — | — | — | 7 | 4 | 1 |
| 10 | — | — | — | — | — | — | — | — | 5 | 2 |
| Form B | Grade Level | | | | | | | | | |
| Paragraph | 1 | 2 | 3 | 4 | 5 | 6 | 7 | 8 | 9 | 10 |
| 1 | 9 | 1 | | | | | | | | |
| 2 | 13 | 2 | 1 | | | | | | | |
| 3 | — | 6 | 3 | 2 | 2 | | | | | |
| 4 | — | — | 5 | 3 | 1 | 1 | | | | |
| 5 | — | — | — | 4 | 3 | 1 | 1 | | | |
| 6 | — | — | — | — | 4 | 3 | 2 | 1 | | |
| 7 | — | — | — | — | — | 5 | 3 | 1 | 2 | |
| 8 | — | — | — | — | — | — | 5 | 3 | 1 | 2 |
| 9 | — | — | — | — | — | — | — | 4 | 3 | 1 |
| 10 | — | — | — | — | — | — | — | — | 5 | 2 |

**Table B-3. Correlation Between the Love Form A and Two Other Oral Reading Tests.**

| Tests | Accuracy | Comprehension |
|---|---|---|
| Love A—Gilmore | .81 | .87 |
| Love A—Gray | .84 | |
| Love B—Gilmore | .90 | .85 |
| Love B—Gray | .79 | |

Table B-4. Pearson Product-Moment Correlation Between
the Love Diagnostic Reading Inventory and the SRA Test.

| Tests | Love Comprehension | r |
|---|---|---|
| SRA Level B | Form A | .89 |
| SRA Level B | Form B | .74 |
| SRA Level C | Form A | .82 |
| SRA Level C | Form B | .71 |

Table B-5. Reliability Data for the Love Diagnostic Reading Inventory

| | | r | | Standard Error of Measurement | |
|---|---|---|---|---|---|
| Grade | N | Accuracy | Comprehension | Accuracy | Comprehension |
| 3 | 17 | .96 | .77 | 2.3 | 3.0 |
| 5 | 31 | .88 | .81 | 4.0 | 3.8 |

## Word Recognition Subtest

**Grade Ratings.** The grade ratings for raw scores are recorded at the end of the test. The grade ratings were derived from the actual mean grade level of students. These ratings provide a convenient way to compare the grade levels of students with other students of a similar age or in a similar grade. However, student, teacher, and community expectations fluctuate according to social concerns. These ratings are valid and reliable indicators of achievement and the child can be identified for instructional placement by these ratings.

The split-half correlation coefficients and standard error of measurement (SE) are summarized in Table B-6. They were determined on samples of 200 children selected in such a way as to represent probability distributions of achievement based on normative data. The split half measures used were odd-even scores after the test items of each child had been arranged in their order of difficulty. The order of difficulty of the test was determined by an item analysis of 600 records.

To determine the validity of the *Love Word Recognition Sub-test* the scores were correlated with the *Wide Range Achievement Test* (WRAT) and the *SRA Reading Test.* A correlation coefficient (r) of .84 was found to exist between the *Love Word Recognition Subtest* and the WRAT. A correlation coefficient of .78 was found to exist between the *Love Word Recognition Sub-test* and the *SRA Reading Test.*

**Table B-6. Summary of Reliability Coefficients
and Errors of Measurement for the Word Recognition Subtest.**

| Test | Ages | r | SEM |
|------|------|---|-----|
| Word Recognition | 5–16 | .96 | 1.68 |

## Administering the Test and Recording Pupil Responses

Most examiners prefer facing the child across a table of suitable height, but other arrangements are permissible. To be valid the test should be done in a quiet, secluded place.

**Recording.** Use the following system for recording errors in the Examiner's Booklet as the child reads:

In order to illustrate the types of errors and the method of recording them, the following paragraph is included:

The Indians would trade animal skins to the early

settlers for glass beads. Many early Americans earned *(made)*

their living by making glass beads and bottles. A man in

Sandwich. Massachusetts/developed a way of making

dishes, lamps, and candlesticks by pressing molten glass

into iron molds. The Indian/traded for these also, but liked

the glass beads better.

If a word is wholly missed circle it as in the case of "settlers." If a portion of the word is mispronounced underline the part of the word mispronounced. For example, in "developed" the middle part of the word was mispronounced, the "s" was omitted in "skins" and the "in" has been omitted from "into". The word "for" was inserted between "trade" and "animal," and the word "made" (in parenthesis) was substituted for earned. The symbol . should be used when punctuation is disregarded and hesitations should be recorded by a / . Repetitions should be indicated by placing a ⁓ above the word and an X above the word indicates that the word has been omitted. If the examiner pronounces a word for the student . . should be placed above the word.

In case you are not sure that an error was made give the student the benefit of the doubt. The marked errors are very important in devising a remedial plan for the child having a reading disorder.

| ERROR RECORD | Number |
|---|---|
| Substitutions | |
| Mispronunciations | |
| Words pronounced by examiner | |
| Disregard of pronunciation | |
| Insertions | |
| Hesitations | |
| Repetitions | |
| Omissions | |
| Total Errors | |

## Love's Diagnostic Reading Inventory

**Computing The Comprehension Score.** A comprehension score for each of the paragraphs is recorded in the "No. Right (or Credited)" column. One point is given for each question answered correctly. The highest possible Comprehension score for any paragraph is 5 since there are 5 questions for each paragraph. For any paragraph the pupil reads, he is given credit only for the question which he answers correctly. In Figure 1, the pupil's basal level is at Paragraph 3. Since on that paragraph he answered four questions correctly, he is given credit for having answered five questions correctly on Paragraphs 2 and 1.

**Where To Begin.** You should begin testing the child one grade level below his present grade placement; ie, if the child is in the fourth grade begin at the third grade level. If the child scored *four or five at that level* then that will be his basal age. You give him the points below his basal age according to the directions above. If *he scores three or less points at the starting level,* back up one grade and test the child until he gets a basal age. The basal is obtained in order that the examiner will not have to go through the entire test with each child.

**Computing the Accuracy Score.** In the column marked "Errors" in the Test Summary, record the number of errors made by the pupil in each paragraph read. In the "10 Minus No. Errors" column, record the difference between the number of errors made in each paragraph and 10. In Figure 2, two errors were made on Paragraph 4; therefore, for that paragraph, 8 has been recorded in the "10 Minus No. Errors" column. The highest possible score for any paragraph is 10; that is, a score of 10 is obtained if a paragraph is read entirely without error. Full credit (10 points) is given for each unread paragraph below the pupil's basal level. The assumption is made that had the pupil read these paragraphs, he would have done so without error. The sum of the scores in the "10 Minus No. Errors" column gives the Accuracy score for the test.

**Figure B-1. Test Summary**

| PARAGRAPH | ACCURACY | | COMPREHENSION | |
|---|---|---|---|---|
| | Errors | 10 Minus No. Errors | No. Right (Or Credited) | |
| 1 | | 10 | 5 | |
| 2 | | 10 | 5 | |
| 3 | | 10 | 4 | Basal |
| 4 | 1 | 9 | 3 | Level |
| 5 | 3 | 7 | 4 | |
| 6 | 6 | 4 | 3 | |
| 7 | 9 | 1 | 2 | |
| 8 | 12 | 0 | 0 | Ceiling |
| 9 | | | | Level |
| 10 | | | | |

The child reaches his *ceiling level* when he makes *10 or more errors while reading the paragraphs.* In Figure B-2 the child made 12 errors while reading story number 8. Twelve is recorded in the accuracy column and testing is discontinued. A "0" is recorded in the "10 Minus No. Errors" column.

## Directions for Administering the Word Recognition Test

**Finding the Raw Score.** The maximum score for the word recognition subtest is 118 points. One point is awarded for each of the letters; therefore, a total of 30 points can be awarded for recognizing letters of the alphabet. If the part pertaining to the letters is not administered because of a satisfactory word reading readiness they are assumed to be correct and their scores are added to the word recognition score. For each mispronounced word the examiner should circle that word and discontinue the test after eight consecutive misses. The number of words pronounced correctly is the total raw score. Use this score to convert the findings to a grade placement score.

Before administering this test study the pronunciation guide on the next page. The directions follow:

"Look at each word carefully and say it aloud. Begin here (point) and pronounce each word as I point to it." The first time a reading error occurs the child is asked to

Figure B-2. Test Summary.

| PARAGRAPH | ACCURACY | | |
|---|---|---|---|
| | Errors | 10 Minus No. Errors | |
| 1 | | 10 | |
| 2 | | 10 | |
| 3 | 1 | 9 | Basal Level |
| 4 | 2 | 8 | |
| 5 | 3 | 7 | |
| 6 | 6 | 4 | |
| 7 | 9 | 1 | |
| 8 | 12 | 0 | Ceiling Level |
| 9 | | | |
| 10 | | | |

say the word again. If the response is right the child gets credit. If a response is vague or not clearly understandable the examiner may ask the child to repeat the word. The examiner should not help the child by probing for the correct answer. The examiner should be completely objective throughout the test.

**Table B-7. Grade Equivalents Corresponding to Love Comprehension
Raw Scores, Forms A and B.**

| Raw Scores | | Grade Equivalent | Raw Scores | | Grade Equivalent |
|---|---|---|---|---|---|
| A | B | | A | B | |
| 44 | 46 | 10.3 | 24 | 25 | 3.8 |
| 43 | 45 | 10.1 | 23 | 24 | 3.6 |
| 42 | 44 | 10.0 | 22 | — | 3.3 |
| 41 | 43 | 9.9 | 21 | 23 | 3.1 |
| 40 | 42 | 9.8 | 20 | 22 | 2.8 |
| 39 | 41 | 9.5 | 19 | 21 | 2.5 |
| 38 | 40 | 9.1 | 18 | 20 | 2.4 |
| 37 | 39 | 8.9 | 17 | 19 | 2.2 |
| 36 | 38 | 8.5 | 16 | 18 | 2.0 |
| 35 | 37 | 8.1 | 15 | 17 | 1.9 |
| 34 | 36 | 7.7 | 14 | 16 | 1.8 |
| 33 | 35 | 7.3 | 13 | 15 | 1.7 |
| 32 | 34 | 7.1 | 12 | 14 | 1.5 |
| 31 | 33 | 6.7 | 11 | 12 | 1.3 |
| 30 | 32 | 6.3 | 10 | 11 | 1.1 |
| 29 | 31 | 6.0 | 9 | 10 | 1.0 |
| 28 | 30 | 5.7 | 8 | 8 | K.9 |
| 27 | 29 | 5.2 | 7 | 7 | K.8 |
| — | 28 | 4.8 | 6 | 6 | K.7 |
| 26 | 27 | 4.3 | 5 | 4 | K.6 |
| 25 | 26 | 4.1 | 4 | 3 | K.5 |

**Grade Equivalents Corresponding to Love Accuracy Raw Scores, Forms A and B**

| Raw Scores | | Grade | Raw Scores | | Grade |
|---|---|---|---|---|---|
| A | B | Equivalent | A | B | Equivalent |
| 76 | 75 | 10.8 | 40 | 38–39 | 5.0 |
| 75 | 74 | 10.7 | 39 | 37 | 4.9 |
| 74 | 73 | 10.6 | 38 | 36 | 4.5 |
| 73 | 72 | 10.4 | 37 | 35 | 4.4 |
| 72 | 70 | 10.3 | 35–36 | 34 | 4.2 |
| 71 | 71 | 10.0 | 34 | 33 | 3.9 |
| 70 | 69 | 9.8 | 33 | 32 | 3.8 |
| 69 | 68 | 9.6 | 32 | 31 | 3.7 |
| 68 | 67 | 9.4 | 31 | 30 | 3.6 |
| 67 | 66 | 9.3 | 30 | 29 | 3.5 |
| 66 | 64 | 9.2 | 29 | 28 | 3.4 |
| 65 | 63 | 9.1 | 27–28 | 27 | 3.3 |
| 64 | 62 | 9.0 | 26 | 26 | 3.2 |
| 63 | 61 | 8.6 | 25 | 25 | 3.1 |
| 62 | 60 | 8.4 | 23–24 | 24 | 3.0 |
| 61 | 59 | 8.0 | 22 | 23 | 2.9 |
| 60 | 58 | 7.7 | 21 | 22 | 2.8 |
| 59 | 57 | 7.5 | 20 | 21 | 2.7 |
| 58 | 56 | 7.4 | 19 | 20 | 2.6 |
| 57 | 55 | 7.2 | 18 | 19 | 2.5 |
| 56 | 54 | 7.0 | 17 | 18 | 2.4 |
| 55 | 53 | 6.9 | 16 | 16–17 | 2.3 |
| 53–54 | 52 | 6.8 | 15 | 15 | 2.2 |
| 52 | 51 | 6.6 | 14 | 14 | 2.1 |
| 51 | 50 | 6.5 | 12–13 | 13 | 2.0 |
| 50 | 49 | 6.4 | 11 | 12 | 1.9 |
| 49 | 47–48 | 6.3 | 10 | 10–11 | 1.8 |
| 48 | 46 | 6.1 | 9 | 9 | 1.7 |
| 46–47 | 45 | 5.9 | 8 | 7–8 | 1.6 |
| 45 | 44 | 5.8 | 7 | 6 | 1.5 |
| 44 | 43 | 5.7 | 6 | 5 | 1.4 |
| 43 | 42 | 5.4 | 5 | 4 | 1.3 |
| 42 | 41 | 5.3 | 3–4 | 3 | 1.2 |
| 41 | 40 | 5.2 | 2 | 2 | 1.1 |

## GRADE 1 (Form A)

A white mouse ran outside.
He wanted to play.
He saw three kittens.
The mother cat was black.
They played and played.

1. Which animal was white?
2. Which animal wanted to play?
3. What color was the mother cat?
4. How many kittens were there?
5. What did the kittens do?

| ERROR RECORD | Number |
|---|---|
| Substitutions | |
| Mispronunciations | |
| Words pronounced by examiner | |
| Disregard of pronunciation | |
| Insertions | |
| Hesitations | |
| Repetitions | |
| Omissions | |
| Total Errors | |

**GRADE 2 (Form A)**

> A little white dog ran away from home.
> He played with two black dogs.
> The black dogs ran under the house.
> A boy came out of the house.
> The boy had a bowl of milk.
> He gave the milk to the three dogs.

1. Which dog ran away from home?
2. Which dogs ran under the house?
3. Who came out of the house?
4. What did the boy have?
5. Who drank the milk?

| ERROR RECORD | Number |
|---|---|
| Substitutions | |
| Mispronunciations | |
| Words pronounced by examiner | |
| Disregard of pronunciation | |
| Insertions | |
| Hesitations | |
| Repetitions | |
| Omissions | |
| Total Errors | |

## GRADE 3 (Form A)

Four boys went camping by the side of a lake.
They took food to eat and milk to drink.
The boys cooked and ate supper.
In the night, a horse came and ate grass around the boys' tent.
The boys got scared.
They thought it was a bear eating their food.

1. Where did the boys go camping?
2. How many boys went camping?
3. What did they take to drink?
4. What did they think they heard during the night?
5. What did they really hear?

| ERROR RECORD | Number |
|---|---|
| Substitutions | |
| Mispronunciations | |
| Words pronounced by examiner | |
| Disregard of pronunciation | |
| Insertions | |
| Hesitations | |
| Repetitions | |
| Omissions | |
| Total Errors | |

## GRADE 4 (Form A)

Mother likes to cook outdoors in the summer. The family loves picnics during the warm weather. Father builds the fire for Mother. Dick and Jane help Mother cook the delicious meals. The family likes the food cooked in the fresh air. The family next door sometimes eats outside too. The two families often eat together on certain holidays.

Both families hate to see winter come because it is too cold to cook outdoors.

1. When does Mother like to cook outdoors?
2. Who builds the fire for Mother?
3. Who helps Mother cook?
4. When do the two families eat together?
5. What time of the year do the two families hate to see?

| ERROR RECORD | Number |
|---|---|
| Substitutions | |
| Mispronunciations | |
| Words pronounced by examiner | |
| Disregard of pronunciation | |
| Insertions | |
| Hesitations | |
| Repetitions | |
| Omissions | |
| Total Errors | |

**GRADE 5 (Form A)**

During the summer Dick and Mary go to camp. Dick goes to a boy's camp which is located by a clear, deep lake. Mary's camp is located by a sparkling, cold, noisy creek. The boys enjoy swimming, water skiing, back packing in the mountains and overnight camping. On special occasions they fish in the lake and cook the fish by a crackling campfire.

Mary and the other girls also enjoy swimming, camping, nature study and making crafts. Next June Mary is going to be a swimming instructor and stay for the entire month. Dick will not be old enough to stay for a month.

1. Where is Dick's camp located?
2. What do the boys do on special occasions?
3. Which child enjoys nature study?
4. What is Mary going to be next June?
5. Which child is the younger of the two?

| ERROR RECORD | Number |
|---|---|
| Substitutions | |
| Mispronunciations | |
| Words pronounced by examiner | |
| Disregard of pronunciation | |
| Insertions | |
| Hesitations | |
| Repetitions | |
| Omissions | |
| Total Errors | |

**GRADE 6 (Form A)**

A computer is a large instrument made up of miles of electric wire. An operator feeds facts, figures and symbols into the machine. A computer also stores information in its "brain." When the operator wants answers, he asks the machine to make combinations of information stored within it.

Computers are often used for scientific and business calculations, but can also be used for literary purposes. Some computers are used to analyze sentence structure of the English language.

The U.S. Government keeps 500 computers working at hundreds of problems in many areas of operation. Thousands of income tax returns are run through the machine each hour. Taxpayers are either notified of an error or money is returned to them.

1. What type of wire can be found in a computer?
2. In what does a computer store its information?
3. What besides scientific and business calculations are computers used for?
4. How many computers work for the Government daily?
5. What kind of returns are run through the computer?

| ERROR RECORD | Number |
|---|---|
| Substitutions | |
| Mispronunciations | |
| Words pronounced by examiner | |
| Disregard of pronunciation | |
| Insertions | |
| Hesitations | |
| Repetitions | |
| Omissions | |
| Total Errors | |

## GRADE 7 (Form A)

One summer day David and his father decided to go diving for hidden treasure. They knew of an old sunken Spanish ship and there were many stories about gold and silver still being inside the hull. Early one morning they sailed to the secluded spot where they thought the schooner had sunk and dropped anchor just inside two reefs.

About an hour after sunrise they made ready by putting on the diving gear. Father said, "There's plenty of sharks in these waters, so let's be careful."

They went over the side and down. Their weighted boots struck bottom at seventy-five feet. It was too shallow for a sunken ship to be located. Father and David looked around for about thirty minutes and decided to go home and try another day.

1. For what type of treasure were David and his father looking?
2. Where did they drop anchor?
3. What was in the water which made them be careful?
4. At what depth did they strike bottom?
5. Why was the sunken ship not there?

| ERROR RECORD | Number |
|---|---|
| Substitutions | |
| Mispronunciations | |
| Words pronounced by examiner | |
| Disregard of pronunciation | |
| Insertions | |
| Hesitations | |
| Repetitions | |
| Omissions | |
| Total Errors | |

**GRADE 8 (Form A)**

Mary and Tod took a trip by train to the Virginia mountains one beautiful spring morning. The train stopped at 10 A.M. at a large town nestled in the beautiful ridges by a fast moving river. They were to backpack for seven miles until they reached a village store. At the village store Mary and Tod got directions to Coon's Ridge where they were to spend the night with Mrs. Mack, a friend of the family. They left the village store thinking that the rest of the trip would be very easy. They took for granted that the trip from the village store to Coon's Ridge, which was only five miles, was just another hike. However, it wasn't. They had been told that Mrs. Mack lived across a ridge but the ridge turned into a fullgrown mountain.

They had to rest every so often and the rests made the trip take twice as long. When they finally saw Mrs. Mack the sun was gently setting in the sky.

1. Where did Mary and Tod take the trip by train?
2. Where did they get directions?
3. Where did Mrs. Mack live?
4. How far was Coon's Ridge from the village store?
5. What time of the day did Mary and Tod reach Mrs. Mack's house?

| ERROR RECORD | Number |
|---|---|
| Substitutions | |
| Mispronunciations | |
| Words pronounced by examiner | |
| Disregard of pronunciation | |
| Insertions | |
| Hesitations | |
| Repetitions | |
| Omissions | |
| Total Errors | |

## GRADE 9 (Form A)

Mary learned from recent school tests that her interests lie in the area of human study. She has always been interested in the study of man's emotions and thought that she wanted to study some branch of medicine. She learned that psychology is the systematic study of the mind and emotions of man. She also learned that disturbances of human emotions adversely affect the way in which people deal with life's problems.

Mary decided that she would like to study rehabilitation counseling which is an area of psychology. This area of psychology is relatively new and began after World War I when it was recognized that handicapped citizens required special assistance in obtaining employment. The goal of the rehabilitation counselor is to assist severely handicapped people achieve a productive and satisfying life. The rehabilitation process includes interviewing and counseling handicapped persons, arranging for medical services, vocational training, conducting job surveys and placing handicapped persons in job settings.

The rehabilitation counselor works with people in medicine, speech therapy, social work, and recreational therapy to make the life of the handicapped person more rewarding and productive.

1. Where did Mary learn about her vocational interests?
2. What did Mary decide that she would study?
3. Rehabilitation counseling is an area of what field of study?
4. Rehabilitation counseling became a field of study at the end of what event?
5. What is the goal of the rehabilitation counselor?

| ERROR RECORD | Number |
|---|---|
| Substitutions | |
| Mispronunciations | |
| Words pronounced by examiner | |
| Disregard of pronunciation | |
| Insertions | |
| Hesitations | |
| Repetitions | |
| Omissions | |
| Total Errors | |

## GRADE 10 (Form A)

The 1920s were exciting years for Americans—a very long party. Riding high on a wave of economic prosperity, people were blindly optimistic and looked ahead to unlimited progress. Nothing could go wrong. Suddenly everything changed. Almost overnight the nation was faced with disaster. The great economic machine failed and with it failed the fortunes of the superrich and the very lives of the working classes were in danger. The stock market crash "lit" the depression of 1930 causing much suffering and woe among the American people.

In the great depression there were serious effects on employment and wages. When the depression came employment was reduced. People were discharged or laid off. Those who remained at work had their earnings reduced by working shorter days. Wage rates were cut, and those of the unemployed who got new jobs had to take them at lower pay. In 1929, our last prosperous year, the total earnings of those people who worked for wages and salaries amounted to something like 55 billion dollars. The wages and salary payments of the working people were reduced approximately 10 billion dollars before the first year of the depression attained its full force. The effect of unemployment and wage cuts were strongly felt by the American people.

The stock market crash was a major factor in the great depression. September 1929 marked the peak of the market. It started slipping on October 3 and declined throughout the week of October 14, then gave way to panic on 'Black Thursday,' October 24.

1. What years were exciting ones for Americans?
2. What crash lit the depression of 1930?
3. What year was our last prosperous year?
4. What affected Americans the most?
5. What day of the week was called 'Black'?

| ERROR RECORD | Number |
|---|---|
| Substitutions | |
| Mispronunciations | |
| Words pronounced by examiner | |
| Disregard of pronunciation | |
| Insertions | |
| Hesitations | |
| Repetitions | |
| Omissions | |
| Total Errors | |

# Pronunciation Guide for Word Recognition Test

| | | | |
|---|---|---|---|
| 1. me . . . . . . . . . . . . . . . mē | 43. trucker . . . . . . . . . . trŭk´ĕr |
| 2. at . . . . . . . . . . . . . . . ăt | 44. apparatus . . . . . . . . ăp´arā´tŭs |
| 3. go . . . . . . . . . . . . . . gō | 45. comment . . . . . . . . . kŏm´ĕnt |
| 4. an . . . . . . . . . . . . . . ăn | 46. commercial . . . . . . . kŏ mûr´shăl |
| 5. you . . . . . . . . . . . . . yo͞o | 47. gallery . . . . . . . . . . . găl´ĕr ĭ |
| 6. live . . . . . . . . . . . . . līv | 48. amber . . . . . . . . . . . ăm´bĕr |
| 7. how . . . . . . . . . . . . . hou | 49. sundry . . . . . . . . . . sŭn´drē |
| 8. night . . . . . . . . . . . . nīt | 50. blight . . . . . . . . . . . blīt |
| 9. early . . . . . . . . . . . . ûr´lē | 51. wrest . . . . . . . . . . . rĕst |
| 10. about . . . . . . . . . . . a bout´ | 52. daunted . . . . . . . . . dônt´ĕd |
| 11. call . . . . . . . . . . . . . kôl | 53. capacious . . . . . . . . ka pā´shŭs |
| 12. cold . . . . . . . . . . . . . kōld | 54. aspen . . . . . . . . . . . ăs´pĕn |
| 13. fear . . . . . . . . . . . . . fĭr | 55. pretext . . . . . . . . . . prē tĕkst´ |
| 14. much . . . . . . . . . . . . mŭch | 56. intrigue . . . . . . . . . ĭn trēg´ |
| 15. first . . . . . . . . . . . . . fûrst | 57. ascent . . . . . . . . . . . a sĕnt´ |
| 16. together . . . . . . . . . too gĕth´ĕr | 58. acrid . . . . . . . . . . . . ăk´rĭd |
| 17. jump . . . . . . . . . . . . jŭmp | 59. delusion . . . . . . . . . dē lūshŭn |
| 18. road . . . . . . . . . . . . . rōd | 60. binocular . . . . . . . . bĭn ŏk´ū lĕr |
| 19. when . . . . . . . . . . . . hwĕn | 61. conscientious . . . . . kŏn´shĭ ĕn´shŭs |
| 20. town . . . . . . . . . . . . toun | 62. galore . . . . . . . . . . . ga lōr´ |
| 21. between . . . . . . . . . bē twĕn´ | 63. isolation . . . . . . . . . ī´sō lā shŭn |
| 22. pretty . . . . . . . . . . . prĭt´ē | 64. molecule . . . . . . . . . mŏl´ē kūl |
| 23. middle . . . . . . . . . . . mĭd´l | 65. ritual . . . . . . . . . . . . rĭt´u ăl |
| 24. moment . . . . . . . . . mō´mĕnt | 66. jaunty . . . . . . . . . . . jôn´tĭ |
| 25. several . . . . . . . . . . . sĕv´ĕr ăl | 67. zany . . . . . . . . . . . . zā´nĭ |
| 26. drew . . . . . . . . . . . . dro͞o | 68. jerkin . . . . . . . . . . . jûr´kĭn |
| 27. straight . . . . . . . . . . strāt | 69. nausea . . . . . . . . . . nô´shē a |
| 28. decided . . . . . . . . . . dē sīd´ĕd | 70. linear . . . . . . . . . . . lĭn´ē ĕr |
| 29. inept . . . . . . . . . . . . ĭn ĕpt´ | 71. legality . . . . . . . . . . lē găl´ĭ tĭ |
| 30. exclaimed . . . . . . . . ĕks klāmd´ | 72. amnesty . . . . . . . . . ăm´nĕs tĭ |
| 31. amazed . . . . . . . . . . a māzd´ | 73. rotunda . . . . . . . . . rō tŭn´da |
| 32. silent . . . . . . . . . . . . sī´lĕnt | 74. capitalism . . . . . . . . kăp´ĭ tăl ĭz´m |
| 33. entered . . . . . . . . . . ĕn´tĕrd | 75. prevaricate . . . . . . . prē văr´ĭ kāt |
| 34. realized . . . . . . . . . . rē´ăl īzd | 76. superfluous . . . . . . . su pûrflo͞o ŭs |
| 35. scanty . . . . . . . . . . . skăn´tē | 77. piebald . . . . . . . . . . pī´bôld |
| 36. develop . . . . . . . . . . dē vĕl´ŭp | 78. behaved . . . . . . . . . bē havd´ |
| 37. escape . . . . . . . . . . . ĕs kāp´ | 79. appropriation . . . . . a prō´prĭ ā´shŭn |
| 38. grim . . . . . . . . . . . . grĭ | 80. distribution . . . . . . dĭs´trĭ bū´shŭn |
| 39. bridge . . . . . . . . . . . brĭj | 81. situation . . . . . . . . . sĭt´u ā´shŭn |
| 40. served . . . . . . . . . . . sûrvd | 82. federation . . . . . . . . fĕd´ĕr ā´shŭn |
| 41. splendid . . . . . . . . . splĕn´dĭd | 83. resolution . . . . . . . . rĕz ō lū´shŭn |
| 42. abolish . . . . . . . . . . a bŏl´ĭsh | 84. discrimination . . . . . dĭskrĭm´ĭnā´shŭn |

Date _____

Name _____     Age _____

School _____     Grade _____

## Word Recognition Test (Form I)

| | |
|---|---|
| B A G O S T E H P M Z U Q E N | ( 15) |
| Q E H Z P U A M U Z Q S Y W D | ( 30) |
| me at go an you live how night early about | ( 40) |
| call cold far much first together jump road when town | ( 50) |
| between pretty middle moment several drew straight decided inept | ( 59) |
| exclaimed amazed silent entered realized scanty develop escape grim | ( 68) |
| bridge served splendid abolish trucker apparatus comment commercial | ( 76) |
| gallery bridge amber sundry blight wrest daunted capacious aspen | ( 85) |
| pretext intrigue ascent acrid delusion binocular conscientious galore | ( 96) |
| isolation molecule ritual jaunty zany jerkin nausea linear legality | (105) |
| amnesty rotunda capitalism prevaricate superfluous piebald behaved | (112) |
| appropriation distribution situation federation resolution discrimination | (118) |

Date _____

Name _____ School _____

Age _____ Date of Birth _____ Grade _____

**Test Summary Form A**

| PARAGRAPH | ACCURACY | | COMPREHENSION |
| --- | --- | --- | --- |
| | Errors | 10 Minus No. Errors | No. Right (Or Credited) |
| 1 | | | |
| 2 | | | |
| 3 | | | |
| 4 | | | |
| 5 | | | |
| 6 | | | |
| 7 | | | |
| 8 | | | |
| 9 | | | |
| 10 | | | |
| | Acc. Score ("10 Minus No. Errors" Column) | | Comp. Score (Tot. No. Right or Credited) |
| | | | |
| Grade Equiv. | | | |
| | | | |

COMMENTS:

**LOVE'S DIAGNOSTIC READING INVENTORY**

**Raw Scores and Grade Ratings for the Word Recognition Test.**

| Raw Score | Grade | Raw Score | Grade | Raw Score | Grade |
|---|---|---|---|---|---|
| 0 | N.R. | 40 | 2.4 | 80 | 7.1 |
| 1 | N.R. | 41 | 2.5 | 81 | 7.2 |
| 2 | N.R. | 42 | 2.6 | 82 | 7.3 |
| 3 | N.R. | 43 | 2.7 | 83 | 7.4 |
| 4 | N.R. | 44 | 2.8 | 84 | 7.5 |
| 5 | Pre. P. | 45 | 2.9 | 85 | 7.6 |
| 6 | Pre. P. | 46 | 3.0 | 86 | 7.7 |
| 7 | Pre. P. | 47 | 3.1 | 87 | 7.8 |
| 8 | Pri. | 48 | 3.2 | 88 | 7.9 |
| 9 | Pri. | 49 | 3.3 | 89 | 8.0 |
| 10 | Pri. | 50 | 3.4 | 90 | 8.1 |
| 11 | Pri. | 51 | 3.5 | 91 | 8.2 |
| 12 | Pri. | 52 | 3.6 | 92 | 8.3 |
| 13 | Pri. | 53 | 3.7 | 93 | 8.4 |
| 14 | Pri. | 54 | 3.8 | 94 | 8.5 |
| 15 | K | 55 | 3.9 | 95 | 8.6 |
| 16 | K | 56 | 4.0 | 96 | 8.7 |
| 17 | K | 57 | 4.1 | 97 | 8.8 |
| 18 | K | 58 | 4.1 | 98 | 8.9 |
| 19 | K | 59 | 4.2 | 99 | 9.0 |
| 20 | K | 60 | 4.3 | 100 | 9.1 |
| 21 | K | 61 | 4.4 | 101 | 9.2 |
| 22 | K | 62 | 4.5 | 102 | 9.3 |
| 23 | K | 63 | 4.6 | 103 | 9.4 |
| 24 | 1.0 | 64 | 4.7 | 104 | 9.5 |
| 25 | 1.1 | 65 | 4.8 | 105 | 9.6 |
| 26 | 1.2 | 66 | 4.9 | 106 | 9.7 |
| 27 | 1.3 | 67 | 5.0 | 107 | 9.8 |
| 28 | 1.4 | 68 | 5.1 | 108 | 9.9 |
| 29 | 1.5 | 69 | 5.3 | 109 | 10.0 |
| 30 | 1.6 | 70 | 5.4 | 110 | 10.1 |
| 31 | 1.7 | 71 | 5.6 | 111 | 10.2 |
| 32 | 1.8 | 72 | 5.7 | 112 | 10.3 |
| 33 | 1.9 | 73 | 5.8 | 113 | 10.4 |
| 34 | 2.0 | 74 | 6.0 | 114 | 10.5 |
| 35 | 2.0 | 75 | 6.3 | 115 | 10.6 |
| 36 | 2.1 | 76 | 6.5 | 116 | 10.7 |
| 37 | 2.2 | 77 | 6.8 | 117 | 10.8 |
| 38 | 2.3 | 78 | 6.9 | 118 | 10.9 |
| 39 | 2.3 | 79 | 7.0 | | |

# AUTHOR INDEX

## A

Ainsworth, S. H., 156, 167
Allington, R. L., 162, 167
Amon, M. G., 28, 43, 54
Anderson, V., 107
Arnold, R. D., 133

## B

Barbe, W. B., 148, 149
Barnett, A., 110
Barr, R., 89
Barrett, T. C., 199
Baumann, J. F., 103, 167
Bealer, J., 43
Bennett, A., 156, 167
Bereiter, C., 107
Betts, E. A., 133, 149
Birch, J. W., 7, 18
Blatt, B., 156, 167
Bouchard, T. J., 27, 43
Bower, E., 13
Brill, R. D., 10, 18
Brophy, J., 162, 163, 167
Bruner, E. C., 96, 110, 168
Burt, C., 151, 167
Buttery, T., 176, 198

## C

Capobianco, R. J., 160, 167
Capron, C., 23, 43
Cassidy, V. M., 55, 156, 157
Chall, J., 49
Clark, C. R., 94, 110, 162
Coghill, G. E., 47, 55
Cohen, S. B., 174, 178, 198
Cohen, A., 17, 158, 160, 168

## D

Coutinho, M., 14, 18
Cowan, P. A., 156, 168
Cramer, B. B., 56, 170
Culhane, J. W., 149
Cunningham, A. E., 26, 44, 56, 78, 170
Curtis, H. M., 65, 71

Davidson, H. P., 154, 168
Davies, C. O., 94, 110
Dechant, E. V., 132
DeFries, J. C., 25, 43
DeHaven, E. P., 187, 189, 193, 198
Derr, W. K., 71
Disick, R. S., 185, 192, 198
Dolch, E. M., 64, 71, 168
Drew, C. J., 9, 18
Duffy, G., 161, 168
Duyme, M., 23, 43
Dye, H., 22, 44

## E

Egan, M. W., 18
Ekwall, E. E., 79, 129, 131, 161, 168
Elenbogen, M. L., 156, 168
Englemann, S., 96, 110, 168
Evans, H., 25, 181, 184, 192, 193, 198

## F

Farber, E. A., 24, 44
Fernald, G. M., 89, 92, 110
Forness, S., 160, 168
Freeman, D. J., 26, 44, 56
Frye, R. M., 57
Fuchs, D., 149
Fuchs, L. S., 149

# SUBJECT INDEX

**F**

f test, 165–166
Fernald Approach, 88–89, 92–93, 148, 181
Formal Assessment, 111–131
Formal Reading Inventory, 120
Frustration Reading Level, 136–137

**G**

Gates-MacGinitie Reading Tests, 120
Gates-McKillop-Horowitz Reading Diagnostic Test, 119–120
Gillingham Approach, 148–180
Gilmore Oreal Reading Test (New Ed.), 120
Glass Analysis Method, 107–109
Goldman-Fristoe-Woodcock Test of Auditory Discrimination, 42
Goodenough-Harris Drawing Test, 127–128
Gray Oral Reading Test-R, 120
Group Phonics Analysis Test, 130

**H**

Handwriting, 193–195
Hearing Impairments, 9–11
    deafness, 9
    hard of hearing, 10
    prevalence, 11
Hegge-Kirk-Kirk Approach, 103–104

**I**

IDEA, 10, 12, 14, 171
Independent Reading Levels, 136–137
Individualized Reading, 50
Informal Assessment, 132–149
    administration, 75–136
    advantages, 175
    construction, 134–135, 138–139
    definition, 132
    disadvantages, 135
    overview, 133–134
    tests, 146–147
Informal Reading Inventory (2nd Ed.), 139
Initial Teaching Alphabet, 51, 109, 192
Instructional Reading Levels, 136–137
Intelligence, 4, 24, 29
Intelligence Tests, 121

Inventory of Early Development, 119
Iowa Tests of Basic Skills, 117–118
IRA, 6
Item Analysis, 115

**K**

KABC, 126–127
Kaufman Assessment Battery for Children, 126–127
Kinesthetic Approach, 88

**L**

Language, 186
    expressive, 186
    inner, 186
    receptive, 186
Language Experience Approach, 50, 180, 185–188
Lateral Dominance, 158–159
Learning Disabled, 52, 56, 171
Lindamood Auditory Conceptualization Test, 42
Linguistics, 51, 179, 192
Listening, 173, 182–185
Love Diagnostic Reading Inventory, 120–121, 139, 142, 144, 224

**M**

Mainstreaming, 71
Mental Retardation, 4–5
    educable, 171
    moderate profound, 99
Metropolitan Achievement Tests, 118
Metropolitan Readiness Tests, 42, 154
Mildly Handicapped, 171, 174–176, 190
Modality Diagnosis, 140–149
Montessori, 148
Muscular Dystrophy, 13

**N**

National Joint Committee for Learning Disabilities, 6
Nature-Nurture Controversy, 22
Neurological Impress Method, 77, 109